LEGENDS OF JERUSALEM

LEGENDS

OF JERUSALEM

THE SACRED LAND: VOLUME 1

ZEV VILNAY

The Jewish Publication Society of America

PHILADELPHIA

Copyright © 1973
by The Jewish Publication Society of America
All rights reserved
First edition
ISBN 0–8276–0004–6
Library of Congress catalog card number: 72-12180
Manufactured in the United States of America
Designed by Sol Calvin Cohen

First edition, Second impression, 1975

PREFACE

Every nation living on its own soil has a great wealth of legends, traditions, memories, stories, and songs interwoven with each nook and cranny, each plant and flower, each bird and animal to be found within its borders. This treasury of national folklore forms an integral part of the culture of the people. Every farmer and shepherd, living in intimate contact with nature, knows his surroundings and how to tell the stories and legends associated with them. These tales reflect the people's attitudes toward their environment and their country; they express love for its places and personalities, and for the memories connected with them.

Every generation makes its own unique contribution to the ancestral heritage. Every event in the life of the nation leaves its distinctive mark on the mass of lore, which thus grows and develops. National folklore is a precious possession, abounding in vitality and original creation. Its life-span is bound up with that of the people, and with the history of their native land.

Israel, too, when dwelling securely in its own land, had a wealth of folklore, which reflected the characteristics of the people, their relationship to their homeland, and to the various events affecting it. Their love of plants and animals and of the wide world around them was also expressed in it. On the Sabbaths and holidays, as the people of Israel gathered around beneath the shade of the fig or olive trees, the elders would tell their tales, while the young would listen, wide-eyed with awe and wonder. These discourses implanted in their hearts a deep love and devotion for the land of their birth, and for the men and women who dwelt and toiled within it. Men of imagination and vision added the fruits of their talent to the national lore and expanded it. The people's close companionship with nature, their familiarity with the springs and streams, mountains and hills, caves and rocks, plants and animals, was the source for the growth and enrichment of the folklore—the creation of a people in its native land.

In the succeeding generations, centers of learning were established in the settlements of Israel. There, too, among the educated groups national legends began to be created, interpretations of the names of sites or verses found in the Holy Scriptures. These explanations were based on careful observation of the land and close contact with nature. In many of them an echo of the folk tale can be discerned—a product of the countryside reworked in the house of study. On the other hand, creations of the house of learning found their way to the people, spread among them, and became the property of the masses, entwined in the web of national folklore.

Then misfortune descended upon the house of Israel. With the destruction of the nation, the impoverishment of the people in the towns and villages, and the exile of many of them, Hebrew folklore, too, withered and shrank. Creations of generations sank into oblivion. Without a land, a sound folklore cannot exist and grow. The wanderers actually did take remnants of their lore with them, but in exile the legend lost meaning and spirit; it became destitute of the life-force vital to its existence. In time it degenerated into a rootless stock of tales that slowly shriveled, vanished, and were forgotten. In the lands of the dispersion, wholesome, earthy legends took on an otherworldly air, mixed with traditions of a messianic age and heavenly Jerusalem. Israel's creative imagination was fettered by the bonds of exile.

Fortunately, the treasures of national legends were not entirely lost. We find remnants and fragments of them here and there in the ancient literature of Israel, clearly revealing the spirit of the land and the character of its inhabitants. As it happened, these tales were incorporated into the Holy Scriptures and the postbiblical literature: Mishnah, Talmud, and Midrash. It was these remnants of national folklore, embodied in the holy writings, that implanted in the hearts of the exiles a love for the faraway land of their forefathers, a land desolate and forsaken, longing for the return of her children, while they yearned for her.

From earliest times the Arab traditions in Israel incorporated not only Hebrew place-names, but fragments of the ancient Hebrew folklore as well. Much was altered to suit the Arab spirit and outlook, yet their folklore contains legends of places and personalities which are obviously Hebrew in content, and which echo the ancient national tales. It is very important to restore the "lost" lore to its place in Hebrew literature, after it has undergone so many transformations in the course of time.

The return of Israel to its homeland and the rebirth of its national life have replenished the long-barren earth from which their folklore drew its nourishment and vitality. Hebrew life in our times has already given rise to

new folk tales, some based on ancient sources, some rooted
in the modern environment and the native countryside.

In my book *Legends of Jerusalem*, I have tried to collect
all the tales about the different places from the ancient
Hebrew literature: Holy Scriptures, Mishnah, Tosefta,
Talmud, Midrash, and from the writings of the pilgrims
of the Middle Ages. I have also gathered material from
Arabic sources. Some stories come from itineraries and de-
scriptions of Christian pilgrims. I have included, too, current legends created in present-day Israel, Arab tales with
Hebrew content, and a few Arab stories for comparison
with the original Hebrew lore.

Hebrew literature is very rich in legends and tales of
sacred graves, so numerous in the Holy Land and so well
known to the inhabitants. These legends, not included in
this volume, are found in my Hebrew book *Holy Shrines in
the Land of Israel*, published in 1951 by Rav Kook Publication, Jerusalem (second edition, enlarged, 1963).

Legends of the Holy Land (Agadot Eretz Israel) was
first published in Hebrew, in 1929, in London. It contained
150 legends, chiefly about places but a few about plants
and animals. In 1932 an enlarged English translation,
Legends of Palestine, including 217 tales, was published
by the Jewish Publication Society. A new Hebrew edition
containing 600 legends, geographically arranged, was published in Jerusalem in 1949. Since then the book has en-
joyed several printings. The last Hebrew edition, the
seventh, appeared in two volumes in 1970. The text was
rearranged, and many legends were added. All told, it
contains approximately 1,200 folk tales. The present English translation was prepared from the last Hebrew edition,
with slight alterations and additions. It appears in three
volumes, of which *Legends of Jerusalem* is the first. The
second volume contains legends about sites in Judea and
Samaria, including the cities of Bethlehem, Hebron, Jeri-

cho, Beersheva, Tel Aviv–Jaffa, Shechem, and their surroundings. The third volume deals with the Galilee, the
lands across the Jordan, and Sinai with the cities of Haifa,
Acco, Tiberias, and Zefat and the mountains of Carmel
and Hermon.

The many illustrations, ancient and modern, add to the
vividness of the legends—the creation and product
of the country which is cherished by Israel and
all humanity.

I wish to express my gratitude to my wife, Esther, for
her important contribution both in the translation from
the Hebrew original and in the preparation of the English
manuscript for publication.

Jerusalem   Z.V.

CONTENTS

Preface v
Illustrations xxi

I. JERUSALEM—CENTER OF THE WORLD

1. Jerusalem Was the Beginning 5
2. Middle of the Earth 6
3. The Navel of the World 6
4. The Eye of the World 6
5. Who Set Up the Stone? 7
6. Where Is the Source of Springs? 8
7. The "Name" on the Stone ....,............... 8
8. The Stone—Jacob's Pillar 10
9. Where Were the Tablets Hewn? 11
10. The Holy Ark on the Stone 11
11. The Angel above the Stone 13
12. Jonah Saw the Stone 14
13. The Stone and Weaving 15
14. Cherubim above the Stone 15
15. The Crown on the Stone 16

II. DOME OF THE ROCK

1. The Foundation Stone and Paradise 17
2. The Stone Rests on a Whale 19

3. The Stone—Source of Waters 19
4. The Tongue of the Rock 19
5. Muhammad's Footprint 21
6. Enoch's Footprint 22
7. The Foundation Stone Hovers 23
8. The Stone and Messiah 24
9. The Holy Cavern 25
10. The Well of the Souls 26
11. The Stone of Eden 27
12. When the Candelabrum Fell 29
13. Why Does the Dome Tarnish? 29
14. The Crescent on the Dome 30
15. The Birds Which Turned into Stone 33
16. The Candles at the Temple Site 34
17. Sighs from the Temple Site 35
18. Voices from the Temple Site 36

III. THE TEMPLE COURT TODAY

1. Solomon's Study House 37
2. Between the Pillars 38
3. Prayer Place of Zechariah 40
4. King David's Tribunal 41
5. The Scales of Judgment 43
6. The Throne of Solomon 44
7. King Solomon's Stables 46
8. The Crypt of the Devils 46
9. The Fragment of the Rock 47
10. The Well of the Leaf 49
11. Weeping from the Well 49
12. The Pool of Israel 50
13. The Holy Nettle Tree 50

IV. GATES OF THE TEMPLE COURT

1. Prayer in the Gates 52
2. The Gate of Mercy 54
3. The Graveyard around the Gate 57
4. Through the Gate of Mercy 57
5. Supplication at the Gate 58
6. Who Built the Gate of Mercy? 58
7. Gate of Eternal Life 60
8. The Golden Gate (Porta Aurea) 60
9. The Golden Gate in the End of Days 61

10. The Gate of the Tribes 62
11. The Gate of Sin 62

V. MORIAH—THE MOUNT OF GOD

1. Height of Israel 64
2. Mount of Myrrh 65
3. Mount of Light 66
4. Mount of Awe 66
5. Mount of Instruction 66
6. Mount of Appearance 67
7. Mount of Exchange 67
8. Mount of Spices 68

VI. PATRIARCHS ON MOUNT MORIAH

1. Where Was Adam Created? 69
2. The Abode of Adam 70
3. Noah on Mount Moriah 70
4. Abraham on Mount Moriah 71
5. Isaac's Sacrifice 71
6. Moriah in the Exodus 72
7. Benjamin and Mount Moriah 74
8. Temples in Benjamin's Portion 75
9. The Purchase of Mount Moriah 75

VII. THE TEMPLE IN ITS GLORY

1. Why Was the Temple on Mount Moriah? 77
2. The Foundation of the Abyss 78
3. King David and the Abyss 80
4. Building the Temple 80
5. Stones Built the Temple 81
6. How Did the Temple Appear? 81
7. Cedars in the Temple 82
8. Light from the Temple 82
9. The Curtain at the Entrance 83
10. The Golden Candlestick 83
11. The Vine on the Entrance 84
12. The Sapphire on the Roof 85
13. The Raven Destroyers 85

VIII. BUILDINGS AROUND THE TEMPLE

1. The Sanhedrin in the Center 87
2. The Bath of the High Priest 88

3. The Chamber of Parvah 88
4. The Chamber of Secrets 89
5. Chamber of the Hearth 89
6. Chamber of the Incense-maker 90

IX. THE SERVICE IN THE TEMPLE

1. The Fire on the Altar 92
2. Who Kindled the Fire? 93
3. Wood for the Temple 94
4. The Offering of Firstfruits 95
5. Census in Israel 96
6. Passover of the Crushed 96
7. Cries from the Temple 97

X. GATES OF THE TEMPLE

1. When Did the Gates Open? 98
2. The Eastern Gate 99
3. Shechina at the Eastern Gate 99
4. The Eastern Gate on Sabbath 100
5. Gate of Nicanor 100
6. Gates of Bridegrooms and Mourners 101
7. The Shushan Gate 102
8. The Water Gate 103
9. Gate of the Sun 104
10. The Gate with Seven Names 104
11. The Gates Sunk 105

XI. NAMES OF THE TEMPLE

1. Ariel—Lion of God 107
2. Devir—The Word 107
3. Hadom Adonai—God's Footstool 108
4. Levanon—Lebanon 109
5. Yedidut—Loving Friendship 110
6. Lev Haolam—The Heart of the World 110
7. Af Haolam—The Nose of the World 111
8. Zavar Haolam—The Neck of the World 111
9. Talpiot—Hill of Mouths 111
10. Apirion—Palanquin 111

XII. DESTRUCTION OF THE TEMPLE

1. Signs of Destruction 113
2. The Portals Opened by Themselves 114

 3. Square—An Omen of Destruction 115
 4. A Thread of Crimson 115
 5. Angels Lit the Fire 116
 6. Where Are the Keys? 116
 7. The Divine Presence Leaves 117
 8. The Divine Presence Is as a Bird 117
 9. The Divine Presence Rebukes 118
10. Ariel Destroyed and Rebuilt 118
11. When Was the Temple Destroyed? 119
12. From the Day of Destruction 120
13. Mourners for the Temple 121
14. Woe to Us That It Is Destroyed 121

XIII. FATE OF THE TEMPLE VESSELS

 1. The Holy Ark 122
 2. The Holy Curtain 124
 3. The Golden Menorah 124
 4. Pillars from the Temple 125
 5. The Golden Plate 126
 6. King Solomon's Throne 126
 7. Vessels in Babylon 126

XIV. THE TEMPLE OF HEAVEN

 1. The Temple of Heaven and of Earth 128
 2. The Heavenly Temple 129
 3. Service in the Celestial Temple 129
 4. Moses in the Temple of Heaven 130
 5. David in the Temple of Heaven 132

XV. ANCIENT JERUSALEM

 1. Possession of the Tribes 133
 2. How Did David Conquer? 133
 3. Customs and Manners 134
 4. Markets in Jerusalem 134
 5. The Spice Market 135
 6. Regulations in Ancient Jerusalem 135
 7. The Coin of Jerusalem 136
 8. The Golden City 136
 9. What Shall Be Sold? 137
10. Stone of Inquiry 137
11. Lodge of Accountants 138
12. Court at Beth Yaazek 138

13. The Armory of Jerusalem 139
14. Tower of the Hundred 139
15. Tower of the Ovens 140
16. Pilgrims in Jerusalem 140
17. Oath in Holy Jerusalem 140
18. Wonders of the Walls 141
19. Watchmen on the Walls 141

XVI. THE DESTRUCTION OF JERUSALEM

1. King of Babylon to Jerusalem 142
2. The Fate of the Destroyer of Jerusalem 143
3. An Angel Broke Through 145
4. From the Wall to the Temple 145
5. Within the Straits 146
6. Why Was Jerusalem Destroyed? 147
7. Rending the Garments 148
8. The Mourners for Jerusalem 149
9. The Comforting of Jerusalem 150

XVII. JERUSALEM IN THE END OF TIME

1. When Will Jerusalem Be Restored? 153
2. Jerusalem in the Future 155
3. The Celestial Jerusalem 156
4. Living Waters in Jerusalem 157
5. The Pilgrimage in the Future 158

XVIII. KOTEL HA-MAARAVI—THE WAILING WALL

1. The Everlasting Wall 159
2. The Wall and the Sultan 160
3. Uncovering the Wailing Wall 162
4. The Ring and the Divine Presence 163
5. Who Saw the Divine Presence? 165
6. God Is behind the Wall 166
7. The Hill of God 166
8. "My House" Engraved on the Wall 169
9. The Wall Sheds Tears 169
10. A Lamentation 170
11. A Prayer at the Wailing Wall 171
12. The Mourning Dove 172
13. Rabbi Shalom at the Wailing Wall 173

14. The Wall and the Nails 174
15. A Missive to the Wall 174
16. The Merits of a Missive 176
17. The Wall of the Poor 177
18. The Stone of Idolatry 179
19. The Stone Which Hinders Redemption 180

XIX. PRAYERS AND SYNAGOGUES

1. God Prays in Jerusalem 182
2. All Hearts toward Jerusalem 183
3. How Many Synagogues? 183
4. The Importance of Prayer in Jerusalem 183
5. The Merits of Prayer in Jerusalem 184
6. Jerusalem Opposite the "Holy Opening" 185
7. The Winds Worship in Jerusalem 186
8. The Synagogue of Rabbi Yohanan 188
9. The Synagogue of Elijah the Prophet 189
10. The Miracle in Elijah's Synagogue 191
11. The Istanbuli Synagogue 194
12. Bethel—Center of the Mystics 195
13. The Fig Tree in the Courtyard 196
14. The Birthplace of Ha-Ari the Holy 198
15. The King and the Dome 199
16. The Synagogue of the Karaites 200
17. Soil from Jerusalem 203
18. Stone from Jerusalem 203
19. The Synagogue "Altneu-Shul" 204

XX. JERUSALEM—THE OLD CITY

1. The Turkish Conquest 206
2. Entrance into Jerusalem 207
3. Fate of the Architects 208
4. Hannah's Lane 208
5. Zela—The Karaite Quarter 209
6. Drought in Jerusalem 209
7. The Protruding Stone 210
8. In the Shops 210
9. The Bath of Healing 212
10. Golgoltha—Golgotha 212
11. Golgotha—Center of the World 213
12. Melchizedek and Abraham 214

XXI. GATES AND TOWERS

1. Why Were the Gates Closed? 215
2. The Gate of Lions 216
3. The Dung Gate 219
4. The Gate of Flowers 219
5. The Tower and the Pool 220
6. Goliath's Fortress 223

XXII. JERUSALEM—THE NEW CITY

1. Where Ezra Wrote the Torah 224
2. The Stoning Place 225
3. Ashes of the Sacrifice 226
4. Monastery of the Cross 227
5. Why Was It Called Meah Shearim? 227
6. Agrippas Street—Beileh Path 228
7. The Assyrian Camp 229
8. The Finger of Og 230
9. Why the Name Mamilla? 231
10. Why Is It Called *Abu-Tor*? 231
11. Mount of Abraham 232
12. Valley of Rephaim 233
13. The Valley of Baca 234
14. Hostel for the One Hundred and Forty-Four Thousand 235
15. Tent of the Messiah 235
16. Rod of the Messiah 237

XXIII. CAVES IN JERUSALEM

1. The Cave of Zedekiah 238
2. Those Who Dared Enter the Cave 240
3. King Solomon's Quarries 241
4. Where Does the Cave Lead? 241
5. Jeremiah's Court of the Guard 242
6. The Cave of Ha-Ramban 243
7. The Cave of the Lion 246
8. The Cave of the Amorites 247
9. The Wondrous Cavern 247

XXIV. ALONG THE BROOK OF KIDRON

1. The Pillar of Absalom 249
2. The Fate of Absalom's Pillar 252

3. The Shelter of King Azariah (Uzziah) 254
4. The Well of the Maids 256
5. King Pharaoh in Kidron 256
6. King Solomon's Mint 257
7. Kidron—Place of Refuse 257
8. Ophel and Kidron 259

XXV. VALLEY OF JEHOSHAPHAT

1. The Judgment in the End of Time 261
2. The Judgment of the Nations 262
3. Israel in the Valley of Jehoshaphat 263
4. The Two Bridges 264
5. From the Sea to the Valley 264
6. Witnesses in the Valley of Jehoshaphat 265
7. The Pillar of Muhammad 266
8. The Valley of Jehoshaphat-Gehenna 266
9. Valley of Decision 268

XXVI. GEHINNOM—PLACE OF THE WICKED

1. The Gate of Hell 269
2. Valley of Hinnom—Tophet 270
3. Idolatry in the Valley of Hinnom 271
4. Why Is It Called Tophet? 272
5. Valley of Slaughter 272

XXVII. SPRINGS AND FOUNTAINS

1. Adam in the Waters of Gihon 274
2. Solomon by the Fountain of Gihon 274
3. Who Sealed up the Gihon? 275
4. Who Unsealed the Gihon? 276
5. The Bath of the High Priest 277
6. The Pool of Siloam 277
7. Siloam in the End of Days 279
8. Siloam on the Sabbath 279
9. Whence the Waters of Siloam? 279
10. Ein Rogel—Fuller's Spring 280
11. The Well of Job 281
12. Well of Job—Well of Joab 282
13. The Well of Nehemiah 283

XXVIII. THE MOUNT OF OLIVES AND SCOPUS

1. The Place of Resurrection 285
2. The Wandering of the Divine Presence 287
3. The Consoler on the Mount of Olives 288
4. Privileges on the Mount of Olives 288
5. No Worms in the Mount of Olives 289
6. Judgment on the Mount of Olives 289
7. Earth from the Mount of Olives 291
8. The Land of the Living 292
9. The Rolling in Tunnels 293
10. Resurrection on the Mount 293
11. The Procession on the Mount 294
12. Mount of Anointment—Mount of Corruption 295
13. The Dove and the Olive 296
14. Flares on the Mount 297
15. Cedars and Cinnamon Trees 297
16. Jeremiah on Mount Scopus 298
17. Whoever Sees Jerusalem 299

XXIX. ROADS TO JERUSALEM

1. Daughters in the Vineyards 302
2. The Roads of Zion Mourn 303
3. The Highways Lie Waste 305
4. Thorns on the Roads 305
5. Where Are the Stones from? 306
6. Ye Mountains of Israel 307

The Ancient Sources 309
The Sources of the Legends 315

ILLUSTRATIONS

1. Map of the world with Jerusalem at its center. From a manuscript, *Psalterium Latinum*, in British Museum, London, Ms. Add. 28681. 4

2. The world in the shape of a cloverleaf. From H. Buenting, *Itinerarium Sacrae Scripturae*, c. 1580. 7

3. The Foundation Stone in the Dome of the Rock. 10

4. The Foundation Stone viewed from above. 12

5. The Dome of the Rock (Mosque of Omar). 18

6. The Dome of the Rock represents the Temple. From *Zebah Pesah* (Passover Sacrifice), 1545. 20

7. The Dome of the Rock represents the Temple. From H. ben Attar, *Rishon Le-Zion* (First of Zion), 1750. .. 20

8. The small turret on the Foundation Stone. 22

9. Interior view of the Dome of the Rock. 23

10. The holy cavern in the Foundation Stone. 25

11. Moslem chieftains—guardians of the Temple site. From B. Noë, *Viaggio da Venetia al S[ancto] Sepulcro*, 1640. 27

12. Stone of the Garden of Eden. From *Palestine Exploration Fund, Quarterly Statement*, 1900, p. 103. 28

13. Southern entrance to the mosque. 32

14. Two birds turned into stone. 33

15. The Dome of the Rock. From *Yehus Abboth Ve-Nebiim,* ed. Hottingero, 1659. 38

16. The pair of pillars. 39

17. Tribunal of David. 42

18. The pillars with the arches. 43

19. The site of the throne of King Solomon. 45

20. Dome of the Fragment of the Rock. 47

21. Dome of the Fragment of the Rock (interior). 48

22. Branch of the nettle tree. From Crowfoot-Baldensperger, *From Cedar to Hyssop,* 1933, p. 104. 51

23. Jewish worshiper praying opposite Temple court. 53

24. Gate of Mercy (Golden Gate). 55

25. Gate of Mercy (*Shaar ha-Rehamin*). 55

26. The coming of the Messiah to Jerusalem. From *Haggadah* of Passover, printed in Venice, 1629. 56

27. Gate of Mercy (Golden Gate), interior view. 59

28. The sacrifice of Isaac on Mount Moriah. From E. L. Sukenik, *Beth-Alpha Synagogue.* 73

29. Jerusalem and the Temple. From *Haggadah* of Passover, printed in Amsterdam, c. 1629. 79

30. The vine over the entrance to the Temple. From J. Fergusson, *The Temple of the Jews,* 1878. 84

31. View of the Temple. 86

32. Drawing of the Temple, sixth century. From Saller, *Mount Nebo.* 93

33. The burial case (ossuary) of Nicanor. 102

34. The Temple. From Mordekhai Yaffe, *Levush Haora,* (Garb of the Light), printed in Prague, 1604. 108

35. Armed battalions encompassing Jerusalem. From *Yosifon* (Yiddish), printed in Basel, 1743. 114

36. A lion—symbol of the month of Av. 119

37. The Temple's vessels—Arch of Titus, Rome. 125

38. Model of a liver from Megiddo. 143

39. Jerusalem. 144

40. Jerusalem and its walls. 151

41. Jerusalem and the arrival of the Messiah. 154
42. The Messiah and Elijah approaching Jerusalem. From *Haggadah* of Passover, printed in Frankfurt on the Oder, 1753. 155
43. The Western Wall. From Yehudah Poliastro, *Zicharon Be-Yerushalaim*, (Remembrance in Jerusalem), printed in Constantinople, 1743. 160
44. The Western Wall and surrounding buildings. From J. Schwarz, *Tevuot Haaretz* (English translation), Philadelphia, 1850. 161
45. Jewish pilgrims praying at the Western Wall. From P. Lortet, *La Syrie d'aujourd'hui*, 1884. 164
46. Worshiper at the Western Wall. 167
47. Prayer at the Western Wall. From John P. Newman, *From Dan to Beersheba*, 1864. 168
48. Jews praying at the Western Wall. 170
49. Begging alms at the Western Wall. 179
50. A seal picturing the Western Wall. 180
51. The land of Israel opposite the "holy opening." From A. Azulai, *Hesed Le-Abraham*, 1685. 186
52. Synagogue of Yohanan ben Zakkai. 187
53. Lattice in the synagogue of Yohanan ben Zakkai. 188
54. Synagogue of Elijah the Prophet. 190
55. The form of the "skull" in the synagogue. 193
56. The stone with the divine Name. 193
57. Synagogue Bethel. 196
58. Synagogue *Or ha-Haim*—Light of Life. 197
59. Synagogue Tifereth Israel. 199
60. Synagogue Tifereth Israel. 200
61. Synagogue of the Karaites. 201
62. *Al-Tenai* Synagogue (Altneu-Shul), in Prague. 205
63. Sultan Salim of Turkey. 207
64. The protruding stone—Robinson's Arch. 211
65. The Navel of the World. 213
66. The Gate of Lions. 216
67. The Tower of David. 221

68. The Tower of David and the Pool of Bathsheba.
From G. Sandys, *The Relation of a Journey*, 1610. 222

69. The angel smites the Assyrians. From *Yosifon* (Yiddish), printed in Basel, 1743. 229

70. The finger of Og, king of Bashan. 231

71. The cave of Zedekiah. 239

72. Court of the guard of Jeremiah. 243

73. Cave of Ha-Ramban (Nahmanides). 244

74. Synagogue of Ha-Ramban. From C. Roth, *The Casale Pilgrim*, London, 1929. 245

75. A cave in the vicinity of Jerusalem. From *Palestine Exploration Fund, Quarterly Statement*. 248

76. The Monument of Absalom. From W. F. Lynch, *Expedition to the River Jordan and the Dead Sea*, 1849. 250

77. Upper portion of the Monument of Absalom. 251

78. The Hand of Absalom. From Z. Vilnay, *The Holy Land in Old Prints and Maps*, 1965, p. 95. 252

79. The Monument of Absalom. From O. Dapper, *Beschryving . . . Palestyn*, 1677, II, p. 526. 253

80. Beth ha-Hofshit in Brook of Kidron. 254

81. Entrance to Beth ha-Hofshit. 255

82. Monument of Zechariah the prophet. 257

83. Monument of the daughter of Pharaoh. 258

84. Mount of Olives and Mount Moriah. 262

85. Pillar of Muhammad. 267

86. Stairs to the Fountain of Gihon. 275

87. Tunnel to the Pool of Siloam. 278

88. Ein Rogel. 281

89. The Mount of Olives. 286

90. The Jewish cemetery on the Mount of Olives. 290

91. The dove and the olive leaf. From J. W. Crowfoot, *Churches at Jerash*. 296

92. The ways leading to Jerusalem. From *Le Pelerin véritable de la Terre Saincte*, 1615. 300

LEGENDS OF JERUSALEM

I

JERUSALEM
—CENTER OF THE WORLD

*"Thus saith the Lord God: This is Jerusalem! I
have set her in the midst of the nations, and
countries are round about her."*

On mountain heights commanding wide horizons stands
Jerusalem—the city of God, the capital of Israel and the
sanctuary of its spiritual life, "fair in situation, the joy of
the whole earth." Jerusalem was the home of great prophets; here they expressed their inspired thoughts, which
became part of the main religions of humanity. Therefore
she is holy and is venerated by Jews, Christians, and Moslems. The ancients believed that Jerusalem is the heart
of the universe and the foundation of the whole world
(fig. 1).

FIG. 1. MAP OF THE WORLD WITH JERUSALEM AT ITS CENTER (c. 1250)

This map is attached to Latin manuscript of Book of Psalms; hence it is known as Map of Psalms. It serves to illustrate words of psalmist: "Yet God is my King of old, working salvation in the midst of the earth" (Psalms 74:22).

On the map three continents are drawn. At left, below, is Europe; at right, Africa; above, Asia; and in center of a double circle is Jerusalem—*Jherusalem*.

At right of Jerusalem: Mount Zion—*m[ons] sion*; below: Bethlehem—*be[t]lehem*; above: Jerusalem, Brook of Kidron—*torrens cedron*.

1 / JERUSALEM WAS THE BEGINNING

"The Lord by wisdom founded the earth;
By understanding He established the heavens."

Within old Jerusalem rises Mount Moriah, upon which stood the Holy Temple—the shrine of the people of Israel. On the summit lies a big rock, the Foundation Stone—in Hebrew *Even ha-Shetiyah*—the base of the whole world and its very center.

The sages of Israel commented: "And it was called the Foundation Stone, because the world was founded on it. For Isaiah the prophet said: 'Thus saith the Lord God: Behold I lay in Zion for a foundation a stone . . . a costly corner-stone of sure foundation.'"

"The Almighty, blessed be He, dropped a rock in the waters, and from thence the world expanded."

While pondering over the creation of the world, the sages asked: "From where did He create it? And the answer is 'From Zion.' For the psalmist sang: 'Out of Zion, the perfection of beauty,/God hath shined forth.'

At right of Bethlehem: Jericho—*jerico*, Well of Joseph—*puteus josef*. On east is Jordan, which, according to map, originates in mountains of Lebanon—*m[ons] liban[o]s*, from two springs: Yeor—*jor*—and Dan—*fl. dan*. Therefore, says medieval legend, river was called Jordan.

Jordan flows to Lake of Kinnereth (Sea of Galilee) where fish is drawn. Above is name Ginosar—*genesar*. On its shores are cities of Tiberius—*thiberadis*—and Bethesda—*bethesida*. At its side, Corazim—*coroza*. From Kinnereth, Jordan flows into Dead Sea—*mare mortuum*. Beneath Jordan mountain is drawn on side of Dead Sea, and it is written: "The high mountain where the Devil tempted the Lord [Jesus Christ]"—*m[ons] excelsus ubi deabolus statuir D[omi]n[u]m*. This mountain is known as Mount of the Forty, in Arabic *Jebal Karantal*. It rises above Jericho, Jordan, and Dead Sea.

On Mediterranean coast are cities of Acre—*acaron*—and Caesarea—*cesaria palestinae*. Opposite coast are several islands.

Hand-written copy of map is preserved in Library of British Museum in London.

"And when the Holy One, blessed be He, shall renew the world, He shall renew it out of Zion. For Isaiah prophesied: 'And it shall come to pass in the end of days,/That the mountain of the Lord's house shall be established as the top of the mountains,/And shall be exalted above the hills.' "[1] *

2 / MIDDLE OF THE EARTH

The sages of Israel, in the third century, made this interpretation of the prophet Ezekiel's words "that dwell in the middle of the earth": "The land of Israel—is the middle of the earth. Jerusalem—is the middle of the land of Israel. The Temple—is the middle of Jerusalem. The holy of holies—is the middle of the Temple. The holy ark—is the middle of the holy of holies. And the Stone of Foundation—is in front of the holy of holies."

In medieval maps Jerusalem is the center of the universe, and therefore it is called in Latin *Umbilicus Mundi* —"Navel of the World"[2] (fig. 2).

3 / THE NAVEL OF THE WORLD

The sages of Israel relate: "The Almighty created the world in the same manner as a child is formed in its mother's womb. Just as a child begins to grow from its navel and then develops into its full form, so the world began from its central point and then developed in all directions."

The "navel" of the world is Jerusalem, and its core is the great altar in the Holy Temple.[3]

4 / THE EYE OF THE WORLD

Rabbi Shemuel the younger, of the first century, compared the form of the world, with Jerusalem at its center, to the eye: "This world is like unto the human eye, for the white is the ocean which girds the earth; the iris is the

* Superior numerals refer to Sources of the Legends.

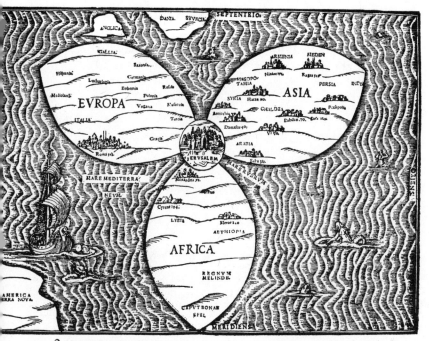

FIG. 2. WORLD IN SHAPE OF CLOVERLEAF WITH JERUSALEM IN ITS CENTER (C. 1580)

From Jerusalem, in center, the three continents spread out; right: Asia; left: Europe; below: Africa. In lower left-hand corner is America, the new land—*America, Terra Nova,* discovered about one hundred years before map was drawn. Above Europe is England—*Anglica*; next to it is Denmark—*Dania*. Between Europe and Africa is Mediterranean Sea—*Mare Mediterraneum*. Between Africa and Asia is Red Sea—*Mare Rubrum*.

earth upon which we dwell; the pupil is Jerusalem, and the image therein is the Temple of the Lord.

"May it be built speedily in our day and in the days of all Israel. Amen!"[4]

5 / WHO SET UP THE STONE?

The holy *Zohar,* the book of the mystics, relates: "When the Holy One, blessed be He, was about to create the world, He detached one precious stone from underneath His throne of glory and plunged it into the abyss; one end of it remained fastened therein, whilst the other end stood out above . . . out of which the world started, spreading itself to the right and left and into all directions.

"That stone is called in Hebrew *Shetiyah*—Foundation.

"Now the earth's expansion around the central point was complete in three concentric rings. . . .

"The second expansion embraces the whole of the land of Israel, the land which was declared holy.

"The third expansion comprehends the rest of the earth, the dwelling place of all the other nations, and the great ocean which surrounds the whole."[5]

6 / WHERE IS THE SOURCE OF SPRINGS?

Some of the wise men of Israel say that this stone was called *Shetiyah*, which in Hebrew also means "drinking," because beneath it is hidden the source of all the springs and fountains from which the world drinks its water.[*]

The psalmist refers to it in his song: "His foundation is in the holy mountains./The Lord loveth the gates of Zion/More than all the dwellings of Jacob/Glorious things are spoken of Thee, O city of God. Selah . . . All my thoughts are in thee!"[6]

7 / THE "NAME" ON THE STONE

"He who pronounces the 'Name' letter by letter forfeits his share of the world to come."

There is a Hebrew legend that the divine Name, Jehovah, was inscribed on the Foundation Stone.

In the Book of Ecclesiastes it is said: "He hath made

* See legend II:3.

everything beautiful in its time; also He hath set the world in their heart, yet so that man cannot find out the work that God hath done from the beginning even to the end."

The Aramaic translator adds: "This hints of the divine Name on the Foundation Stone.

"The divine Name was engraved on the Foundation Stone, and the Lord guarded it in great secrecy, so as not to arouse the 'evil inclination' in the hearts of men, who would desire to know, with its help, all that shall come to pass in the end of time, until eternity."

When King David had dug the foundation for the Temple, he found a stone resting on the mouth of the abyss with the divine Name on it. He put this stone into the holy of holies in the Temple. The sages of Israel began to fear lest some young men might learn the divine Name and destroy the world. To prevent this, they made two brazen lions which they placed on iron pillars by the door of the holy of holies, one on the right and the other on the left. If anyone entered and learned the divine Name, these lions would roar at him when he came out, so that through terror and fright, the Name would be utterly driven out of his mind and forgotten.

Jesus of Nazareth went secretly to Jerusalem and entered into the Temple, where he learned the holy letters of the divine Name. He wrote them on parchment, and, uttering the Name to prevent pain, he cut his flesh and hid the parchment therein. Then, again pronouncing the Name, he caused the flesh to grow together. As he left the door, the lions roared and the Name was erased from his mind. When he went outside the city, he cut his flesh again and drew out the parchment, and when he had studied its letters, he learned the Name again.

Thus was he able to perform all his miracles and wonders[7] (fig. 3).

FIG. 3. FOUNDATION STONE IN DOME OF THE ROCK
Above Foundation Stone is great dome, supported by pillars and arches.

8 / THE STONE—JACOB'S PILLAR

When Jacob the patriarch woke from his dream at Bethel, he erected a pillar to the Lord, using the stone which had been his pillow. Then he poured oil upon the top of it as a libation. The legend relates that this is the Foundation Stone. "Jacob fell down before the Stone of Foundation and prayed to the Holy One, blessed be He, saying: 'Master of the universe, if Thou shalt return me to this place in peace, then shall I offer up to Thee sacrifices of thanks.' "

The Torah records of Jacob: "And he lighted upon a certain place." That place is Jerusalem where the Temple was built; here Jacob prayed, saying in his terror: "How dreadful is this place." Why did he say this? Because he saw in his vision the Holy Temple built, destroyed, and restored to its full perfection. In addition Jacob saw two Jerusalems, one of earth and one of heaven. And he said: "Surely the Lord is in this place." He saw the divine Presence hovering over Mount Moriah, the site of the Temple, and therefore he called it Bethel—the House of God.

Many Christian pilgrims in the Middle Ages gave the name of Bethel to the Temple site in Jerusalem and believed that there the patriarch Jacob rested from his journeys and dreamt his dream. They believed, furthermore, that the Foundation Stone is the very stone which he set up. John of Würzberg, who visited the Holy Land in 1170, writes of the inscriptions on the Foundation Stone: "This is holy ground. Here he saw the ladder; here he built his altar." "Jacob, this thy land shall be, and thy children's after thee."[8]

9 / WHERE WERE THE TABLETS HEWN?

Moses the lawgiver ascended Mount Sinai to receive from the Almighty the two tablets of the covenant, as the Torah records: "Two tables of the testimony, tables of stone, written with the finger of God."

It is said that these tablets were hewn from the Foundation Stone in the Holy City (fig. 4).[9]

10 / THE HOLY ARK ON THE STONE

The elders of Israel related: "And there was a stone [in the Temple] from the time of the first prophets, and "Foundation" was its name . . . and at the beginning, the

FIG. 4. FOUNDATION STONE (VIEWED FROM ABOVE)
In Foundation Stone is hole penetrating into hole cavern (fig. 10).
At top right-hand corner is small turret (fig. 8).

holy ark rested on it. When the holy ark was removed, they used to burn incense there."

The high priest of Israel entered the holy of holies in the Temple. "Before the ark was removed, he entered and left by the light that the holy ark issued forth. And when the ark was removed, he groped his way out in the dark."[10]

11 / THE ANGEL ABOVE THE STONE

On the heights of Mount Moriah was the threshing floor of Ornan the Jebusite. Here the angel of God who was sent to destroy Jerusalem revealed himself to David the king. For David had numbered the people of Israel, and thus provoked the wrath of God.

The Book of Chronicles relates: "And David lifted up his eyes and saw the angel of the Lord standing between the earth and the heaven, having a drawn sword in his hand stretched out over Jerusalem. Then David and the elders, clothed in sackcloth, fell upon their faces.

"And David said unto God: 'Is it not I that commanded the people to be numbered? even I it is that have sinned and done very wickedly; but these sheep, what have they done? let Thy hand, I pray Thee, O Lord, my God, be against me and against my father's house.'

"Then the angel of the Lord commanded . . . that David should go up, and rear an altar unto the Lord in the threshing-floor of Ornan the Jebusite."

"And David built there an altar unto the Lord, and offered burnt-offerings and peace-offerings, and called upon the Lord; and He answered him from heaven by fire upon the altar of burnt-offering."

King Solomon, son of David, erected the Temple of the Lord over Ornan's threshing floor, as it is written in the Book of Chronicles: "Then Solomon began to build the house of the Lord at Jerusalem in mount Moriah, where [the Lord] appeared unto David his father; for which provision had been made in the Place of David, in the threshing-floor of Ornan the Jebusite."

The well-known historian of the Crusades, Wilhelm of Tyre, about 1175 describes the Temple in Jerusalem: "In the center of the Temple, within the inner row of columns, is a rock, not very high, which contains a cavern. Here it was, according to tradition, that the angel sat when he struck down the people by the Lord's command, in punishment for David's presumption in numbering them."[11]

12 / JONAH SAW THE STONE

The prophet Jonah calls out in his prayer: "And I said 'I am cast out/From before Thine eyes';/Yet I will look again/Toward Thy holy temple. . . ./I went down to the bottoms of the mountains; . . ./And my prayer came in unto Thee,/Into Thy holy temple."

When Jonah was swallowed by the fish, he had the privilege of seeing, among other things, the base of the Foundation Stone, which lies beneath the Temple of the Lord in Jerusalem.

There was a certain pearl embedded in the bowels of the fish. This pearl gave forth light for Jonah as does the sun at noontime, and illumined for him all that is in the sea and the abyss.

The fish addressed Jonah: "Do you not know that I am to be eaten by the whale today?"

Jonah replied: "Lead me to him!"

When they arrived, Jonah said to the whale: "It was because of you, to survey your abode, that I descended; for I am destined to put a rope through your tongue, raise you from the waters and sacrifice you for the great feast of the righteous in paradise." And the whale fled before Jonah.

Said Jonah to the fish: "Since I have saved you from the whale, show me all that is found in the sea and the abyss." And it showed him the Foundation Stone set in the abyss below the Temple of the Lord.

The fish said to Jonah: "Behold, you are now below the Lord's Temple. Pray, and you will be answered."

And Jonah began to pray before the Holy One, blessed be He, whereupon the Lord signaled to the fish, and it threw Jonah upon the shore.[12]

13 / THE STONE AND WEAVING

The divine blessing, emanating from the Foundation Stone, was bestowed upon Israel from the holy of holies. With the destruction of the Temple, this benediction was lost, to the lasting sorrow of Israel.

There is a legend which relates the Hebrew word *shetiyah* in the name *Even ha-Shetiyah*—Foundation Stone —to the Aramaic *shetiyah,* which means "weaving."

Accordingly, a custom grew up among Jewish women to refrain from weaving during the nine days of mourning, from the first day of the month of Ab to the ninth day (Tisha be-Av), which commemorate the destruction of the Temple. They believed that there would be no blessing on their work in these sad days. The ancients found a hint of this in the saying of the psalmist: "When the foundations are destroyed,/What hath the righteous wrought?"

The sages interpret this to mean: "Since the Temple is destroyed, what have the righteous achieved?"[13]

14 / CHERUBIM ABOVE THE STONE

The principal work of the cabalists, the *Zohar,* relates that groups of angels and cherubim hover above the Foundation Stone, and that from there all the world is blessed. "At the time of the sunrise, these cherubim stand in this place, raise their wings upward and spread them, and the sound of the melody of their wings is heard."

And what song did they sing at this hour? "They that

trust in the Lord/Are as mount Zion, which cannot be removed, but abideth forever./As the mountains are round about Jerusalem,/So the Lord is round about His people/ From this time forth and for ever."

And the stars and the planets in the heavens joined in the song.

The angels above, and Israel below, all hold fast to the stone, and it rises in heaven and rests among the righteous. And the Holy One, blessed be He, comes to frolic with them in the Garden of Eden.[14]

15 / THE CROWN ON THE STONE

*"And I will lay My vengeance upon Edom
by the hand of My people Israel."*

In the days to come there will be ten portents, presaging the arrival of the Messiah of Israel.

The seventh portent—the king of Edom shall enter Jerusalem. All the sons of Ishmael shall flee before him and go to Teiman. A great army shall be formed, headed by a man named Hoter, who shall be King. Hoter shall slay many Edomites until the king of Edom shall flee before him.

Then Hoter shall die and the king of Edom will return, for the second time, to Jerusalem. He shall enter the Temple, remove the golden crown from his head, place it upon the Foundation Stone, and say: "Lord of the universe, I have repaid what my ancestors took."

The eighth portent—the Holy One, blessed be He, shall suddenly cause Nehemiah son of Hushiel, who is the Messiah son of Joseph, to go forth. And he shall war with the king of Edom and slay him. Then he shall wear the crown returned by Edom's king to Jerusalem. And the name of Nehemiah shall go forth in the world.

The name Nehemiah means "consolation of God."[15]

II
DOME
OF THE ROCK

1 / THE FOUNDATION STONE AND PARADISE

*"Paradise longs for Jerusalem,
And Jerusalem longs for Paradise."*

The Foundation Stone is known in Arabic as *es-Sakhra* —the Rock; hence the Mosque of Omar is called *Kubbat es-Sakhra*—the Dome of the Rock (fig. 5). On the western façade of the Dome of the Rock is the following Arabic inscription on a slab of porcelain: "The Rock of the Temple —from the Garden of Eden."

The northern gate of the mosque, facing the Foundation Stone, is named the Gate of Paradise; in Arabic *Bab ej-Jinah.*

A Moslem sage relates: "The Rock of the Temple is of the stones of the Garden of Eden. At resurrection day, the Kaaba Stone, which is in holy Mecca, will go to the Foundation Stone in holy Jerusalem, bringing with it the inhabitants of Mecca, and it shall become joined to the Foundation Stone. When the Foundation Stone shall see

FIG. 5. DOME OF THE ROCK (MOSQUE OF OMAR) ON HEIGHTS
OF MOUNT MORIAH (VIEWED FROM NORTH)
Within Dome of the Rock is Foundation Stone.

the Kaaba Stone approaching, it shall cry out: 'Peace be to the great guest!'" (figs. 6 and 7).[16]

2 / THE STONE RESTS ON A WHALE

The Foundation Stone rests upon the crown of a palm, which grows by one of the rivers of Eden. By this stream sits Pharaoh's wife and Miriam, sister of Moses, in the shade of the palm, weaving garments for the dwellers of Eden, in preparation for the resurrection of the dead.

The whole world rests upon a mighty whale, whose head is at the place of the rising of the sun and whose tail is at the setting thereof. The Foundation Stone, the Rock of paradise, rests on the very center of the back of this giant whale.[17]

3 / THE STONE—SOURCE OF WATERS

Arab tradition relates that all the sources of the world's rivers and clouds lie concealed beneath "the Rock," the Foundation Stone.

The Moslem Abu-Huraira said on the authority of the prophet Muhammad: "All rivers and clouds, vapors and winds come from under the holy Rock in Jerusalem."

"Jerusalem is provided with dew and rain ever since Allah created years and days." All the fresh waters of the world have their origin under the holy Rock. Hence everybody who drinks water at night should say: "O water of the Holy City, I salute you!"* [18]

4 / THE TONGUE OF THE ROCK

When Muhammad, the prophet of Islam, rode to Jerusalem astride his marvelous mare, he perceived the Foundation Stone in the Temple, and recalled all that had befallen it: the binding of Isaac at the hands of Abraham his father, and the altar of David and King Solomon. The

* See legend I:6.

FIG. 6. DOME OF THE ROCK IN HEBREW ART (C. 1545)
Dome of the Rock mosque represents the Temple. Above dome are
the words of the prophet Haggai: "The glory of this house shall be
great, . . . saith the Lord of hosts." This picture is included in
several Hebrew books printed in seventeenth and eighteenth centuries.

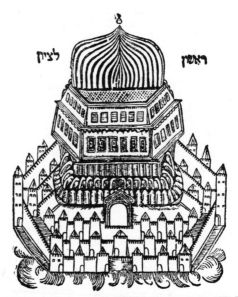

FIG. 7. DOME OF THE ROCK REPRESENTS THE TEMPLE
(C. 1750)

sight of the Rock roused his emotions and he cried out with fervor: "*Salem Aleik Ya Sakhrat Allah*—Peace be unto you, Rock of Allah!"

Upon seeing Muhammad and hearing his benediction, the Rock, too, was seized with emotion; it put forth from itself a tongue and said: "*Salam Aleik Ya Rassul Allah*— Peace be unto you, messenger of Allah!"

To this very day the tongue protrudes from the south-eastern side of the Foundation Stone. Its name in Arabic is *Lisan es-Sakhrah*—Tongue of the Rock (fig. 6).

When the hour came for Muhammad to ascend to heaven, he placed himself upon the Foundation Stone, which had begun rising toward the opened heavens. The Foundation Stone continued to rise and intended to enter heaven with the prophet. At that moment the angel Gabriel descended, clutched the Foundation Stone on both sides with all his strength, and cried: "Your place, O Stone, is on earth. You have no part in the prophet's Garden of Eden."

At the edges of the Foundation Stone may be seen long ridges. These are the traces of Gabriel's fingers as he clutched the Foundation Stone and fastened it to its place on earth.[19]

5 / MUHAMMAD'S FOOTPRINT

A small turret rises at the corner of the Foundation Stone. Within it may be seen on the Foundation Stone the imprint of Muhammad's heel. The Arabs call this mark *Kadam en-Nabi*—Heel of the Prophet—or *Kadam esh-Sharif*—Heel of the Noble One, that is, Muhammad (fig. 8).

A silver box containing three hairs is guarded in this small turret. It was given to the mosque by the Turkish sultan, Ahmad I, in 1609. Moslems say these hairs are from the beard of Muhammad. Once a year, on the twenty-

FIG. 8. SMALL TURRET AT CORNER OF FOUNDATION STONE
Within the turret is preserved a box which contains hairs attributed
to Muhammad, prophet of Islam.

seventh day of the feast month of Ramadan, these hairs
are shown to the assembled worshipers—and the sight
causes great excitement among them.* [20]

6 / ENOCH'S FOOTPRINT

On the surface of the Foundation Stone, by its margin,
a sign is carved. The Arabs believe that this is the imprint
of Idris the holy, who is sanctified by the Moslem tradition.
This sign is called in Arabic *kadam saydna Idris*—the footprint of our master Idris. Next to it is his praying place.
By the virtue of his prayer on this holy spot, Idris ascended
to heaven. Idris the holy is mentioned by the Koran, and
according to an ancient Moslem tradition he is none
other than Enoch of the Torah.

It is told in the Book of Genesis: "All the days of Enoch
were three hundred sixty and five years. And Enoch walked
with God, and he was not; for God took him."[21]

* An anonymous Christian pilgrim in the twelfth century attributes the
footprint to Jacob the patriarch; others relate it to Jesus. Seawulf writes
in 1102: "There still are seen in the rock the footsteps of our Lord."

7 / THE FOUNDATION STONE HOVERS

During the Middle Ages the legend was widespread among Jews and Arabs that the Foundation Stone hovers in the air and instills fear and astonishment into the hearts of all who see it (fig. 9).

FIG. 9. INTERIOR VIEW OF DOME OF THE ROCK
Cross-section of mosque, from north to south: under dome are Foundation Stone—the Rock—and cavern in the Rock (fig. 10).

The Moslem judge Mujir ed-Din, an inhabitant of Jerusalem, bore witness about 1496 that a certain Arab who lived at the end of the eleventh century saw the Foundation Stone hovering in the air.

A Karaite voyager, Samuel son of David, who visited Jerusalem in 1641, tells of the hovering Foundation Stone in the Dome of the Rock: "And it is said that there is within it a big stone, known as the Foundation Stone, which hovers between heaven and earth. In recent times walls were built surrounding the Foundation Stone, but not touching it. And the reason for building these walls, it is said, was that pregnant women, upon perceiving the hovering stone, would miscarry. And therefore the walls were raised."

Rabbi Moses Hagiz, a Jerusalemite of the seventeenth century, describes the Dome of the Rock thus: "Within it a stone hovers in the air, known by us as the Foundation Stone. Hence, greater sanctity is observed in that chamber and one is forbidden to enter it, if only for the purpose of lighting the oil candles which burn there day and night."* [22]

8 / THE STONE AND MESSIAH

If the Foundation Stone which hovers in the air should fall to the surface of the earth, it would be a sign and an omen that the Messiah is approaching, bringing redemption to Israel, his people.

Rabbi Binyamin Lilienthal, who went to the Holy Land in 1847, writes his impressions of his visit to Jerusalem and to the site of the Holy Temple on which a mosque, the Dome of the Rock, has been erected. He says: "In one of the mosque's hall there is, according to the general belief, the Foundation Stone, which is not fastened but is suspended above the floor. The Turks hold that when the stone falls, it will be the sign that the Messiah comes. Therefore they [the Turks] have built it a base and a support. And thus do the Turks hope to prevent the advent of the Messiah of Israel."[23]

* The Samaritan legend tells of Ahidan, the grandson of Tubal-Cain, who is mentioned in the Torah. Ahidan, they say, built Zion: "And he placed there a stone suspended [in the air] for worship." Maimonides tells of a temple in the land of Babylon in which was a golden image in the form of the sun. "This image was suspended between earth and heaven." A similar legend exists among the Arabs concerning the grave of Muhammad, in the city of Medina, in Arabia. The grave reputedly hovers in the air, between heaven and earth.

9 / THE HOLY CAVERN

A small cavern is carved into the Foundation Stone. It is entered by descending several stairs from the hall of the Dome of the Rock. Arabs indicate various spots in the cave where important personages in Israel's history have worshiped. They believe that their souls gather here from time to time to pray. In consequence, the cave plays an important role in their lives, and many Arabs come here to supplicate Allah, the merciful and compassionate (fig. 10).

One corner marks a place of worship named after the

FIG. 10. HOLY CAVERN IN FOUNDATION STONE IN DOME OF THE ROCK
In cavern are places of prayer named for the patriarch Abraham, King David, King Solomon, the prophet Elijah, and others.

patriarch Abraham, another after King David. Nearby are worshiping places bearing the names of King Solomon, the prophet Elijah, and the angel Gabriel. There is a depression in the cave's ceiling which was formed, Arabs say, by the head of Muhammad as he prayed in the cave.

David ha-Reubeni, who came from Arabia and proclaimed himself the Messiah of Israel, visited the Holy Land at the beginning of the Turkish reign. In 1523 he entered the Dome of the Rock, and he relates: "When I came to the sanctuary, all the Ishmaelite guardians came to bow before me and to kiss my feet, and said to me: 'Enter, O blessed of the Lord, our Lord, the son of our Lord!'

"And the two chiefs among them came and took me to the cavern which is in the Foundation Stone and said to me: 'Here prayed Elijah the prophet, and here King David; in this place prayed King Solomon, and in that, the patriarchs Abraham and Isaac; and here prayed Muhammad!'

"I said to the chieftains: 'Now that I know all this, go your way, for I wish to pray here alone.' I remained in the Temple, and I fasted five weeks; no bread did I eat, and no water passed my lips, except on the eve of Sabbath" (fig. 11).[24]

10 / THE WELL OF THE SOULS

In the floor of the holy cavern in the Foundation Stone, which serves as a prayer place for the Moslems, there is a big round marble slab. It is said that this slab rests upon the entrance to another cave, sealed and hidden in the depths. All who step on the slab hear a dull echo emanating from the hollow cave. The Arabs call it *Bir al-Aruah*— Well of the Souls or Spirits. They say that here the souls of the dead gather to pray and worship.

Since all who descended into the cave immediately perished, it was sealed up. Rabbi David ben-Zimra

FIG. 11. MOSLEM CHIEFTAINS (C. 1600)
These chieftains were guardians of the Temple site, Jerusalem.

(Radbaz), who lived in Jerusalem in the sixteenth century, tells: "A cave is to be found under the Dome [of the Rock], into which the first kings sent their men, and they perished. And then it was sealed with earth."

It is said that in this sealed cave were hidden many of the treasures of the Temple. In 1911, during the scientific excavations in the city of David, at the edge of Mount Moriah, a rumor spread that the English excavators had penerated at night, by hidden labyrinths, into the sealed cave in the depths of the Foundation Stone, and had absconded with the Temple treasures. The rumor caused great excitement in Jerusalem for many days.[25]

11 / THE STONE OF EDEN

In the floor of the Dome of the Rock, at the side of the Foundation Stone, a square green slab of jasper was inserted. The Arabs call it the Stone of Eden, because it rests above one of the gates to the Garden of Eden. The entrance to the mosque facing the stone is therefore called the Gate of the Garden of Eden—in Arabic, *Bab ej-Jinah* (fig. 12).

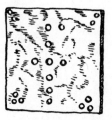

FIG. 12. STONE OF GARDEN OF EDEN (1900)
Stone is almost square. Its length is about half a meter. It has nineteen holes.

There are nineteen holes in the stone which apparently once served as a place to nail a plaque to. The nails still remain in several holes. The stone possibly dates back to the Crusades in the twelfth century and held a plaque sanctified in Christian tradition.

When Muhammad appeared in Jerusalem and entered the Temple, he put nineteen gold nails into the Stone of Eden as a memorial of his visit and set the angel Gabriel to guard them, saying to him: "Remember that should all these nails be removed, the world would return to nothingness. Guard them well!"

But the accursed Satan, desiring the destruction of the world, would steal in from time to time and remove a nail. At length he succeeded, by his cunning, in removing many of them. But when he came to remove the sixteenth nail, the angel Gabriel felt his presence, attacked him, and drove him away. In his bewilderment and haste, Satan withdrew only half a nail—and three and a half nails remained in the stone.

Others say that Satan withdrew the nails while attempting to raise the stone in order to enter the Garden of Eden.

The Arab judge Mujir ed-Din, who lived in Jerusalem at the end of the fifteenth century, gives the Stone of Eden the Arabic name *Balattat es-Saudah*—the Black Slab. He says that the grave of Solomon lies beneath this slab.

A Moslem pilgrim who visited Jerusalem in the seventeenth century, Abd al-Ghani al-Nablusi, tells us: "And we stood upon the black slab and saw silver nails fixed in it. People believe that one nail disappears yearly, and that when all of them shall have disappeared, the eternal resurrection shall have come. It is also called the Stone of the Garden of Eden."

During World War I, in 1916, Jamal Pasha, Turkish high commissioner and commander of Turkish forces in Palestine, removed the Stone of Eden from the Dome of the Rock. Its whereabouts are now unknown.[26]

12 / WHEN THE CANDELABRUM FELL

In the Middle Ages there hung in the Dome of the Rock a large, beautiful candelabrum with hundreds of branches. During the hours of prayer it would illuminate the whole mosque brightly. In 1060, when Moslems ruled in Palestine, the candelabrum suddenly fell, and all five hundred branches broke into splinters. The Moslems interpreted this as an evil omen.

About forty years later, Jerusalem was conquered by the Crusaders, and the Dome of the Rock mosque was converted into a Christian church, called *Templum Domini* —Temple of our Lord (Jesus).[27]

13 / WHY DOES THE DOME TARNISH?

Green is the holy color of Islamic tradition. Moslems whose headgear is a green turban claim to be able to trace their origin back to the prophet Muhammad. The Moslems are accustomed to painting the domes of their mosques green. This is also the color of the dome crowning the Great Mosque in the city of Acre (Accho) on the coast.

It is told that the Dome of the Rock, which is erected on the site of the Temple of the Jews, was painted green when it was built. It gradually began to tarnish and blacken. The legend explains this as a sign of mourning for the destruction of the Holy Temple, which in ancient times had stood in its place with all its splendor.[28]

14 / THE CRESCENT ON THE DOME

The round shape of the crescent, symbol of Islam, is fixed atop the Dome of the Rock. Legend says that occasionally the crescent turns of itself and changes its direction. And this is an ominous portent.

Rabbi Moses Bassola, who visited the Holy Land in 1522, in the time of the Turks, reported that the "rumor concerning the crescent is, that an overturned crescent, facing south, protrudes from a big column of metal at the head of a dome which the Arabs have in the Temple. It is said that during the Feast of Tabernacles [Sukkoth] in 1519 it turned eastward. The Arabs believed this to be a portentous omen. They attempted to turn it southward, in the direction of Mecca, the holy city of Moslems in Arabia, and a tree, growing in the Temple court since the days of Muhammad, fell. Thus have I heard."

David ha-Reubeni, a false Messiah of Israel, went to Jerusalem from Arabia. He was on his way to Rome to petition the pope for help in his endeavor to restore the Jewish people to their land. In 1523, he entered the Dome of the Rock, and he relates:

"Now on the top of the dome there is a crescent which faces westward. On the first day of the Feast of Pentecost [Shebuoth], this crescent was seen to face the east, and when the Arabs saw this, they shouted in great alarm. I asked them, 'Why do you shout?' They answered, 'Because of our sins this crescent has turned toward the east, which is an evil omen to the Arabs.'

"A workman climbed to the dome and turned the crescent to its former position, but on the next day it was facing the east. And the Arabs continued to shout and to weep as they vainly tried to turn the crescent.

"Then I knew that it was time to leave Jerusalem, for the wise men had told me, 'When you behold this sign, it is time to proceed to Rome.' "

A Christian traveler who visited Jerusalem in 1652 tells of the crescent having changed its position, and of the fear this instilled in the inhabitants of Jerusalem: "The leaden crescent on the summit of the dome of their Great Mosque—an object large, thick, massive, weighing more than three hundred pounds, and so firmly fixed that neither winds nor storms can move it—on this day, ninth of April, it had of its own accord turned four times from south to west, and had been restored as many times to its former position by a dervish who had ascended for this purpose.

"A council (it was alleged) had been held to determine the significance of this miracle. Some had supposed that God and Muhammad were wroth against them [the Moslems] because they had allowed the monks to build [a convent], and that they needs must demolish the whole to avert the threats and the punishments of heaven.

"Others said that this prodigy had yet a further significance—that it was a promise that their [Turkish] empire —so long flourishing in the east—was now to stretch to the west; that all Christians were to become Turks; and that they should begin with those who were in Jerusalem— compel them to accept their law, or else expel and exterminate them.

FIG. 13. SOUTHERN ENTRANCE OF DOME OF THE ROCK
Above man's head there is black-bordered stone set into wall of mosque. On it is image of birds turned to stone by King Solomon (fig. 14).

"Yet another party said that the monks were whispering in the convent that it was a good omen—that the [Turkish] empire was coming to an end; that the Westerners and the Franks were to arrive in a short time to make themselves masters of the Holy Land and of the whole East."[29]

15 / THE BIRDS WHICH TURNED INTO STONE

A black-bordered slab, veined with red- and rose-colored lines in the likeness of two birds facing each other, is fixed on the entrance to the Dome of the Rock (figs. 13 and 14).

Why were these birds transformed into stone?

FIG. 14. TWO BIRDS TURNED INTO STONE
Stone tablet is set into wall of Dome of the Rock to right of southern entrance (see fig. 13).

King Solomon, wisest of mankind, understood the language of all animals, as it is told in the Book of Kings: "He spoke also of beasts, and of fowl." One day, he sat at the entrance to his palace on the Temple Mount, delighting in the bright sky and clear daylight. Before him two cooing birds caressed each other, twittering merrily.

As the king looked up he heard one bird say to his spouse: "Who is this man seated here?" And she answered: "This is the king whose name and fame fill the world." Then the bird answered in mocking pride, "And do they call even him mighty? How is his power sufficient for all these palaces and fortresses? Did I so desire I could overthrow them in a second by fluttering one wing."

His spouse encouraged him, saying: "Do so, and show your valor and power, if you have the strength to carry out your words."

And Solomon, listening to the conversation in astonishment, signaled to the bird to approach, and asked him the cause of his overweening pride. Terrified, the trembling bird answered the august king: "Let my Lord the king grant me forgiveness out of his loving-kindness and goodness of heart. I am naught but a poor powerless bird who can do him no evil. All that I said was only to please my wife and raise myself in her esteem." And Solomon laughed to himself and sent the bird back to his spouse.

She, meanwhile, stood on the roof waiting for her mate to return and tell her why the king had sent for him. When he came back, she asked excitedly: "What did the king want?" And his chest swelling with pride, he answered: "The king heard my words and entreated me not to bring destruction upon his court and not to carry out my purpose."

When Solomon heard this, he grew wroth with the brazen birds and changed them both into stone slabs, to warn others to refrain from vain bragging and empty boasting, and to teach womenfolk not to incite their chosen ones in their vanity to undertake foolish and foolhardy deeds.[30]

16 / THE CANDLES AT THE TEMPLE SITE

In the Dome of the Rock there are many lamps and candles which serve the worshipers during the nights, especially those of feasts and holidays. Hebrew legend relates that on the night of the ninth of the month Ab (Tisha be-Av), the day commemorating the destruction of the Temple, the lamps would be extinguished of themselves, and all efforts to relight them would be of no avail.

Rabbi Meshullam of Volterra (Italy), who visited the

Holy Land in 1481, writes about the Dome of the Rock mosque: "There are Arab servants who keep themselves in strict purity. Inside the mosque they light seven candles. Remember, gentle readers, that what I am about to relate is no myth. Every year when the Jews go to their synagogues on the eve of Tisha be-Av, all candles in the mosque go out of their own accord, and it is impossible to rekindle them. And the Arabs know when it is Tisha Be-Av, and therefore they keep it, as the Jews do. This is clear and well known to everybody, without the slightest doubt."

In 1489 Rabbi Obadiah of Bertinoro, Italy, writes from Jerusalem: "You ask me about the miracles which are said to take place at the Temple Mount. . . . What can I tell you, my brother, about them?

"I have not seen them. As for the lights on the site of the Temple, of which you have heard that they always cease to burn on the ninth of Ab, I have been told that this is the case, but I cannot speak with certainty respecting it."[31]

17 / SIGHS FROM THE TEMPLE SITE

Rabbi Joseph, an inhabitant of Jerusalem, in his Hebrew book *Kessef Razuf* (Pure Silver) reports: "When I was in the Holy City, in Jerusalem, may she be built and established, sitting quietly and peacefully at home, I heard it said that on the eve of the ninth day of the month Ab, a voice of mourning and sighing goes forth from the Temple that all may hear.

"I wanted to hear for myself, so after prayers on the eve of the ninth of Ab, I sat down at my window which overlooks the Wailing Wall. And then I heard the noise of great lamenting issuing out of the Temple, and my hair stood on end, and I was seized with much weeping until I fainted."

In a letter sent by the heads of the Eastern Jewish communities, it is related: "Let your brothers tell you of the signs of our redemption in words that are good and consoling and faithful, that in the year 5214 after the creation of the world [1454 C.E.], one night in the month of Ab—may God turn the sorrow of Ab into happiness!—we heard many loud voices from the mountain on which stood the Temple. And the Arabs, too, heard them and were greatly frightened, for never had they heard any like them. Many Jews understood the message in these voices, and they said that they heard in them the words of Isaiah the prophet: 'Awake, awake, put on strength, . . ./Awake, as in the days of old, The generations of ancient times. . . ./Awake, awake, Put on thy strength, O Zion;/Put on thy beautiful garments, O Jerusalem, the holy city.' "[32]

18 / VOICES FROM THE TEMPLE SITE

Many signs will announce the coming of the Messiah of Israel: "And it was in the year five thousand one hundred and fifty-three after the creation of the world, in the year one thousand three hundred and fifteen after the destruction of the Temple [1393 C.E.], may it quickly be rebuilt even in our own lifetime . . . and there was heard the voice of heaven crying out from the Temple: 'Leave you my house! Let my sons return!'

"The Ishmaelites were smitten with fear . . . and from amongst them, one arose and descended into the cavern that was nearby and said that he saw three old men, wrapped in prayer shawls. . . . He fell at their feet. . . . They said: 'Arise,' and he arose.

"He asked them: 'Who may you be?' and they answered: 'Of the sons of Israel are we; and now, go and tell the Ishmaelites to leave the Temple, for their time is up. Tell them that thus were you commanded by Abraham the Hebrew, and Moses the lawgiver, and Elijah the prophet!' "[33]

III

THE TEMPLE COURT TODAY

1 / SOLOMON'S STUDY HOUSE

In the southern section of the Temple court there stands a large mosque called, in Arabic, al-Aksa. Jews call this mosque by the Hebrew name: *Midrash Shelomo ha-Melech* —King Solomon's Study House. In that place he used to study the Torah, and there he composed his Song of Songs, Proverbs, and Ecclesiastes (fig. 15).

Why was it named al-Aksa—the Farther? In the Koran, in the chapter "Night Journey (The Children of Israel)" is written: "Praise be unto Him who transported His servant [Muhammad] by night from the sacred temple [mosque of Mecca in Arabia] to the farther temple. The circuit of which we have blessed, that we might show Him some of our signs."

Moslem tradition has it that the farther temple mentioned is one located on Mount Moriah, and it is "farther" in relation to the central mosque in Mecca. The words of the chapter "Night Journey" are inscribed on the exterior of the Dome of the Rock.

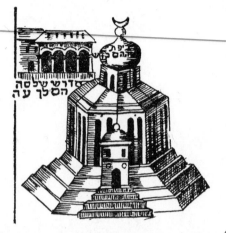

FIG. 15. DOME OF THE ROCK AS THE TEMPLE (BETH HA-
MIKDASH) AND AL-AKSA MOSQUE AS KING SOLOMON'S STUDY
HOUSE (MIDRASH SHELOMO) (C. 1537)

Muhammad rode from the central mosque in Mecca to
the farther mosque in Jerusalem on his winged steed, al-
Burak—Lightning, so named because of his swift pace.

This bears resemblance to the story of King Shabur of
Persia, who promised to send to the Messiah of Israel,
instead of a donkey, a lightning horse (*susa beraka*).*[34]

2 / BETWEEN THE PILLARS

In the al-Aksa mosque there is a large prayer hall, in
which there are two rows of pillars. In one part of the hall
stand two pillars, very close to each other (fig. 16).

It was believed that anyone who could squeeze through

---

* When Muhammad went to the farther mosque, he left his horse,
al-Burak, in the narrow street of the Wailing Wall, which thereby got
its Arabic name: *Hosh al-Burak*—Courtyard of al-Burak. At the side of
the Wailing Wall, buried and concealed in the ground, is a small gate
called by the Arabs *Bab al-Burak*—Gate of al-Burak. The ring to which
al-Burak was tied was formerly displayed here. The steps leading to the
Dome of the Rock from the eastern side are called: *Daraj al-Burak*—
Stairs of al-Burak.

FIG. 16. PAIR OF PILLARS IN AL-AKSA MOSQUE

the narrow space between them was assured of a place in the Garden of Eden. Naturally, many came to try their luck; with great effort, some succeeded in squeezing through.

Once a Moslem of Jerusalem went to al-Aksa to pray, and like most of the faithful, he was very anxious to know his lot in the next world. He girded his loins and squeezed between the pair of pillars. But the man was too fat, and the effort sapped all his strength. Right in the middle, between the pillars, the pressure was too great, and his soul left his body. But where did it go—to the Garden of Eden or, heaven forbid, to hell?

Since then, bars have been erected between the pillars, and no one may try to assure his fate in the world to come by trying to squeeze through them.[35]

3 / PRAYER PLACE OF ZECHARIAH

In the hall of the al-Aksa mosque, a prayer niche in the wall is named after Zechariah the prophet—in Arabic *a-Nabi Zakariah*. It recalls the fate of the prophet Zechariah in ancient days.

The Book of Chronicles tells of Zechariah's death in the courtyard of the Temple: "And the spirit of God clothed Zechariah the son of Jehoiada the priest; and he stood above the people, and said unto them: 'Thus saith God: Why transgress ye the commandments of the Lord, that ye cannot prosper? because ye have forsaken the Lord, He hath also forsaken you.' And they conspired against him, and stoned him with stones at the commandment of the king in the court of the house of the Lord."

On the day Zechariah was slain, his murderers committed seven transgressions: they killed a priest and a prophet; they profaned the Sabbath and the Day of Atonement; they worshiped heathen idols; they desecrated the Temple; and they neglected the perpetual light.

An anonymous Christian traveler who visited Jerusalem in 333 tells us: "And in the building itself, where stood the Temple which Solomon built, they say that the blood of Zacharias which was shed upon the stone pavement before the altar remains to this day. There are also to be seen the marks of the nails in the shoes of the soldiers who slew him, throughout the whole enclosure, so plain that you would think they were impressed upon wax."

The Christian scholar Jerome, who lived in Bethlehem in the fourth century, and translated the Bible into Latin, tells about red stones said to be stained with the blood of Zechariah, shown between the ruins of the Temple and the altar or in the outlets of the gates which lead to the Pool of Siloam in the Brook of Kidron.*[36]

4 / KING DAVID'S TRIBUNAL

East of the Dome of the Rock is a small domed building which is known in Arabic as *Mahkamet en-Nebi Daud*— the Tribunal of the Prophet David. It is also called *Kubbat es-Silsila*—Dome of the Chain, to commemorate the chain that once hung there, which was used by David to test the honesty of the people who stood before him for judgment (fig. 17).

In ancient times, when Israel dwelt in his land, a great chain was suspended from this dome. Litigants or witnesses about to take an oath took hold of this chain; if any man lied a link would fall from the chain, so that the falsehood stood revealed.

Once there was a dispute between two men. One had left a number of gold coins with the other. When he went to get them back, the other refused to return them, saying they had already been returned. So they brought the matter to court. The judge heard their pleas and told them to come to the tribunal of the Dome of the Chain the next day in order to be sworn.

The defendant knew of the chain and planned a trick.

---

* The Christian tradition calls the father of Zechariah who was killed in the Temple by the name of Barachias: "The blood of Zacharias son of Barachias, whom ye slew between the temple and the altar." This refers either to the prophet mentioned in the Bible, or to the Zechariah son of Baruch killed in the Temple by the Zealots, during the Jewish revolt against Rome.

The Moslem tradition used the name a-Nabi Zakariah—the prophet Zechariah—for both the Zechariah mentioned in the Bible and the Zacharias who was the father of John the Baptist, mentioned in Christian sources and also in the Koran: Zakaria ibn Yahia. Christians tell that this Zacharias and his wife, Elisabeth, lived in the town of Ain-Kerem, near Jerusalem.

FIG. 17. TRIBUNAL OF KING DAVID ON MOUNT MORIAH
At left: part of Dome of the Rock, with its eastern entrance.

He pierced a hole in his walking staff and placed in it the requisite number of gold coins. The next day, when he had to take the oath, he gave his staff to the plaintiff for a while and, taking hold of the chain, said: "I swear on my honor that I have put the money into the hands of this my comrade."

The judge, seeing nothing happen to the chain, was about to pronounce judgment in favor of the perjurer when a voice from heaven was heard, crying, "Let the chain be hid from this day forth, that it should not cause justice to stumble by reason of the cunning and deceit of men."*37

* The legend says that the chain is concealed in the village Gush Halab (Jish), in the upper Galilee. In commemoration of the chain, the

5 / THE SCALES OF JUDGMENT

On the heights of Mount Moriah, at the top of the steps
leading up to the Dome of the Rock, stand high pillars
which support beautiful arches. The Arabs call these
pillars and arches *al-Mizan*—the Balances (fig. 18).

FIG. 18. PILLARS WITH ARCHES—THE BALANCES
Behind pillars Dome of the Rock with its crescent can be seen.

The Arabs say that on the day of the resurrection of the
dead, the great Judgment Day, when all the souls will
gather on Mount Moriah to stand before the seat of
justice, from these pillars will hang huge balances, on

most important gate leading to the Temple area today is still called in
Arabic *Bab es-Silsila*—Gate of the Chain. Likewise, the marketplace
which starts at this gate and extends westward is known in Arabic as *Suk
es-Silsila*—Market of the Chain.

whose scales will be weighed the good and evil deeds of each and every one; on the right-hand scale, the good deeds, and on the left, the evil. Blessed is the man whose good deeds will tip the right scale in his favor.

"One whose scales are heavy/A pleasant life shall spend/But one whose scales are light/To the abyss shall descend."[38]

6 / THE THRONE OF SOLOMON

In the Temple area there is a small chamber called in Arabic *Kursat Sulaiman*—the Throne of Solomon. The chamber is sacred to the Arabs, who come here and tie pieces of cloth to the windows, as is the custom in their holy places. These pieces are torn from the clothing of sick people, and are tied to the window in the belief that this will bring about a cure for their illness (fig. 19).

It is said that the royal throne of King Solomon once stood there. When the day of Solomon's death drew near he feared that it might become known to the demons who served him. So he seated himself on the throne and, leaning on his staff, passed into eternal slumber. All who approached thought the king slept. Many days passed. At length a worm came along; it gnawed through the staff until it was entirely consumed within; the staff gave way, and the body toppled from the throne. And only then did the people know that King Solomon was dead.

The staff of Solomon was made from the wood of a carob tree, which is called in Hebrew *harub*. One day King Solomon noticed in his garden a young plant unknown to him. He said to the plant, "Of what use art thou?" "To destroy thy works," replied the plant. "What is your name?" "*Harub* [carob]," answered the plant. In Hebrew *harub* means "destroyed."

Solomon dug up the carob and planted it in an isolated corner of his garden, to prevent its doing any harm. When

FIG. 19. ROOM BUILT ON SITE OF THRONE OF KING SOLOMON

it was full grown, he cut it down and fashioned it into a staff for himself. This is the staff he was leaning on when he passed into eternal slumber. And now that the worm had hollowed the staff and the body of Solomon had fallen to the ground, the demons knew that the king whom they had feared was dead. They therefore proceeded to destroy his works.[39]

In a corner of the Temple courtyard, by the side of the Al-Aksa mosque, there is a big building completely buried underground. The Jews call it Solomon's Stables—in Arabic *Astabel Sulaiman.** In these stables, King Solomon kept his numerous horses and his magnificent chariots.

Narrow steps lead down to the gloom of the long halls below, which stretch over a great area. Square pillars support the roof; some of them are perforated in their corners, and through these holes, it is told, the horses' reins were tied. In the Middle Ages there were shown, too, the troughs from which the horses fed.

In bygone days Jewish and Christian pilgrims entered Solomon's Stables through a small gap opening outside the Temple area. A Christian monk, Felix Fabri, who visited this spot in 1483, tells of the Jews who guided him in this way. They put up heaps of stones to record their visits and told him that they expected redemption to come soon to the Holy Land. Jewish pilgrims from faraway countries do the same and hope to come to this place after the great resurrection in the end of time. The heaps of stones will bear witness to their pilgrimages and to the prayers they offered in these holy places.† [40]

8 / THE CRYPT OF THE DEVILS

An anonymous French pilgrim from Bordeaux, France, who visited Jerusalem in 333, describes the buildings in the Temple courtyard which existed in his time, and says: "There is also here a crypt, in which Solomon used to tor-

---

*The Arabic word *astabel* is derived from the Latin *stabulum*, meaning "stables." The crusaders called Solomon's Stables by the name *Stabulum Solomonis.*

† A stone projects from the wall in Solomons Stables. The Arabs name it *Mahed Issa*—the Cradle of Jesus. In the Middle Ages it was commonly believed that Jesus' cradle was here, although it was well known that it stood in the Church of the Nativity, in Bethlehem, where it is held in great veneration by the Christians.

ture devils. . . . There also is the chamber in which he sat and wrote the *Book of Wisdom*. This chamber is covered with a single stone."[41]

9 / THE FRAGMENT OF THE ROCK

In the Temple court there is a small, round, domed building. From its floor projects a small rock. Therefore

FIG. 20. DOME OF FRAGMENT OF THE ROCK
This dome is built in the Temple court. In background are Dome of the Rock and the Balances (on left).

the building is called in Arabic *Kubbat es-Sakhra a-Saghire* —the Dome of the Small Rock, or *Kubbat Shakfet es-Sakhra*—the Dome of the Fragment of the Rock (figs. 20 and 21).

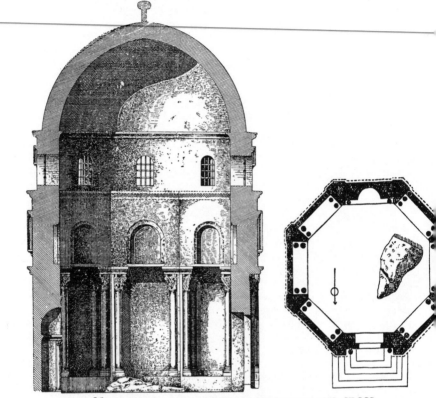

FIG. 21. DOME OF FRAGMENT OF THE ROCK AND CROSS-SECTION OF MOSQUE
Left: under dome, above floor, fragment of the Rock protrudes; right: plan of dome and fragment of the Rock.

After the capture of Jerusalem, Nebuchadnezzar, king of Babylon, entered the Temple ruins and found the Foundation Stone before him. He was excited by its grandeur and holiness and ordered his men to break off a fragment of the rock and take it to Babylon with the Temple treasures, in memory of his glorious victory in the Holy City of Jerusalem.

When the Jews returned from Babylon, they brought

with them the sacred vessels of the Temple, together with this fragment, and bore them to Mount Moriah in great joy.

There they set the rock on the very spot where King Solomon had stood and prayed when he dedicated the holy sanctuary to God. Therefore the site is sometimes called in Arabic *Kubbat Sulaiman*—Dome of Solomon.[42]

10 / THE WELL OF THE LEAF

In the Temple area are to be found great wells and cisterns which hold rainwater. Near the al-Aksa mosque there is a big well called in Arabic *Bir al-Waraka*—Well of the Leaf.

Why is it so called?

Once a sheikh was drawing water from this well, when his bucket slipped from his hand and fell to the bottom. Since there was only a little water in the well, he descended in order to search for the bucket. After wading for some distance along the bed of the well, he suddenly saw an opening, from which a bright light streamed. He passed through and walked on, deriving great pleasure from all he saw, till he came to the gate to Eden. Trembling, he entered, hastily plucked a leaf from a tree, and then rushed forth again and returned to his friends. He told them all that had befallen him and showed the leaf as evidence. Wise men examined the leaf and found it was of a kind known to grow only on the trees of Eden. So others went down the same well to discover the gate to Eden, but they did not succeed in finding it.

And the well has been called the Well of the Leaf ever since.[43]

11 / WEEPING FROM THE WELL

Some of the wells in the Temple court are very ancient. Legend tells us that Jews threw themselves into one of these wells at the time of the Temple's destruction, to escape the wrath of the enemy.

In 1481 a rabbi wrote from Jerusalem, describing buildings in the Temple yard: "There is a well where youths and maidens cast themselves to evade the sword. The Arabs tell that even today, in the night of the ninth of the month of Ab [the memorial day of the destruction of the Temple], a great weeping is heard from this well."[44]

12 / THE POOL OF ISRAEL

Outside the wall surrounding the Temple courtyard, there is a large cistern which has been filled in the past decades with debris and garbage. The Arabs call it *Birkat Israil*—the Well of Israel. Near the cistern is a gate to the courtyard called in Hebrew *Shaar Shivtei Yisrael*—the Gate of the Tribes of Israel.

Moslem geographers in the Middle Ages said that the cistern was built by King Solomon. Ali al-Hiransi, who visited Jerusalem in 1173, tells of the Well of the Sons of Israel: "It is told that Nebuchadnezzar filled it with the heads of the children of Israel that he slaughtered."[45]

13 / THE HOLY NETTLE TREE

In addition to the olive and cypress trees which grow on Mount Moriah in the Temple area, there are also a few nettle trees (*Celtis australis*). They are lofty, with handsome crowns and longish pointed leaves. Their fruit is small and grape-shaped (fig. 22).

The first foundations of the Temple as laid out by King Solomon were destroyed by some hidden hand. He laid them anew and found them destroyed again. This puzzled the king sorely, and only after much investigation did he discover that the evil eye rested upon his work and that evil spirits were wreaking vengeance upon him. He sought for means to keep these at a distance from

Mount Moriah. By planting nettle trees round the area he succeeded in driving away the demons, for such trees ward off the evil eye.

Today you still find Arabs plucking small twigs of the nettle trees and making charms out of them. The most

FIG. 22. BRANCH OF NETTLE TREE
Scientific name of nettle tree is *Celtis australis*; Hebrew name *maish*; Arabic name *meis*. On branch are berries; at right, its flowers are shown.

effective is one plucked after sunset on the twenty-seventh day of the fast month of Ramadan. The twig is usually placed in a blue bead and hung as a charm around the neck of man or beast.

At night you sometimes see an Arab traveling with his donkey over a forsaken road, wearing a bead containing such a charm. And if fear seizes him and he imagines that demons are coming after him, he recites these words: "O demon! O demon! Dost thou not see the bead and the twig of the nettle tree?"[46]

IV
GATES OF
THE TEMPLE COURT

1 / PRAYER IN THE GATES

Today there are several gates opening into the Temple court on Mount Moriah. Some of them are built on the site of gates which were famous in ancient times.

It was the custom of Jewish pilgrims in the Middle Ages to stand outside the Temple court and to pray at the entrances leading to it. The Arab masters of the area did not permit non-Moslems to enter the court or to view the holy shrines. Thus the worshipers halted at the gates and gazed from afar at the site of the Temple, the heart and soul of the people of Israel. Today the names of many medieval Jewish pilgrims may still be seen engraved on the gates (fig. 23).

Jews and Karaites used to offer special prayers in these gates, in memory of the Temple—Mother of Israel. "We come to learn how fares our mother./Standing on her threshold—we weep./There the guards find us—they beat us and wound us./'Away, defiled ones!,' they call./We lift our voices in mourning/For the desecration of Mount

FIG. 23. JEWISH WORSHIPER PRAYING OPPOSITE TEMPLE
COURT
Within court is Dome of the Rock, built on site of Temple.

Moriah,/For our mother—desolate/And none remain to revive her."

This is one of the prayers that the Jews used to recite on beholding the site of the Temple, the inheritance of Israel, in the hands of strangers:

"I offer thanks to Thee, O Lord my God, for Thou hast given me life and filled my days with grace; for Thou hast given me strength, and I am privileged to ascend and view Thy holy Temple, which all Thy people Israel wait to see rebuilt, and hope to ascend unto it, to visit in the shade of its walls, and to roll in its dust and ashes.

"And upon me, Thy servant, son of Thy handmaid, Thou hast bestowed the blessing of seeing that for which I have waited, and I have gazed upon what I longed for, and have sung what I yearned to, and I have had the privilege to stand opposite Thy Holy Temple. And although it is desolate, it is perfected by Thy holiness, and glorified by Thy divine Presence; and if strangers have defiled it with their abominations and have soiled it with their filth, yet is it pure with Thy nobleness, and exalted above all places.

"May it be Thy will, O Lord my God, and God of my fathers, that Thou shalt number me among those privileged to view the fulfillment of Thy promises, and gaze upon Thy pleasantness, so that I may see Thy Temple built and perfected, praised and gloried. . . . And may the remnants of Thy people be gathered and the dispersed be united, so that they may attain their desires, and ascend together unto this place, which is the chosen of the world . . . unique among sites, pleasure of souls, sanctified above all holiness."[47]

2 / THE GATE OF MERCY

"Thus saith the Lord:
I am returned to Jerusalem
with mercies My house shall be built in it."

In the wall which surrounds the Temple area a closed gate can be seen. It faces east toward the Mount of Olives. The Jews call it *Shaar ha-Rehamim*—the Gate of Mercy—and the Christians call it the Golden Gate. This gate has been blocked for many generations (figs. 24 and 25).

The Jewish traveler Rabbi Petahia, who visited Jerusalem in 1187, relates the following: "At Jerusalem there is a gate, and its name is the Gate of Mercy. The gate is full of stone and lime. No Jew, much less a gentile, is permitted to go there. One day the gentiles wished to open this gate, but the whole of Palestine shook from one end to the other, and there arose a great tumult in the city until they ceased. There is a tradition among the Jews that the divine Presence first departed through this gate, and that by the same gate the divine Presence will return.

When the resurrection comes, those who arise will see distinctly the eternal Spirit returning to Zion through that gate, and therefore it is on this spot that prayers are offered.

FIG. 24. GATE OF MERCY (GOLDEN GATE)
In east wall of Temple court. Gate has two sealed entrances; at right, Entrance of Mercy; at left, Entrance of Repentance.

שערי
רחמים

FIG. 25. GATE OF MERCY (SHA'AREI REHAMIM) (C. 1537)

Samuel son of David the Karaite, who visited Jerusalem in 1641, tells of the Gate of Mercy: "And it will not be opened until the eyes of Israel shall be opened in the future redemption. And it is said that several times the Ishmaelites tried to open it, but they could not."

In our time it is told that the Arabs blocked this gate because they believe that in the end of days the Messiah of the Jews and Elijah the prophet will enter through its path, coming from the east to Jerusalem, leading the hosts of Israel (fig. 26).[48]

FIG. 26. COMING OF MESSIAH TO JERUSALEM (C. 1629)
Elijah the prophet is blowing a shofar; after him rides the Messiah, mounted on donkey. They are approaching East Gate of Holy City. From all sides multitudes of Jews flock into Jerusalem extending hands to the Redeemer, as Isaiah prophesied: "Thus saith the Lord:/In an acceptable time have I answered thee,/And in a day of salvation have I helped thee . . . ./To raise up the land,/To cause to inherit the desolate heritages. . . ./Behold, these shall come from far;/And, lo, these from the north and from the west . . ./Lift up thine eyes round about and behold:/All these gather themselves together, and come to thee" (Isaiah 49:8–18).

3 / THE GRAVEYARD AROUND THE GATE

On the slope of the mountain which descends by the Gate of Mercy, and around its blocked entrances, stretches an Arab cemetery (fig. 24).

Legend holds that these graves have been dug by the Arabs purposely to prevent Elijah the prophet, the forerunner of the Messiah, from entering through the Gate of Mercy into the Holy City at the end of days. As Zechariah prophesied: "Behold, thy King cometh unto thee,/ He is triumphant, and victorious,/Lowly, and riding upon an ass,/Even upon a colt the foal of an ass."

The Moslems know that Elijah the prophet is a Cohen, of a priestly family; as such, he is forbidden to walk into a graveyard, lest he become impure. Hence they believe that he shall be unable to enter through the Gate of Mercy and bring to his people Israel salvation and redemption.[49]

4 / THROUGH THE GATE OF MERCY

From the Temple area a few steps lead down to the Gate of Mercy. At the bottom of the steps, iron doors bar the entrance to the Gate of Mercy, which lies in great part buried underground.

In a message sent from Jerusalem in 1523, it is told of the Gate of Mercy and its entrance from its western side: "And it is said that an Ishmaelite tried many times to open it, but to no avail. And they endeavored to block it up with stones from all the sides, but with no success either. And they erected in the ground a building to block up the gate, but they only built it halfway up. And the gate is closed by iron doors. And no man can enter . . . from the forbidden side. Anyway, the Ishmaelites let no one approach it.

"And it is told that at the time when the Turkish king

came here, some Jews were with him and all those who
entered [the gate] died.

"May God lengthen thy days. Amen!"[50]

5 / SUPPLICATION AT THE GATE

In the Middle Ages, Jewish pilgrims were wont to repair to the Gate of Mercy to pray and pour out in front
of it the bitterness of their sorrowful hearts. One of them
writes: "And we have no other consolation but to walk
around the gates, to prostrate ourselves in front of the
Almighty and to beg for clemency and forgiveness, that
He may mercifully return us to the Holy City."

At the beginning of the fourteenth century, Rabbi
Ashtori ha-Parhi reports a prayer which was recited in
front of the Gate of Mercy: "O Thou, the only Lord,
toward this house, the light of the world. This is a poor
man calling, praying and pouring out his bitter heart,
crying all a-tremble, lifting up his hands and stretching
out his palms toward Thee./Toward Thou, O my God,
I set myself awaiting Thy righteousness/And hoping for
salvation through Thee,/With Thy true mercy, O my
God, build Thy house anew;/Attend to salvation, seek
Thy chosen people, satiated with troubles, wandering in
exile./And to the city of Thy holiness, in Thy praised
Temple and palace bring them back kindly and mercifully,/And upon Thy altar there shall be offerings and
Thou shall restore it to Thy praise and glory."[51]

6 / WHO BUILT THE GATE OF MERCY?

The Gate of Mercy was built by King Solomon and has
stood ever since his day. It is set with well-cut stones
which the Queen of Sheba brought him as a present.
It is held that upon the destruction of the first Temple,
and again at the destruction of the second Temple, the
Gate of Mercy remained whole; it merely sank partway
underground (fig. 27).

FIG. 27. GATE OF MERCY (GOLDEN GATE)
Interior view.

An ancient Christian tradition of the end of the fourth century recalls one of the Temple gates in these words: "The Gate of the Temple, named the Beautiful Gate, the praiseworthy fruit of King Solomon's work."

A Persian traveler who visited Jerusalem in 1047 tells of the wall which limits the Temple area, and of the beautiful gate which opens therefrom. "And it is said that it was built by King Solomon son of David, peace be upon him, to honor his father's memory."

The Gate of Mercy has two entrances. One is the Entrance of Mercy (in Arabic *Bab er-Rahma*) and the other the Entrance of Repentance (*Bab et-Tuba*), because here King David repented and was forgiven by the Lord God the sublime and the admirable.

Everyone who came to worship at the Gate of Mercy began his prayer at the Entrance of Mercy, to the right, beseeching the Lord's mercy. He concluded at the left, opposite the Entrance of Repentance, and there awaited the forgiveness in loving-kindness from the Holy One, blessed be He.[52]

7 / GATE OF ETERNAL LIFE

The Arabs also call the Gate of Mercy *Bab ed-Dahariye* —the Gate of Eternal Life, a name mentioned in Arabic literature.

The Gate of Eternal Life was so called because of the Arab belief—stemming from an ancient Hebrew tradition—that around the Gate of Mercy, on the slope of the mountain descending to the neighboring Valley of Jehoshaphat and on the Mount of Olives rising opposite it, is where the dead shall be resurrected in the end of days, and where the eternal life of mankind on earth shall begin. Therefore, surrounding the Gate of Mercy, on the mountain slope opposite the Jewish cemetery on the nearby Mount of Olives, a Moslem cemetery is spread out. It is the most holy and exalted burial ground of the Arabs of Jerusalem.[53]

8 / THE GOLDEN GATE (PORTA AUREA)

According to Christian tradition, in ancient times the Golden Gate stood on the site of the Gate of Mercy. Through this gate Jesus of Nazareth entered the Temple court, followed by his pupils carrying palm branches in their hands. The New Testament describes his passing through a gate, without mentioning its name. "And the multitudes that went before, and that followed, cried, saying: Hosanna to the son of David: Blessed is he that cometh in the name of the Lord. Hosanna in the highest!"

From earliest times, Christian pilgrims used to come to the Golden Gate, palm branches in their hands and intone the psalm: "We beseech Thee, O Lord, save now!/We beseech Thee, O Lord, make us now to prosper!/Blessed be he that cometh in the name of the Lord;/We bless you out of the house of the Lord."

In 614, Chosroes II, king of Persia, broke through the Golden Gate into Jerusalem and drove out the Byzantines and their King Heraclius. In his army were Jews who volunteered in the hope of living in the Holy Land free from persecution and realizing their dream of establishing Jerusalem anew.

After fifteen years Heraclius, king of the Byzantines, succeeded in overpowering the Persians and chasing them from Jerusalem. When Heraclius returned victorious, his intention was to enter the city by way of the Golden Gate. Attired in robes all glittering with royal gems, and followed by a long train of courtiers and nobles, he advanced with gladness and was about to enter through this splendid gate, when an invisible hand pushed him back. He tried with all his strength to pass, but he could not succeed against this unseen and mysterious power.

Suddenly he heard a voice from heaven calling: "O emperor, remove thy jeweled garments and armor; put on a simple dress, and enter humbly, like Jesus your Lord."

The emperor hastened to comply, and the invisible hand ceased to obstruct his way into the Holy City.[54]

9 / THE GOLDEN GATE IN THE END OF DAYS

The name Golden Gate is mentioned in a Jewish legend, which tells of the revelation of Jerusalem and its Temple to the people of Israel at the end of time.

"And all Israel shall find favor in the eyes of the Lord. In place of destroyed Jerusalem, He shall lower from the skies eternal Jerusalem which is built in heaven . . . and the Temple shall be established.

"A pillar of fire shall burst forth from inside the House of God and shall be a sign to all who witness it. . . .

"And at God's command two angels shall lift up the Golden Gate which lies hidden in the earth; and they shall raise it back to its first place.

"Abraham the patriarch, peace be upon him, shall stand to its right and Moses the man of God, peace upon him, with the Messiah son of David, peace be upon him, shall stand to its left, and all Israel shall come forward."[55]

10 / THE GATE OF THE TRIBES

"Our feet are standing
Within thy gates, O Jerusalem. . . .
Whither the tribes went up, even
the tribes of the Lord."

In the corner of the Temple court, not far from the Gate of Mercy (Golden Gate), there is a gate called in Arabic *Bab al-Asbat*—Gate of the Tribes. These are the tribes of Israel.

The Moslem tradition also tells that through this gate the tribes of Israel passed as they ascended in pilgrimage to the holy sanctuary for the high festivals.

Close by this gate is a pool called in Arabic *Birkat* (*Bani*) *Israil*—Pool of (the Children of) Israel, which can be seen to this day. The nearby tower of the mosque is called *Madenat Bani Israil*—Minaret of the Children of Israel. A small Moslem monastery of dervishes which existed here in the Middle Ages was called *Zawiyat el-Lawi*—the Corner of the Levites, in memory of the Levites who served in the Temple in olden days.[56]

11 / THE GATE OF SIN

One of the northern entrances to the Temple court is called by the Arabs *Bab al-Khetta*—the Gate of Sin.

Why was this gate so named?

When the children of Israel sinned in the wilderness, rebelling against God's words, He commanded them: "When ye come unto Jerusalem ye shall stand before Mount Moriah and for the sins that ye committed in the wilderness, shall ye proclaim: 'Khett! Khett!'—sin! sin! Then shall ye be forgiven."

But when the children of Israel came to Jerusalem, they stood before Mount Moriah and instead of crying: "Khett!" they cried: "Hitta! Hitta!"—wheat! wheat! And the Lord was angry with them and a grievous plague fell upon them which slew many and never ceased until they cried: "Khett! Khett!"

On the same spot where the children of Israel uttered aloud these words, a gate was erected which was called the Gate of Sin. It is believed that anyone who passes this gate and says: "O Lord, may I be relieved from the burden of my sin" will be completely forgiven.

It is said that the panels of this gate were brought from one of the gates of Jericho which sank into the earth in the days of Joshua the son of Nun.[57]

V

MORIAH
—THE MOUNT OF GOD

Jerusalem is situated on the heights of mountains. The most important and sacred of them is Moriah—mountain of the Lord of hosts. Upon it stood the Temple in all its glory—the abode of the living God. Therefore it was known as the Mount of the House of the Lord, or simply, the House Mount (*Har Habayit*).

The prophets Micah and Isaiah call: "But in the end of days it shall come to pass,/That the mountain of the Lord's house shall be established as the top of the mountains" and "It shall come to pass in the end of days,/That the mountain of the Lord's house shall be established as the top of the mountains,/. . . And many peoples shall go and say:/'Come ye, and let us go up to the mountain of the Lord,/To the house of the God of Jacob."

Atop Moriah was the holy center for all the tribes of Israel, and they called it the holy mount. In the words of Isaiah: "And they shall bring all your brethren out of all the nations for an offering . . . to My holy mountain Jerusalem." Ezekiel says: "For in My holy mountain, in the mountain of the height of Israel . . . there shall all the house of Israel, all of them, serve Me in the land."

Daniel calls the mountain "beauteous holy mountain," in Hebrew *Har Zebi Kodesh*—the deer holy mount. The deer is a symbol of glory and beauty. Its name was applied to the entire country of Israel: *Eretz ha-Zebi*—Land of the Deer.[58]

2 / MOUNT OF MYRRH

The legend seeks to derive the name Moriah from the Hebrew word *mor*, meaning "myrrh," a fine perfume burnt as incense in the Temple on this mountain. Rashi, the famous Bible commentarian of the twelfth century, explains: "It was known as Moriah because of the incense burnt on it, which contained myrrh, nard [spikenard], and other perfumes."

Abraham the patriarch came to Mount Moriah to sacrifice his son Isaac to God. The Book of Genesis relates: "And He said: 'Take now thy son, thine only son, whom thou lovest, even Isaac, and get thee into the land of Moriah.'" The sages of Israel add: "To the Mountain of Myrrh."

The ancients find a hint of the sacrifice of Isaac in the words, "a mountain of myrrh" from the Song of Songs. In the same song it is said: "I will get me to the mountain of myrrh and to the hill of frankincense." This refers to Mount Moriah.

Samuel son of David, describing his visit to the Holy City in 1641, writes: "My soul yearned for the courtyard of the Lord—longed to ascend unto the Mount of Myrrh . . . to kneel and offer thanks . . . in the midst of Jerusalem, may she be built and established speedily in our day, Amen."[59]

There is a legend which finds in the name Moriah, the Hebrew word *orah,* meaning "light." When the world was created, it was from this mountain that light first shone forth upon all the world and mankind.

Light was created at the site of the Temple, for it is written (in Ezekiel's prophecy): "And behold, the glory of the God of Israel came . . . and the earth did shine with His glory." "His glory" refers to the Temple on Mount Moriah.

When His light (the light of the Holy One, blessed be He) shone over the land of Israel, it shone first in the Temple, and from there illumined the entire world, for the psalmist said: "Out of Zion, the perfection of beauty."[60]

4 / MOUNT OF AWE

The Hebrew word *mora,* meaning awe, fear, and reverence, is taken by some to be a component of the name Moriah: Mora-iah—Awe of God. The mountain of Moriah is identified as "the place from which the fear of God went forth into the world." For the ancient psalmist sings: "Awful [*mora*] is God out of thy holy places;/the God of Israel, He giveth strength and power unto the people."

Others derive the name Moriah from the Hebrew word *yirah,* which also stands for awe and reverence: "It was called Mount Moriah because the reverence [*yirah*] of the Holy One, blessed be He, caused it to form into a mountain."[61]

5 / MOUNT OF INSTRUCTION

There is a legend which finds in the name Moriah the Hebrew word *horaha* (*horaiah*), which means instruction, from the root *moreh*—teacher and instructor, and the same root in the word Torah.

From Mount Moriah the instruction of the Torah, law of Israel, spread forth, as told by the prophet Isaiah: "For out of Zion shall go forth the law [Torah],/And the word of the Lord from Jerusalem."

Rabbi Shimon son of Yohai finds in Moriah the Hebrew word *raui*—worthy: "That place is worthy to be opposite the Temple in heaven."[62]

6 / MOUNT OF APPEARANCE

Some think that in the name Moriah is the Hebrew word *yerahe*—to be seen or to appear. As it is written in the Book of Genesis: "And Abraham called the name of that place Adonai-jireh [God will see]; as it is said to this day: 'In the mount where the Lord is seen.'" Rashi adds: "In this mount God, blessed be He, will appear to his people."

Pilgrims of Israel came to the Holy Temple on Mount Moriah during the holidays to worship God, according to the commandment of the Torah: "Three times in the year shall all thy males appear before the Lord, thy God, in the place which he shall choose."

The pilgrimage to the Temple and the offering of first-fruits there is known as the command of appearance (*reayah* or *reayon*). The sages of Israel said: "All are subject to the command of appearance, excepting deaf mutes, imbeciles, and children."[63]

7 / MOUNT OF EXCHANGE

Others find in the name Moriah the Hebrew word *temurah*—exchange or recompense. For on this mount Abraham our patriarch came to sacrifice his son Isaac, and according to the Lord's command, he offered in exchange the ram He sent, which was thereby sanctified.

The Torah said about the sacrifice: "He shall not alter it, nor change it . . .; and if he shall at all change . . . then both it and that for which it is changed shall be holy."[64]

The poet of the Song of Songs concludes his verses, calling: "Make haste, my beloved,/And be thou like to a gazelle or to a young hart/Upon the mountains of spices."

The legend finds in "mountains of spices" a hint of Mount Moriah in Jerusalem. The Aramaic translator of the Song of Songs says of this: "A mountain in Jerusalem where the priests used to offer incense and spices."

Rashi explains the words of the Song of Songs thus: "To hasten the redemption, and to spread the divine Presence over the mountains of spices—that is Mount Moriah and the Holy Temple, may it be built speedily in our day, Amen."[65]

VI
PATRIARCHS
ON MOUNT MORIAH

1 / WHERE WAS ADAM CREATED?

In the Book of Genesis it is written: "Then the Lord formed man of the dust of the ground." The Aramaic translator adds: "And He gathered dust from the site of the Temple, and from all the waters of the earth." Adam was created from the earth of Mount Moriah, from the place where the Holy Temple was built in later generations.

When the Holy One, blessed be He, created man, He collected his dust from the four directions of the world, and made his bones on the site of the earthly Temple. Then He breathed into him a soul from the heavenly Temple.

Some say that on the place from which the dust for the creation of Adam was taken, there was built the altar of the Temple.

Adam's body was taken from Babylon, his head from the land of Israel, and his limbs were taken from the rest of the lands.

God loved Adam with deep affection, for He created him from such a pure and holy site.[66]

2 / THE ABODE OF ADAM

In the Book of Genesis it is written: "So He drove out the man; and He placed at the east of the garden of Eden the cherubim."

Legend tells that the place referred to is Mount Moriah.

After Adam's expulsion from the Garden of Eden, "he lived on Mount Moriah, because the gate of the Garden of Eden was close to Moriah. From that place God took him, and to that place He brought him back."

On Mount Moriah, Adam and his sons, Cain and Abel, erected an altar to the Lord, and on it they offered their sacrifices.

"Adam sacrificed an ox—with one horn on its forehead."[67]

3 / NOAH ON MOUNT MORIAH

When Noah the righteous left the ark, after the waters of the flood had receded and the face of the earth was revealed, he came with his sons first to Mount Moriah. There they sacrificed a thank offering to the Lord, on the same spot where Adam had sacrificed and where Abraham, generations later, brought his offering.

It is told that when Abraham and Isaac reached Mount Moriah, the Holy One, blessed be He, pointed out the altar to Abraham and said: "There is the altar! Upon this altar did Adam, Cain, and Abel place their offerings! Upon this altar did Noah and his sons place their offerings!"

On a nearby hill, Shem, the son of Noah, interred the skull of Adam, which he had taken with him into the ark and guarded during the flood. Since then the hill is called Golgoltha (Golgotha)—the Skull.[*][68]

* See legend XX:10.

4 / ABRAHAM ON MOUNT MORIAH

The holy One, blessed be He, revealed himself to our father Abraham: "And [He] said unto him: 'Abraham'; and he said: 'Here am I'; And He said: 'Take now thy son, thine only son, whom thou lovest, even Isaac, and get thee into the land of Moriah, and offer him there for a burnt-offering upon one of the mountains which I will tell thee of. And Abraham . . . went unto the place of which God had told him. On the third day, Abraham lifted up his eyes, and saw the place afar off."

The sages wondered how this place looked from afar, and they said: "We learn that at the beginning the place was low; whereas the Almighty, blessed be He, chose it to set His divine Presence and to build His Temple thereon. He said: 'The King should not dwell in low places, but in lofty and sublime regions which appear to the eyes of all.' Forthwith, the Almighty, blessed be He, prompted the hills around the valley to foregather in one place to form a high mountain for the seat of the divine Presence. Wherefore it is called the Mountain of Moriah, for it was created through reverence [*yirah*] for God the Almighty."

"And [Abraham] saw the place afar off. . . .—What did Abraham see?—He saw a pillar of fire reaching from earth to heaven. He said to Isaac: 'My son, dost thou see anything over one of yonder hills?' Isaac answered: 'Yes, father!' 'What dost thou see?' 'I see a pillar of fire reaching from earth to heaven.'

"Then Abraham knew that God had accepted and pardoned the youth Isaac as an offering."[69]

5 / ISAAC'S SACRIFICE

Father Abraham started on his journey to Moriah with his ass, two of his young men, his son, Isaac, and wood for burning the offering. It is written in the Book of Genesis that Abraham "cleaved the wood for the burnt-offering."

The sages of Israel say: "Wherewith our father Abraham cleaved the wood . . . his reward was that God should cleave [divide] the [Red] Sea before his descendants [the children of Israel, after they left Egypt], as it says [in the Book of Exodus]: And the waters were divided."

Abraham went to Moriah, built there an altar, and placed the wood on it, intending to slay Isaac for God. And an angel of the Lord called unto him: "Abraham, Abraham . . . Lay not thy hand upon the lad . . . for now I know that thou art a God-fearing man. . . . And Abraham lifted up his eyes, and looked, and beheld behind him a ram caught in a thicket by his horns. And Abraham went and took the ram, and offered him up for a burnt-offering in the stead of his son" (fig. 28).

The ancients tell, in praise of the ram that appeared to Abraham, that no part of this ram was wasted:

His ten veins became the ten strings for the harp upon which King David played.

His two horns became shofars. With the left horn the Holy One, blessed be He, blew on Mount Sinai. The right horn, larger than the left, is destined to be blown in the days to come at the time of the ingathering of the exiles of Israel.

The ram's hide was used to gird the loins of Elijah the prophet.

An Arab historian of the Middle Ages tells of the ram's horn which was guarded on the Temple site. About 730 it was taken from Jerusalem, from the Dome of the Rock, and taken to Mecca, the holy Moslem city in Arabia.[70]

6 / MORIAH IN THE EXODUS

When the children of Israel left Egypt, on their way to the promised land, they came to the Red Sea, which was divided for them, and they crossed over on dry land.

FIG. 28. SACRIFICE OF ISAAC ON MOUNT MORIAH
A picture in mosaic floor of ancient synagogue at Beth-Alpha, Israel, from sixth century. Left: donkey and two young men, as told in Torah: "And Abraham rose early in the morning, and saddled his ass, and took two of his young men with him, and Isaac his son." Abraham stands in center; above him his name is written in Hebrew. In one hand he holds knife, in other hand is Isaac, whose name is written above him. In front of him is altar with sacrificial fire. "And Abraham built the altar there, and laid the wood in order. . . . And Abraham stretched forth his hand, and took the knife to slay his son. And the angel of the Lord called unto him out of heaven and said: 'Abraham, Abraham. . . . Lay not thy hand upon the lad.'" Above Abraham is seen a hand extending from heaven, and below it is written: "Lay not thy . . ." Beside Abraham, on his left, is a ram; above it is written "Here is the ram." His horns are caught in the thicket, as the Torah tells: "And Abraham lifted up his eyes, and looked, and beheld behind him a ram caught in a thicket by his horns."

At the moment when the Israelites approached the shore of the sea, Mount Moriah began to move from its place, and rested on the bottom of the sea.

And Moses prayed, asking for salvation.

Then God said to Moses: "Moses, My children are in distress, the sea forming a bier, the enemy pursuing, and you stand so long praying!"

And Moses asked Him: "What should I be doing?"

Then He said to Moses: "Lift up thy rod! . . ." And the sea was opened before the children of Israel, and they passed it, on Mount Moriah.

It is told that the men of the tribe of Benjamin were the first to enter the sea. What reward did the tribe of Benjamin receive for this courageous deed? The divine Presence rested in his portion on Mount Moriah in the land of Israel.[71]

7 / BENJAMIN AND MOUNT MORIAH

The psalmist sings: "A mountain of God . . ./A mountain of peaks. . . ./Why look ye askance, ye mountain peaks,/At the mountain which God hath desired for His abode?/Yea, the Lord will dwell therein for ever." A tradition says that this refers to the choosing of Moriah, the hill of God, as the abiding place for the divine Presence.

When King Solomon announced that he would build the Holy Temple, the tribes of Israel began to strive and quarrel among themselves. One said: "It shall be built within my borders." And another said: "It shall be built within my borders."

The Holy One, blessed be He, said: "Tribes, why do you argue? You are all righteous. But all of you participated in the sale of Joseph, your brother—except Benjamin, who did not take part. Therefore, God desires to dwell in the hill placed in his portion."

Moses blessed the tribes of Israel, and of Benjamin he said: "The beloved of the Lord shall dwell in safety by him, and the Lord shall cover him all the day long, and he shall dwell between his shoulders."

The sages of Israel explain this blessing:

"Cover him"—that is the first Temple.

"All the day"—that is the second Temple.

"Shall dwell between his shoulders"—that refers to the end of time when the Messiah of Israel will appear.

The words of Jacob's blessing to his son, "Benjamin is a wolf that raveneth; In the morning he devoureth the prey," are interpreted by the rabbis: "These are the sacrifices offered in the Temple, which is in his portion."[72]

8 / TEMPLES IN BENJAMIN'S PORTION

Why did the divine Presence choose to rest on the Mount of Moriah in the portion of Benjamin? Because all the other tribes were born outside the land of Israel, but Benjamin was born in the land of Israel. Therefore, Benjamin was privileged to become the abode of the divine Presence.

After the destruction of the first Temple, Jews returned from exile and built in its place the second Temple.

The legend finds a hint of the destruction of both Temples in the words of Joseph to his brother Benjamin, when they met in Egypt: "And he [Joseph] fell upon his brother Benjamin's neck, and wept." In the Hebrew text the word neck is in the plural form: *zavarei*—necks.

How many necks did Benjamin have? Joseph wept in anticipation of the two sanctuaries that were to be destroyed in the inheritance of Benjamin.

And where does the word neck stand for sanctuary? It is written in the Song of Songs: "Thy neck is like the tower of David." The sages say: "'Thy neck'—this is the Temple."*[73]

9 / THE PURCHASE OF MOUNT MORIAH

In the Torah is written: "Unto the place which the Lord your God shall choose out of all your tribes to put His name there." "Out of all your tribes" refers to Jerusalem, of which all the tribes have a share.

King David bought the threshing floor on Mount Moriah

* See legend XI:8.

from Ornan (Araunah) the Jebusite, with money that he collected from all the tribes of Israel.

How do we know this? In the Book of Samuel it is written: "So David bought the threshing-floor . . . for fifty shekels of silver." And the Book of Chronicles says: "So David gave to Ornan for the place six hundred shekels of gold by weight."

How can this be? One says fifty and the other, six hundred.

David took fifty shekels from each tribe; from all twelve tribes he collected a total of six hundred shekels. For this payment, Ornan sold to him the threshing floor upon which the Temple was built.

When the exiles of Babylon returned to Israel, they found under the Temple altar the skull of a man. It is told that this was the skull of Ornan the Jebusite.[74]

VII
THE TEMPLE IN ITS GLORY

1 / WHY WAS THE TEMPLE ON MOUNT MORIAH?

*"And the Lord measured all the cities,
and He found no city in which to erect His Temple,
only Jerusalem."*

King David prepared Mount Moriah as the site of the Temple, on the place called the threshing floor of Ornan; King Solomon erected the first Temple. In the Book of Chronicles it is told: "Then Solomon began to build the house of the Lord at Jerusalem in mount Moriah, where [the Lord] appeared unto David his father, . . . in the Place of David, in the threshing-floor of Ornan the Jebusite."

Israel Kosta, a printer and bookseller in the middle of the nineteenth century, relates that the site on which the Holy Temple was built was once the property of two brothers. One had a wife and children, the other did not. They lived together in one house—happy, quiet, and satisfied with the portions which they inherited from their father. Together they worked the fields with the sweat of their brows.

And the harvest came. The brothers bound their sheaves and brought them to the threshing floor. There they divided the crops of the field in two parts equally between them, and left them.

That night, the brother who had no family lay on his bed and thought: I am alone . . . but my brother has a wife and children. Why should my share be equal to his? And he rose from his bed, went stealthily out into the threshing floor, took from the stalks of his own sheaf, and added them to the sheaf of his brother.

That same night, the other brother turned to his wife and said: "It is not right that we have divided the crop into two equal parts, one for me and one for my brother. He is alone and has no other joy or happiness, only the yield of the field. Therefore, come with me, my wife, and we will secretly take from our share and add to his." And they did so.

In the morning, the brothers went out into the threshing floor, and they wondered that the sheaves were still equal. Each one decided to himself to investigate. During the night each one rose from his bed to repeat his deed. And they met each other in the threshing floor, each with his sheaves in his arms. Thus the mystery was explained. The brothers embraced, and kissed each other.

And the Lord looked with favor on this threshing floor where the two brothers conceived their good thoughts . . . and the children of Israel chose it for the site of their Holy Temple (fig. 29).[75]

2 / THE FOUNDATION OF THE ABYSS

The ancients believed that a great abyss lay deep beneath the Foundation Stone and that the bases of the Temple on Mount Moriah were laid in the depths of the

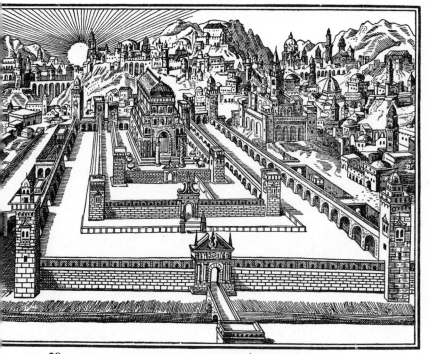

FIG. 29. JERUSALEM AND THE TEMPLE (C. 1629)
Below picture (not shown) is written (in Hebrew): "The form of the Temple and the city of Jerusalem, may it be speedily rebuilt and established in our day, Amen, may it be Thy will."

earth, above the great abyss. The idea of building the Temple was, according to legend, one of the "seven things which were contemplated before the creation of the world." And its foundations were prepared during the six days of creation, by the hands of the Holy One, blessed be He.

The Torah starts with the Hebrew words *Bereishith Bara Elohim*—"In the beginning God created. . . ." "Do not read: 'Bereishith'—In the beginning, but read: 'Bara Shith'—Created the foundation. This refers to the foundation of the Temple."

When King David began to dig the foundations of the Temple, the waters of the abyss burst forth and hastened to cover the whole world. David took a fragment of pottery and wrote on it the divine Name, then threw it into the abyss. Immediately the abyss receded sixteen thousand cubits into the depths. When David saw this he said: "The closer the abyss is to the earth, the more the earth drinks of its waters and is blessed thereof."

What did he do? He sang the fifteen Songs of Degrees of the Book of Psalms, and the abyss rose again fifteen thousand cubits. And it remained one thousand cubits beneath the surface of the earth.[76]

3 / KING DAVID AND THE ABYSS

When King David came to dig the foundations for the Temple around the Foundation Stone, he dug to a depth of fifteen hundred cubits. At length he found a projecting stone which he wished to remove. But the stone said to him: "This thou canst not do."

David asked: "Why not?" and it answered: "I cover the mouth of the abyss!"

"Since when?" asked the king. "Since the day when I heard the voice of the Lord upon Mount Sinai saying, 'I am the Lord thy God!' Then the earth shook and was almost swallowed in the depths of the abyss; I hastened and closed it and so I saved the earth."

But David would not hearken and wished to remove the stone; and as he tried, the waters of the abyss rose in great torrents which appeared to be about to flood the world. Then David began to sing the Song of Degrees from the Book of Psalms, and the waters of the abyss returned to their place.[77]

4 / BUILDING THE TEMPLE

The second Temple of Israel was built in the time of King Herod. "While the Temple was being constructed, the rains came down only during the nights. In the morning the wind blew, the clouds dispersed, the sun shone—and the people went out to their tasks." For the Almighty, blessed be He, did not want to disturb the workers who were establishing the Temple for Him.

And the workers knew that they were participating in the work of heaven.[78]

5 / STONES BUILT THE TEMPLE

In the Book of Kings, the building of the Temple is described in these words: "For the house, when it was in building, was built of stone made ready at the quarry; and there was neither hammer nor axe nor any tool of iron heard in the house."

"The stone moved of its own accord and arose, set itself in the wall of the Temple, and erected it."

King Solomon said in his prayer at the consecration of the Temple: "I have surely built Thee a house of habitation,/A place for Thee to dwell in for ever."

Legend adds: "I have constructed a building, and the stones flew and rose up by themselves."[79]

6 / HOW DID THE TEMPLE APPEAR?

"He who has not seen the Temple in its full construction, has never seen a glorious building in his life."

"He who has not seen the Temple of Herod, has never seen a beautiful building. Of what did he build it? Of yellow and white marble. Some say: Of blue, yellow, and white marble. Alternate rows of the stones projected, so as to leave a place for cement.

"Herod originally intended to overlay the marble with gold, but the rabbis advised him not to, because it was more beautiful as it was, looking like the waves of the sea."[80]

7 / CEDARS IN THE TEMPLE

The interior of the Temple was paneled with trees of cedar, that Hiram, king of Tyre, sent from the mountains of Lebanon to King Solomon, as it is told in the Book of Kings: "And he built the walls of the house within with boards of cedar; from the floor of the house unto the joists of the ceiling." The Temple was therefore also called House of Cedars.

When Solomon placed the ark in the Temple, all the trees were watered, and the cedars there gave forth fruit, as it is written in the Book of Psalms: "Planted in the house of the Lord,/They shall flourish in the courts of our God./ They shall still bring forth fruit . . . full of sap and richness."

The words of Zechariah the prophet: "For the cedar is fallen,/Because the glorious ones are spoiled" are interpreted by the sages: "The cedar is fallen—this is the Temple."[81]

8 / LIGHT FROM THE TEMPLE

"Jerusalem—light of the world."

In the walls of the Temple were distinctive windows, as is described in the Book of Kings: "And for the house, he [Solomon] made windows broad within, and narrow without."

The ancients said: "Whoever builds windows in his house, makes them wide outside and narrow inside, that they should bring in the light. Not so in the Temple; because there the light was within, and shone forth onto the whole world."

"As oil gives light—so the Temple gives light to the world, as Isaiah prophesied: 'And the nations shall walk at thy light, and kings to the brightness of thy rising.'"

"Why were our forefathers called 'a leafy olive tree'? In the words of Jeremiah: 'The Lord called thy name a leafy olive-tree, fair with goodly fruit' because the light of their faith illuminated all."[82]

9 / THE CURTAIN AT THE ENTRANCE

The curtain of the entrance to the holy of holies in the Temple was exceedingly beautiful. "The veil was one handbreadth thick and was woven on [a loom having] seventy-two rods, and over each rod were twenty-four threads. Its length was forty cubits, and its breadth twenty cubits: it was made by eighty-two young girls, and they used to make two in every year, and three hundred priests immersed it."

The Torah tells about the curtains of the tabernacle: "Moreover thou shalt make the tabernacle with ten curtains: of fine twined linen, and blue, and purple, and scarlet, with cherubim the work of the skilful workman shalt thou make them." In another chapter the curtain is described: "Of blue, and purple, and scarlet, and fine twined linen, the work of the weaver in colours."

The rabbis related this to the curtain of the Temple, on which there were embroidered different shapes: a pair of lions, an eagle, and so on.[83]

10 / THE GOLDEN CANDLESTICK

In Jerusalem there once dwelt a queen, Helene, who had come from the land of Adiabena (part of Iraq today) and had accepted the Jewish faith. Her burial cave is known as "the tomb of the kings."

It is told of Helene and her family that they donated precious vessels to the Temple. Helene herself gave "a golden candlestick over the door of the sanctuary. When the sun began to shine, sparkling rays proceeded from the candlestick, and all knew that the time had arrived for the reciting of the morning prayer."[84]

11 / THE VINE ON THE ENTRANCE

At the entrance to the sanctuary, there was a vine arbor covered with leaves and clusters of grapes, all made of gold, which were donated by the worshipers. "Once three hundred priests tried to remove this vine with its leaves and grapes" (fig. 30).

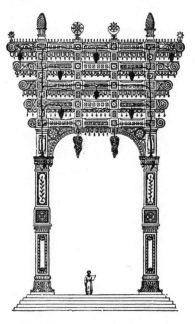

FIG. 30. VINE OVER ENTRANCE TO THE TEMPLE

Legend holds that the vine with the branches and clusters which Joseph saw in his dream referred to Jerusalem and to Israel:

"The vine" is Jerusalem.

"The three branches" are the Temple, the king, and the high priest.

"The clusters of grapes" are the tribes of Israel.[85]

12 / THE SAPPHIRE ON THE ROOF

Arab lore describes the greatness and splendor of King Solomon's Temple. The building was vast; it was so high that as its shadow fell to the east it reached Jericho, and on hot, sunny days women of this town found shelter in its shade.

Another tale pictures this shadow as being even bigger and reaching to Beit-Haram, in the eastern Jordan valley at the foot of the mountains of Moab.

On the roof of the Temple was set an enormous sapphire —*yacut* in Arabic—which glittered in the night and shone over great distances, even to the mountains of Gilead beyond the Jordan.

"The women of Gilead were wont to spin their wool at night by the bright light from the sapphire of the Temple."[86]

13 / THE RAVEN DESTROYERS

Spiked sheets of metal were placed on the roof of the Temple to prevent birds from alighting thereon and soiling it. These sheets were called raven-destroyers, because they were intended especially against the raven—an unclean bird which was, according to the ancient belief, an omen of evil.

The Torah prohibited the Jews to eat of the raven: "And these ye shall have in detestation among the fowls; they shall not be eaten, they are a detestable thing. . . . Every raven after its kinds."

The rabbis taught: "If one says: 'Behold, I vow iron [as a donation to the Temple] . . .' he must not give less

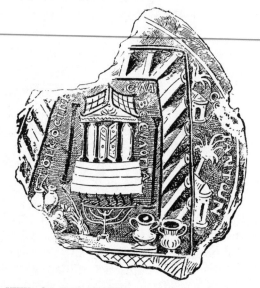

FIG. 31. VIEW OF THE TEMPLE
Drawing on a plate, from third or fourth century. Below: candelabrum and vessels of the Temple; center: holy of holies. Plate was
found in catacomb in Rome. It is preserved in Vatican Library.

than a square cubit [of sheet iron]. What is this fit for?
To ward off the ravens."

Josephus Flavius also tells about these bird-destroyers
on the Temple's roof.[87]

VIII
BUILDINGS
AROUND THE TEMPLE

1 / THE SANHEDRIN IN THE CENTER

The Sanhedrin, the Supreme Court of ancient Israel, met in a special building which was named the Chamber of Hewn Stone (*Lishkat ha-Gazith*). It was situated in the Temple courtyard.

"The Great Sanhedrin sat in the rear of the Temple, and it was the jewel thereof."

The rabbis add to the words of the Torah: "Justice, justice, shalt thou follow!"—"Follow the Sages in the Chamber of the Hewn Stone."

The poet of the Song of Songs says: "How beautiful are thy steps. . . ./Thy navel is like a round goblet.

" 'Thy navel'—that is the Sanhedrin. Why was it called navel?—Because it sat in the centre—the navel of the world.

" 'A round goblet'—in Hebrew: *Agan ha-Sahar*. . . . 'Agan' resembles the word 'Megin'—to defend. Because the Sanhedrin defends the rights of the whole world.

" 'Ha-Sahar'—means in Hebrew: Moon. Because the

members of the Sanhedrin sat during their sessions in a circle—like the disk of the moon."[88]

2 / THE BATH OF THE HIGH PRIEST

In the Temple courtyard there was a bathhouse for the high priest. He used to immerse himself in water on the eve of the Day of Atonement, before he entered the holy of holies, fulfilling the words of the Torah: "He shall put on the holy linen tunic, and he shall have the linen breeches upon his flesh. . . . They are holy garments; and he shall bathe his flesh in water, and put them on."

To the bathhouse flowed water from the spring called Ein Eitam, which is in the mountains of Bethlehem, close to the Pools of Solomon of today. The rabbis said: "The Eitam fountain was twenty-three cubits above the ground of the Temple court."

The rabbis describe the bath of the high priest: "They spread a linen sheet between him and the people. He stripped off his clothes, went down and immersed himself, came up and dried himself. They brought him raiments of gold and he put them on and sanctified his hands and his feet. . . .

"In the morning he was clothed in Pelusium linen . . . and in the afternoon, in Indian linen. . . . These were at the charge of the congregation, and if he was minded to spend more he could do so at his own charges. . . .

"If the high priest was aged or infirm—they prepared for him hot water which they poured into the cold water to abate its coldness. . . .

"Lumps of wrought iron were heated on the eve of the Day of Atonement and were cast into the cold water to mitigate the coldness."[89]

3 / THE CHAMBER OF PARVAH

One of the many chambers in the courtyard of the Temple was the Chamber of Parvah (*Lishkat ha-Parvah*).

"The high priest underwent five immersions and the sanctification on that day, all of them on holy ground in the Chamber of Parvah, with the exception of the first, which took place on profane ground on top of the Water Gate, lying at the side of his private cell."

What does Parvah mean? It is the name of a magician who built the chamber by sorcery, and it was named after him.

Parvah had dug a cave under the ground of the sanctuary, so that he might watch the high priest in the holy of holies, at the service of the Day of Atonement. The sages noticed the digging, found this hidden cave, and hence they named the chamber after him.[90]

4 / THE CHAMBER OF SECRETS

"There were two chambers within the Temple: one—the Chamber of Secrets, and the other—the Chamber of Utensils.

"Into the Chamber of Secrets the devout used to put their gifts in secret, and the poor of good family received support thereof in secret.

"The Chamber of Utensils—whoever made a gift of any article used to cast it therein, and every thirty days the treasurers opened it.

"Any article which they found of use for the Temple fund, they left there; the rest was sold and the price fell to the chamber of the Temple fund."[91]

5 / CHAMBER OF THE HEARTH

The Book of Chronicles tells about the guards of the Temple: "And they lodged round about the house of God, because the charge was upon them, and the opening thereof every morning pertained to them."

The rabbis relate: "The Chamber of the Hearth was vaulted; it was a large chamber, and around it ran a raised stone pavement. There the eldest of the father's house used to sleep with keys of the Temple court in their hands. The young priests had each his mattress on the ground.

"The Chamber of the Hearth was called after the fire which burnt continuously within it, and the priests warmed themselves there, because they walked barefoot on the marble floors."[92]

6 / CHAMBER OF THE INCENSE-MAKER

In the Temple courtyard was a special building in an upper story, which was called the Chamber of Abtinas, the name of a family whose members were great experts in preparing incense for the sacred service in the Temple.

"The house of Abtinas were expert in preparing the incense, but would not teach [their art].

"The sages sent for specialists from Alexandria of Egypt, who know to compound incense as well as they, but did not know to make ascent as well as they. The smoke of the former ascended [as straight] as a stick, whereas the smoke of the latter was scattered in every direction.

"When the sages heard thereof, they said: The house of Abtinas may return to their place!

"The sages sent for them, but they would not come. Then they doubled their hire, and they came.

"The sages said to them: What reason did you have for not teaching [your art]? They said: They knew in our father's house that this house is going to be destroyed and they said: Perhaps an unworthy man will learn [this art] and will serve an idol therewith.

"And for the following reason was their memory kept in honor: never did a bride of their house go forth perfumed. And when they married a woman from elsewhere, they expressly forbade her to do so, lest people say: From the preparation of the incense they are perfuming themselves. . . .

"Rabbi Ishmael son of Luga relates: One day I and one

of there descendants [of the house of Abtinas] went to the field to gather herbs, and I saw him laughing and crying.

"I said to him: Why did you cry?—He answered: I recalled the glory of my ancestors!—And why did you laugh happily?—He replied: Because the Holy One, blessed be He, will restore it to us!

"And what caused you to remember?—He said: There is a smoke-raiser [the name of a plant for incense] before me!

"Show it to me!—He said to me: We are bound by oath not to show it to any person!

"Rabbi Yohanan son of Nuri relates: Once I came upon an old man, who had a scroll.

"I asked him: Whence are you?—He said: I come from the house of Abtinas!

"What have you in your hand?—He replied: A scroll [containing prescriptions] for frankincense.

"Show it to me!—He said: As long as my father's house was alive, they would not surrender it to anyone, but now, here it is; but be very careful about it."[93]

IX

THE SERVICE IN THE TEMPLE

1 / THE FIRE ON THE ALTAR

In the Temple stood the altar; upon it was a pile of wood, and a fire burnt there continually. The ancients said: "The rain never quenched the fire of the woodpile, and no wind prevailed over the pillar of smoke."

"Five things were reported about the fire of the woodpile on the altar: it was lying like a lion; it was clear as sunlight; its flame was of solid substance; it devoured wet wood like dry wood; and the smoke arising from it, though all the winds of the world might blow, would not move from its place.

"On the night following the last day of the Festival of the Tabernacle [Sukkoth], all the people stood gazing upon the smoke rising from the pile of wood.

"If it inclined northward—the poor rejoiced and the people of means were sad, because the rains of the coming year would be abundant, and their fruits would rot [hence they would have to sell them quickly and cheaply].

"If it inclined southward—the poor were depressed and

the men of means rejoiced, for there would be little rain that year and the fruits would be preserved.

"If it inclined eastwards—all rejoiced, because it meant average rainfall, plenty of fruit, without danger of rotting.

"If westward—all were depressed, because the wind from this direction dries up the seed and causes famine."[94]

2 / WHO KINDLED THE FIRE?

Whence came the fire of the woodpile on the Temple altar?

"When King Solomon approached the altar to offer the first sacrifice to God the Almighty, a hidden ember fell upon it and kindled the pile of wood" (fig. 32).

The sages of Israel say: "Although a fire descends from

FIG. 32. DRAWING OF THE TEMPLE

In a mosaic floor on Mount Nebo, Jordan. From sixth century. Center: entrance to holy of holies; within it is ark of the covenant. Below: a fire burning on the altar.

heaven, the duty of sacrificing falls on the layman as well."

"The glowing ember which fell from the sky in Solomons' day, and remained on the altar till Manasseh [the king of Judah] came and removed it, was like a crouching lion."

An Arab legend tells us: "When Solomon sacrificed for the first time on the Temple rock, a fire descended from heaven, and afterwards a phoenix (*hol*) emerged and transported the sacrifice to heaven."

"Aaron's sons used to enter the Temple, and a stream of olive oil would pour down from heaven, filling the lamps. Likewise, a fire would come down from heaven, move over the Mount of Olives like a wild beast, go on through the Gate of Compassion, and enter the Temple Mount."[95]

3 / WOOD FOR THE TEMPLE

From the area around Jerusalem, the Israelites used to bring logs for the woodpile of the Temple altar. The rabbis noted which type of wood was used for this purpose: "Are all kinds of wood suitable for the altar fire?—All kinds are suitable, except olive and vine. . . . Rabbi Eliezer adds also wood from the nettle tree [*maish**] and the oak and the date and the carob and sycamore. . . ."

In the Book of Chronicles are mentioned, among the families of the tribe of Judah, "the sons of Salma . . . the Netophathites." Salma is similar to the Hebrew word *sulam*—ladder. The legend explains why they are called after a ladder.

"Once the ruling power [Greeks] decreed that Israel should not bring wood to the altar of the Temple, and they placed guards on the roads leading to Jerusalem, to prevent Israel from going on pilgrimage.

"What did the godfearing men of that generation do?—

* See fig. 22.

They took the logs of wood and made them into a ladder, which they carried on their shoulders, and proceeded on their journey.

"When they reached the guards, they were asked: Whither are you going?—They replied: We are going with the ladder on our shoulders to take down young pigeons from the dovecote at a place farther on.

"When they had gone out of sight of the guards, they dismantled [the ladders] and brought them to Jerusalem. And they offered them as fuel for the altar, for the sacrifices."[96]

4 / THE OFFERING OF FIRSTFRUITS

At the festivals, the children of Israel used to make a pilgrimage to the Temple, and bring their *bikkurim*—the firstfruits of their land. The Torah commands the Israelites: "Three times in a year shall all thy males appear before the Lord thy God, in the place which He shall choose . . . and they shall not appear before the Lord empty. Every man shall give as he is able, according to the blessing of the Lord thy God which He hath given thee."

When the Greeks ruled over the Holy Land, they forbade the offering of firstfruits, and they posted guards along the roads to prevent the pilgrims from reaching Jerusalem. Of course this caused great sorrow in Israel. However, some men found a way to trick the guards and to pass with the *bikkurim* for the Temple.

The rabbis tell: "It is reported that once the ruling power issued a decree that Israel should not bring wood to the altar, nor bring their firstfruits to Jerusalem. And they placed guards on the roads, to prevent Israel from going on pilgrimage.

"What did the pious and sin-fearing men of that generation do?—They took their baskets of the firstfruits and covered them with dried figs, and carried them with a pestle on their shoulders.

"When they reached the guards, they were asked: Whither are you going?—They replied: With the pestle on our shoulders we are going to make two cakes of pressed figs, in the mortar we have yonder.

"After they had passed the guards, they decorated their baskets, and brought them to Jerusalem."[97]

5 / CENSUS IN ISRAEL

To take a census in Israel was regarded as an unfortunate omen. Since every male in Israel was obliged to make a pilgrimage to the Temple in Jerusalem on the Passover festival, and each brought with him a sacrifice for the priests, it was possible to count the number of offerings and thus learn the size of the population.

"Once King Agrippas desired to know what was the number of his people. He said to the Temple priests: 'Separate for me one kidney from each Passover sacrifice!'

"And the priests found six hundred thousand pairs of kidneys."[98]

6/PASSOVER OF THE CRUSHED

Great throngs used to come to Jerusalem at the festivals; they wandered about the holy shrines and gathered together in the Temple. Yet despite the size of the crowd, no one was ever crushed there.

During prayer time, too, each pilgrim had enough space about him.

Only once did an accident occur there, and it was remembered for generations. "The rabbis taught: No man was ever injured in the Temple court, except on one Passover in the days of Hillel."

An old man was then crushed by the crowd, and they called it "The Passover of the Crushed" (in Hebrew *Pesah Meuchin*).[99]

7 / CRIES FROM THE TEMPLE

The rabbis relate: "Four cries did the Temple court cry out.

"The first cry: Cause the sons of Eli: Hophni and Phineas, to depart hence, for they defiled the Temple!

"The second cry: Open, O ye gates, and let Yohanan the son of Nidbai, the disciple of Pinkai, enter and fill his stomach with the divine sacrifices.

"It was told of the son of Nidbai that he used to eat four measures [*seah*] of young birds as a dessert in the Temple.

"The third cry: Lift up your heads, O ye gates, and let Elishama the son of Pinkai, the disciple of Phineas, enter and serve in the office of the high priesthood!

"The fourth cry: Open, O ye gates, and cause Issachar of Kefar-Barkai to depart from hence, for he honors himself and treats with contempt the divine sacrifices.

"What used he to do?—He used to wrap silk over his hands, and thus perform the service."[100]

X
GATES
OF THE TEMPLE

1 / WHEN DID THE GATES OPEN?

"The Lord loveth the gates of Zion
More than all the dwellings of Jacob."

When Solomon built the Temple, he wished to take the ark into the holy of holies, but the gates thereof cleaved to each other and would not open. He uttered twenty-four psalms, but was not answered.

He then further supplicated: "Lift up your heads, O ye gates,/And be ye lifted up, ye everlasting doors;/That the King of glory may come in./'Who is the King of glory?'/ 'The Lord strong and mighty,/The Lord mighty in battle.'" And still he was not answered.

Then he said: "Now therefore arise, O Lord God, into Thy resting-place, Thou, and the ark of Thy strength. . . ./ O Lord God, turn not away the face of Thine anointed;/ Remember the good deeds of David Thy servant." And immediately the gates opened.[101]

2 / THE EASTERN GATE
"The gates of Zion are called: beloved."

One gate, because of its location on the eastern side of the Temple court, was called *Shaar ha-Kadim*—the Gate of the East.

Ezekiel the prophet narrates: "He brought me to the gate, even the gate that looketh toward the east; and behold, the glory of the God of Israel came from the way of the east, and His voice was like the sound of many waters; and the earth did shine with His glory. . . . And the glory of the Lord came into the house by the way of the gate whose prospect is toward the east."

"Then He brought me back the way of the outer gate of . . . the east; and it was shut. And the Lord said unto me: 'This gate shall be shut, it shall not be opened, neither shall any man enter in by it, for the Lord, the God of Israel, hath entered in by it; therefore it shall be shut.' "

The sages of Israel commanded: "No man should be negligent of the eastern gate, which faces toward the holy of holies."

"In the days to come, the Almighty, blessed be He, shall make the Gate of the East out of one single pearl."[102]

3 / SHECHINA AT THE EASTERN GATE

Ezekiel the prophet describes in his vision the glory of the Lord: "Then a spirit lifted me up, and brought me unto the east gate of the Lord's house." "And the glory of the Lord went forth from off the threshold of the house, and stood over the cherubim. And the cherubim lifted up their wings, and mounted up from the earth in my sight when they went forth, and the wheels beside them; and they stood at the door of the east gate of the Lord's house; and the glory of the God of Israel was over them above."

The Gate of the East—*Shaar ha-Kadim*—was also known as *Shaar ha-Kadmoni*; after the destruction of the Temple, the divine Presence rested thereon as it wandered from the holy of holies. The sages of Israel relate: "Ten stations did the Shechina make . . . from the cherubim [of the altar] to the eastern gate; from the eastern gate to the Temple courtyard, and from the wall to the town."[103]

4 / THE EASTERN GATE ON SABBATH

Ezekiel, in describing the Temple, says: "The gate of the inner court that looketh toward the east shall be shut . . . ; on the sabbath day it shall be opened, and in the day of the new moon [first day of the month] it shall be opened."

On the eve of Sabbath, the people of Israel stood there and saw the gate open by itself. Then they knew that the Sabbath had arrived, and they sanctified it.

On the day of the new month, too, the gate opened of is own accord; the people watching knew that at the very moment of its opening, the new moon was born, and they blessed the month.

Seeing the gate open by itself, Israel knew that the divine Presence of the Holy One, blessed be He, rested thereon.[104]

5 / GATE OF NICANOR

In the Temple court was a gate named for its donor— Gate of Nicanor. It was the holiest gate; therefore it is said: "Wherever it is written in the Bible 'before God'— it means at the Gate of Nicanor."

"To the east was the Nicanor Gate, and it had two wickets, one to the right, and one to the left."

The doors of Nicanor's Gate were made of special

bronze, and the ancients praised it highly. Josephus says: "Its height reached unto fifty cubits, its doors were forty cubits high—and in the richness of its beauty, it exceeded all the other gates, and it was overlaid with silver and pure gold."

The rabbis said: "All the gates there [of the Temple] had been changed into gold—save only the doors of the Nicanor Gate. Its bronze shone like pure gold."

On the heights of Mount Scopus in Jerusalem, an ancient burial cave was discovered. Inside, the coffin of Nicanor was found, with these words engraved in Greek: "The bones of Nicanor of Alexandria, who built the gate," and in Hebrew *Nicanor Alexa* (an abbreviated form of Alexandria, Egypt, the city of Nicanor).

The cave is now located in the courtyard of the Hebrew University, and it is called the Cave of Nicanor (fig. 33).[105]

6 / GATES OF BRIDEGROOMS AND MOURNERS

When King Solomon built the Temple of God, he prepared two gates—one for bridegrooms and one for mourners and excommunicates.

The crowds of Israel would go on the Sabbath and sit between these two gates. And when a man entered through the Bridegrooms' Gate, they knew that he was newly wed, and they would bless him, saying: "May the Lord of this house make thee rejoice in many sons and daughters!"

And one who came through the Mourners' Gate, his mouth covered, they recognized as a mourner, and to him they would say: "May the Lord of this house comfort thee!"

And one who came by the Mourners' Gate, his mouth uncovered, they ascertained to be under anathema, and they would address him thus: "May the Lord of this house console thee, and plant obedience in thy heart, that thy friends may welcome thee!"

FIG. 33. BURIAL CASE (OSSUARY) OF NICANOR THE
ALEXANDRIAN
This stone burial case from the first century was found in a cave on
Mount Scopus, Jerusalem, and is now preserved in British Museum
in London.

In such fitting way did Israel practice the virtue of
benevolence.

The Jewish pilgrims of the Middle Ages believed the
Gate of Mercy, with its two portals, to be the gates built
by King Solomon—one for bridegrooms and one for
mourners.[106]

7 / THE SHUSHAN GATE

On one of the gates leading to the courtyard of the
Temple was a drawing of the city of Shushan, the ancient

capital of Persia, famed also as the place where Queen Esther and her uncle, Mordecai the righteous, dwelt. From Shushan, the prophet Nehemiah went to Jerusalem to start the rebuilding of the Temple. He built a wall around the city, and the gates on all sides leading into it.

The rabbis tell: "Shushan ha-Bira [the capital] was portrayed on the eastern gate. What was the reason for this? —One said: 'So that they [the Jews] be ever mindful whence they came'—from the exile in Persia, and so would offer thanks to God for their deliverance."

"Another said: 'So that the fear of the dominant power be ever before them.'"

Rabbi Obadiah of Bertinoro, Italy, in his commentary says: "When the Jews returned from the Diaspora, the king of Persia commanded them to draw Shushan the capital, on the gates of the Temple, that they not forget their fear of the earthly kingdom—and they drew it on the East Gate."

According to Jewish tradition, Shushan stood where Hamadan now stands in Iran. There the Jews show the graves of Mordecai the righteous and Queen Esther, holy to the Jewish communities of Persia and the neighboring countries.

Among the Persian Jews residing in Jerusalem, many of whom originated in Hamadan, the family name Shushani is frequently found. They have founded a quarter in the New City of Jerusalem which they have called "Shushanat Zion."[107]

8 / THE WATER GATE

In the wall of the Temple court was a gate called by the ancients *Shaar ha-Mayim*—the Gate of Water. And why was it so named? Because through it was brought the flagon with water for the libation at the Feast of Tabernacles.

How was the libation performed? They would fill a

golden flagon with water at the Fountain of Siloam. When they reached the Gate of Water, they blew the trumpets, cheered loudly, and blew the trumpets again.

"Rabbi Eliezer the son of Jacob said: Through it [the gate] the waters trickle forth, and hereafter they will issue out from under the threshold of the house."

Zechariah prophesies: "And it shall come to pass in that day,/That living waters shall go out from Jerusalem."*[108]

9 / GATE OF THE SUN

In the Temple court was a gate called *Shaar ha-Harsith*. Jeremiah the prophet refers to it: "Thus said the Lord: Go and get a potter's earthen bottle, . . . and go forth unto the valley of the son of Hinnom, which is by the entry of the gate Harsith." The English translation renders it the East Gate.

The name Harsith is derived from the Hebrew word *heres*—the sun. The rabbis said: "How hard did the early prophets labor to make Shaar ha-Harsith face directly opposite the rays of the sunrise in winter and summer alike."[109]

10 / THE GATE WITH SEVEN NAMES

The eastern gate of the Temple court had seven other names which are mentioned in the Holy Scriptures:

Gate of Sur. Sur means "turn aside or depart." The unclean were forbidden to approach the gate and had to turn aside, as it is written in the Book of Lamentations: "Depart, ye unclean! . . . Depart, depart, touch not!"

Gate of the Foundation. There the Elders of Israel established the law.

Gate of the Sun. The gate faced toward the sunrise (see above).

---

* See legend XVII:4.

Gate of the Entrance. It was the entrance and the exit to the Temple.

The Middle Gate. It was built between two other gates.*

The New Gate. There the scribes of Israel renewed the law.

The Upper Gate. It was the highest gate in the Temple courtyard. [110]

11 / THE GATES SUNK

The Book of Lamentations expresses great sorrow at the destruction of Jerusalem and the Temple, and for the fate of its gates: "Her gates are sunk into the ground; /He hath destroyed and broken her bars."

The gates of the Temple sank into the earth and were hidden away in its depths. The gates paid honor to the ark of the covenant, and for that reason the enemy had no power over them.

The Gate of Mercy is among the gates which sank into the earth upon the destruction of the Temple.

In the end of days, when Israel is redeemed, the sunken gates will rise above the surface, around the glorious Temple.

In a Hebrew letter sent in 1456, and signed by the scribe of the community in Jerusalem, it is told of the various portents that will announce the approach of the Messiah: "The Gates of Mercy which are sunk in the earth with the Western Wall and with much remains from the Temple enclosure, will rise more than six cubits above the ground, and the Ishmaelites will wonder and quake with fear."[111]

* The Hebrew name of the Middle Gate is *Shaar ha-Tavech*. The rabbis call it *Shaar ha-Toch*. Legend finds in the name *ha-Toch* the Hebrew word *hatoch*, which means "to cut, to decide": "the place where laws are decided upon."

XI
𝒩𝒜𝑀𝐸𝒮
𝒪𝐹 𝒯𝐻𝐸 𝒯𝐸𝑀𝒫𝐿𝐸

The Holy Temple has many names in the Bible. The most common is *Beth ha-Mikdash:* the House of Holiness, from which the Arabic *Beit el-Makdass* for the whole of Jerusalem is derived. Another version is *Beit Kodesh:* Holy House, hence the Arabic *el-Kuds:* the Holy, as Jerusalem is called by the Moslems today.

The Holy Temple was also known as *Beth Elohim:* the House of God. And since this edifice was the most sanctified site in the life of the Israelites, it was also designated by the name *Habayit:* the House.

Other appellations were *Hazerot Adonai:* Courts of the Lord, *Heichal: Armon* Palace, *Beth Zevul (Zebul):* House of Habitation, *Beth Avotenu:* Our Fathers' House, *Beth Tefila:* House of Prayer, *Beth Menuha:* House of Rest, and *Habayit Haelyon:* the Supreme House.

In postbiblical literature new names appear: *Beth Olamim:* the Everlasting House, a designation which has its source in King Solomon's prayer at the consecration of the Temple: "I have built Thee a house of habitation, and a place for Thee to dwell in forever"; *Beth Habehira:* the Chosen House, since the Almighty chose it for the resting place of the divine Providence in the heart of Jerusalem, as it is called "the city which the Lord had chosen out of all the tribes of Israel," and again, "For the Lord hath chosen Zion, He hath desired it for his habitation"; *Beth Hayenu:* the House of Our Life; and *Beth Meorenu:* the House of Our Light.*

1 / ARIEL—LION OF GOD

The prophet Isaiah exclaimed: "Ah Ariel, the city where David encamped." Legend stresses the first two syllables of Ariel, which form the word *ari*—lion, and adds that as the lion is broad in the chest and small behind, so is the Temple wide in front and narrow at the back. Ariel also designated the whole of Jerusalem; thus the emblem of modern Jerusalem is the side view of a lion raised on his hind legs, on the background of the town's rampart (fig. 34).†[112]

2 / DEVIR—THE WORD

A very common appellation of the Temple was *devir* (*debir*), which first designated the holy of holies: "And the priests brought in the ark of the covenant of the Lord unto its place, into the Sanctuary [*debir*] of the house, to the most holy place, even under the wings of the cherubim." Later it was applied to the Temple in its entirety.

Legend relates the word *devir* to *davar*: Word (Logos), for the holy ark contained the Ten Commandments (in Hebrew *Asseret Hadiberot*: the Ten Words or Decalogue). The sages of Israel explained that it is called *devir* because from it the words (of God) went out to the world.

Others connect the name *devir* with *dever*: plague, and

---

* See legend V:3.
† See legend XII:10.

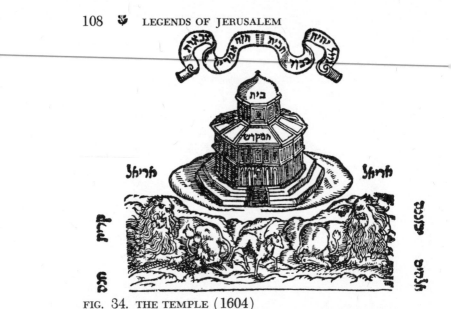

FIG. 34. THE TEMPLE (1604)

Above Temple are written words of prophet Haggai: "The glory of this latter house shall be greater . . . saith the Lord of hosts" (Haggai 2:9); on sides, the prophecy of Isaiah: "Ah, Ariel, Ariel, the city where David encamped!" (Isaiah 29:1); and on right the artist added: "God will restore her." Ariel means lion of God in Hebrew; therefore the artist drew lions in foreground.

say that the plague will be inflicted upon the man, who does not obey the words inscribed on the tablets of the law.[113]

3 / HADOM ADONAI—GOD'S FOOTSTOOL

The Hebrews pictured the heavens as the seat of God, the Master of the universe, and the earth as His footstool, as told by Isaiah: "Thus saith the Lord:/The heaven is My throne,/And the earth is My footstool." Thus the Temple is known as *Hadom Adonai*: the Footstool of God. This expression appears on several occasions in the Bible. David, expressing his desire to build a Temple to the Lord, says: "Hear me, my brethren, and my people; as for me, it was in my heart to build a house of rest . . . for the footstool of our God." The psalmist sings: "Let us go into His dwelling-place,/Let us worship at His footstool."

The Book of Lamentations, bewailing the destruction of the Temple, cries out! "He hath cast down from heaven unto the earth/The beauty of Israel,/And hath not remembered His footstool."[114]

4 / LEVANON—LEBANON

Lebanon, in Hebrew spelled Levanon, is derived from the Hebrew *lavan*: white, which evokes the snowy summits of these mountains.

The cedars used for the upbuilding of the Temple were brought from the mountains of Lebanon. A part of the Temple was named *Beth Yaar Halevanon*: House of the Forest of Lebanon: "And king Solomon made . . . three hundred shields . . . and the king put them in the house of the forest of Lebanon."

Moses, prostrating himself in front of the Lord, humbly expresses his heart's yearning for the promised land: "Let me, I pray, cross over and see the good land . . . , that good hill country, and the Lebanon." Legend explains that Lebanon here refers to the Temple, whose upbuilding the lawgiver foresaw in his vision. The prophet Zechariah said: "Open, thy doors, O Lebanon," and Isaiah prophesied: "And Lebanon shall fall by a mighty one." Levanon, explained the sages, is the Holy Temple whose fall the prophet foresaw. Why was the Temple named Levanon? Because Levanon includes the word *lev*: heart, since all hearts turn toward it and all hearts rejoice in it while praying to the Almighty.

Others explain that Levanon comes from *lavan*: white, because the sanctuary atones, whitens, all the sins of Israel, as Isaiah said: "Though your sins be as scarlet,/They shall be as white as snow."[115]

Our sages, their memory be blessed, used to say that these were called beloved friends:

God the Almighty, as Isaiah said: "Let me sing of my well-beloved";

Abraham the patriarch, as the prophet declares: "But thou, Israel, My servant . . ./The seed of Abraham My friend";

Israel the nation, as Jeremiah proclaims: "I have cast off My heritage, I have given the dearly beloved of my soul";

Benjamin, the son of Jacob, as in Moses' blessing: "beloved of the Lord,/He rests securely beside Him."

King Solomon, known as Jedidiah (Yedidiah), Friend of God: "David comforted Bathsheba his wife . . . and she bore a son, and called his name Solomon. And the Lord loved him . . . , and he called his name Jedidiah."

Jerusalem the capital, as the psalmist sang: "How lovely are Thy tabernacles. . ./My heart and my flesh sing for joy unto the living God."

God said: "The son of a friend, shall build a house to a friend, in the portion of a friend. This means: Israel 'the beloved' will build the Temple, by the hands of Solomon 'the friend of God,' in the portion of Benjamin 'the beloved of the Lord.'"[116]

6 / LEV HAOLAM—THE HEART OF THE WORLD

The wise men of Israel interpreted the words of Jeremiah, "Yea, it reacheth unto thy heart," as relating to the Holy Temple, for at its solemn consecration the Lord vowed to King Solomon: "Mine eyes and My heart shall be there perpetually."

Similarly the holy *Zohar*, the book of the Mystics, mentions the holy of holies as *Lev shel kol haolam*: the heart of all the universe.[117]

7 / AF HAOLAM—THE NOSE OF THE WORLD

The Song of Songs praises the beloved: "Thy nose is like the tower of Lebanon." The sages explained that nose refers to the Temple, for as the nose is set at the top of the human countenance so is the Temple set at the top of the world.[118]

8 / ZAVAR HAOLAM—THE NECK OF THE WORLD

"Thy neck is as a tower of ivory," rejoices the Song of Songs. "Thy neck," say the sages, "is the Temple." "Why is it compared to a neck—because so long as the Temple was standing, Israel's neck was stretched up among the nations of the world; when the Temple was destroyed Israel's neck was bowed." And the Book of Lamentations bewails: "To our very necks we are pursued."

Zavar is also an appellation of Jerusalem used by Isaiah describing the enemy invading the country: "And he shall sweep through Judah. . . ./He shall reach even to the neck." The Aramaic translation writes, instead of neck, Jerusalem.*[119]

9 / TALPIOT—HILL OF MOUTHS

The Song of Songs proceeds: "Thy neck is like the tower of David/Builded with turrets [*talpiot*]"; another version gives "armory."

Legend holds that Talpiot is a contraction of the Hebrew *tel*: hill, and *piot*: mouths, and adds that it is the place toward which all mouths turn while praying to the blessed Almighty.[120]

10 / APIRION—PALANQUIN

The Song of Songs also says: "King Solomon made himself a palanquin/Of the wood of Lebanon . . ./The inside

* See legend VI:8.

thereof being inlaid with love,/From the daughters of Jerusalem."

The sages interpret it thus: Palanquin is the Temple. In later Hebrew literature Apirion became a designation of the Temple rebuilt in the end of time. Nahamanides, the famous rabbi who restored the Jewish community in Jerusalem in the thirteenth century, prays for the revival of all Israel in the land of the ancestors: "Soon may Thee lift up the flag to ingather our exiles, restore the Apirion and renew the days of peacefulness." Above the entrance of the synagogue Hahurva, in the Old City of Jerusalem, following the names of the donors, there was inscribed: "May they be privileged to see the erection of Apirion on Mount Zion, soon, in our times. Amen."[121]

XII

DESTRUCTION
OF THE TEMPLE

1 / SIGNS OF DESTRUCTION

Josephus Flavius, who lived in the time of the Temple's destruction, wrote about the signs which announced the forthcoming catastrophe: "So it was when a star, resembling a sword, stood over the city Jerusalem and a comet which continued for a year. . . .

"And again, when before the revolt and the commotion that led to war, at the time when the people were assembling for the Feast of Unleavened Bread [Pesah] . . . at the ninth hour of the night, so brilliant a light shone round the altar and the sanctuary that it seemed to be broad daylight, and this continued for half an hour. . . .

"For before sunset throughout all parts of the country, chariots were seen in the air and armed battalions hurtling through the clouds, and encompassing the city (fig. 35).

"Moreover, at the feast which is called Pentecost [Shebuoth] the priests, on entering the inner court of the Temple by night, as was their custom in the discharge of their ministrations, reported that they were conscious

FIG. 35. ARMED BATTALIONS HURTLING THROUGH CLOUDS
ENCOMPASSING JERUSALEM (1743)

first of a commotion and a din, and after that, of a voice
as of a host: We are departing hence!"[122]

2 / PORTALS OPENED BY THEMSELVES

"Forty years before the destruction of the Temple, the
western light could not be kindled. And the portals of the
sanctuary used to open by themselves, until Rabbi Yohanan ben Zakkai reproached them, saying: 'Sanctuary!
Sanctuary! Why dost thou frighten thyself! Well do I
know that thy fate is to be destroyed.'"

Josephus Flavius relates: "Moreover, the eastern gate
of the inner court—it was of brass and very massive, and
when closed toward evening, could scarcely be removed
by twenty men; fastened with iron-bound bars, it had
bolts which were sunk to a great depth into a threshold
consisting of a solid block of stone.

"This gate was observed at the sixth hour of the night
to have opened of its own accord. The watchman of the
Temple ran and reported the matter to the captain, and

he came up and with difficulty succeeded in shutting it.

"This again, to the uninitiated, seemed the best of omens, as they supposed that God had opened to them the gate of blessing. But the learned understood that the security of the Temple was dissolving of its own accord, and that the opening of the gate meant a present to the enemy, interpreting the portent in their own minds as indicative of coming desolation."[123]

3 / SQUARE—AN OMEN OF DESTRUCTION

The courtyard of the Temple, on the heights of Mount Moriah, was in the shape of a rectangle, as it is today. On the northern boundary of the yard there stood the Tower of Antonia—a fortress for the Temple's defense. In ancient times there was a belief among the people that if the rectangular court should become squared, whatever the reason, it would be an omen that the destruction of the Temple was at hand.

Josephus Flavius tells of the bloody battles fought in the Temple court between the Jews and the Romans. The Romans captured the northern part, and the Jews fell back to the south. "Now, if anyone considers these things, he will find that God takes care of mankind, and by all ways possible, foreshows to our race what is for their preservation: but that men perish by those miseries which they madly and voluntarily bring upon themselves.

"For the Jews, by demolishing the Tower of Antonia had made their Temple foursquare, while at the same time they had it written in their sacred oracles: That then should their city be taken, as well as their holy house, when once their Temple should become foursquare."[124]

4 / A THREAD OF CRIMSON

A thread of crimson wool was tied to the doors of the sanctuary. If it turned white, this was a sign that the Holy One, blessed be He, had forgiven the sins of Israel, as in the words of Isaiah: "Though your sins be as scarlet/ They shall be as white as snow;/Though they be red like crimson/They shall be as wool."

"Originally they used to fasten the thread of scarlet on the door of the [Temple] court on the outside.

"If it turned white,—the people would rejoice.

And if it did not turn white,—they were sad. . . .

"Forty years before the destruction of the Temple, the thread of crimson never turned white—but it remained red."[125]

5 / ANGELS LIT THE FIRE

It was not enemies of flesh and blood who burnt the Temple, but angels from heaven.

"The foes erected a platform on the Mount of the holy house. They climbed and settled in its center, whereon King Solomon was wont to sit and take counsel of the elders. . . .

"There the enemies consulted,—how to burn the Temple?—They were still considering, when lifting their eyes, they saw four angels descending from heaven, carrying in their hands torches. These they applied to the four corners of the sanctuary and sent it up in flames.

"When the high priest saw the Temple burning, he took the keys and flung them to the heavens, crying: 'These are the keys of Thy house!' "[126]

6 / WHERE ARE THE KEYS?

When the Holy Temple was destroyed the first time, the youngest among the priests gathered on the roof of the sanctuary carrying the keys of the Temple in their hands.

And they cried: "Master of the universe! Since we have not been privileged to become Thy faithful ministers, let these keys be entrusted to Thy hands!"—and they threw them upward into the skies.

And the shape of a hand came out of heaven and received them.

Isaiah the prophet lamented their death in these words: "The burden concerning the Valley of Vision:/What aileth thee now, that thou are wholly gone up to the housetops?/Thou that art full of uproar, a tumultuous city, a joyous town?/Thy slain are not slain with the sword, nor dead in battle."

The young priests said to heaven, when returning the Temple keys: "We were unfaithful guardians of your house, and unworthily ate from the royal treasure.

"And they held one another, jumped into the fire, and were burned together."[127]

7 / THE DIVINE PRESENCE LEAVES

The divine Presence departed from the holy of holies of the Temple, after its destruction: "And the divine Presence kissed the walls and embraced the pillars, sighing: 'Farewell, o my house and my sanctuary! Farewell, o my palace! Farewell, o my dear home! Farewell to you!'

"Blessed by Thy Name, O God, thou who shall return the divine Presence unto Zion."[128]

8 / THE DIVINE PRESENCE IS AS A BIRD

In the Book of Ecclesiastes it is said: "And one shall start up at the voice of a bird," Legend explains that this refers to Nebuchadnezzar, the wicked.

Nebuchadnezzar, king of Babylon, destroyed the first Temple—the nest of the divine Presence. The fate of the divine Presence in the Holy Temple was like that of a bird whose nest has been plundered and her young carried off.

"Like the bird whose brood has been stolen, and nevertheless does not abandon its nest, but sits solitary within, so is the divine Presence. For although the Temple is burnt down, Jerusalem destroyed, and Israel scattered among the nations—the divine Presence still dwells in its place."[129]

9 / THE DIVINE PRESENCE REBUKES

"In the days to come, the Almighty, blessed be He, shall sit on His seat of judgment. He shall call out to heaven and to earth and say: 'In the beginning I created you. . . . How could you behold My divine Presence depart and My house lie in ruins and My sons go into exile among the nations of the world—and refrain from raising your voices and begging mercy for them?

"Then He shall address Himself to the sun and moon in the same words: 'Two large luminaries have I created you. . . . How come you behold My divine Presence depart and My house lie in ruins and My sons go into exile among the nations of the world—and refrain from raising your voices and begging mercy for them?

"Then He shall direct the same reproaches to the stars and constellations, and to the ministering angels. . . . 'Why did you not beseech forgiveness?'

"Finally He shall face the patriarchs and say: 'I have enacted harsh judgments against your own sons, and you have not prayed for pity!' "[130]

10 / ARIEL DESTROYED AND REBUILT

Jerusalem and the Temple were nicknamed Ariel—Lion of God, because the sanctuary on the mount looked like a reclining lion, king of the animals.*

The sages of Israel said of its destruction: "A lion came, in the month of the lion, and destroyed the lion of God."

"A lion came"—that is Nebuchadnezzar the wicked, king of Babylon. As Jeremiah describes his coming: "A lion is gone up from his thicket."

"Month of the lion"—the destruction of the Temple was

* See legend X:1.

in the month of Av, whose symbol was a lion in the
Hebrew Zodiac cycle. As Jeremiah said: "The carrying
away of Jerusalem captive in the fifth month" (fig. 36).

"Destroyed the lion of God" (Ariel)—as Isaiah lamented:
"Ah Ariel, Ariel, the city where David encamped!"

FIG. 36. LION AS SYMBOL OF MONTH OF AV
From mosaic floor of ancient synagogue at Beth-Alpha, Israel. From
sixth century. Above it is written (in Hebrew) *arieh*, lion.

But then the sages add: "And in the end of time, a lion
shall come, in the month of the lion, and rebuild the lion
of God.

" 'A lion shall come'—this is God the Almighty, as He is
called in the prophecy of Amos: 'The lion hath roared,
who will not fear? The Lord God hath spoken.'

" 'Month of the Lion'—as Jeremiah prophesied: 'For I
will turn their mourning into joy,/And will comfort them,
and make them rejoice from their sorrow.' The mourning
day is in Av—the lion's month.

" 'And rebuild the lion of God'—as the words of the
psalmist: 'The Lord doth build up Jerusalem. He gathereth
together the outcasts of Israel.' "[131]

11 / WHEN WAS THE TEMPLE DESTROYED?

The Temple was destroyed on the ninth day of the
month Av. The ninth of Av, Tisha be-Av, is the day of
deepest mourning in Israel.

"On the ninth of Av it was decreed that our fathers should not enter the promised land, and on that day the first and second Temples were destroyed."

"Where it was customary to work on the ninth day of Av, work is allowed; where it was customary not to work, work is forbidden. And in all places, learned men and scholars desist from work."

"Whoever eats and drinks on the ninth of Av, is considered in the same way as if he ate and drank on the Day of Atonement.

"Whoever works on the ninth day of Av does not enjoy reward and blessedness for his efforts ever. . . .

"Whoever performs work on the ninth day of Av, instead of lamenting the fate of Jerusalem, shall see no joy in his life."

"In the end of time, the Almighty, blessed be He, shall restore to Jerusalem all its joy and happiness. . . . Although the ninth of Av is now a day of mourning, in the days to come the Almighty, blessed be He, shall turn it into a holy day, as it is said [by the prophet Jeremiah]: 'For I will turn this mourning into joy,/And I will comfort them,/And make them rejoice from their sorrow.' "[132]

12 / FROM THE DAY OF DESTRUCTION

From the day that the Temple was destroyed, men of sound judgment were cut off. Confusion of thought prevailed, and the heart did not seek after purity, but decided according to appearance. The shedding of blood profanes the holy soil and is an offence against the divine Presence; it was because of the shedding of blood that the Holy Temple was burned.

From the time that the Temple was destroyed, not a day passed without a curse. The rains dried up, and the dew did not yield its blessing; the fruits of the trees lost their taste, neither did they give forth nourishment.

When the offering of the firstfruits for the Temple was

abolished, the fig tree ceased to blossom. When the offering of wine ceased, the vineyards refused to put forth their vines. When the burning of the holy oil ceased, the olive trees would no longer yield their oil.[133]

13 / MOURNERS FOR THE TEMPLE

When the Temple was destroyed, a number of Jews became Nazarites and hermits.

Rabbi Yoshua came to them and said: "My children, why do you refuse to eat meat or to drink wine?"

They answered him: "How can we eat meat which once would have been sacrificed on the holy altar, and which is sacrificed no longer! How can we drink wine which once would have been poured out on the holy altar, and which is poured out no longer!"

The Lord said to Israel: "Ye have caused the destruction of My house and the exile of My children. Pray that peace come back to Jerusalem, and I will forgive you. For Jerusalem is the city of peace!"

"Pray for the peace of Jerusalem. May they prosper that love thee. . . . For my brethren and companions' sakes, I will now say 'Peace be within thee. For the sake of the house of the Lord our God, I will seek thy good.' "[134]

14 / WOE TO US THAT IT IS DESTROYED

"It happened once when Rabbi Yohanan ben Zakkai set out for Jerusalem and Rabbi Yoshua accompanied him. And they saw the Temple lying in ruins.

"Said Rabbi Yoshua: 'Woe to us that the sanctuary is waste, the place where Israel atoned for its sins!'

"Said Rabbi Yohanan: 'My son do not fear! We have just as effective a way of atoning for our sins!'

" 'What is it?'

" 'Charity toward each other, for it is said [by the prophet Hosea]: 'For I desire mercy and not sacrifice!' "[135]

XIII

FATE OF THE TEMPLE VESSELS

"The Holy City, with all its beloved possessions buried and hidden, has become shamed and despised; nothing remains but the exalted Torah."

1 / THE HOLY ARK

What became of the holy ark after the Temple was destroyed?

Some say that it sank in its place on Mount Moriah, into the depths of the earth; others say that the ark was exiled into Babylon along with the children of Israel; yet another opinion held is that it is hidden under the Lodge of Wood, which was in the Temple courtyard.

In the course of his duties in the courtyard, a priest serving in the second Temple perceived in the floor a slab which differed from all the others. He went to tell his friends about it, but before he had finished speaking, his soul departed from his body. Then the priests knew that the holy ark was hidden beneath this peculiar slab.

"The ark was struck with a hammer until a flame was kindled, and it was burnt."

There was a stone in the western part of the holy of holies. Upon it rested the ark, and before it, the flask of manna and the rod of Aaron. Knowing that the Temple would one day be destroyed, when Solomon constructed it he contrived a place of concealment for the ark, in deep and tortuous caches.

When the ark was hidden, along with it were hidden the bottle containing the manna and the one containing the sprinkling water, the staff of Aaron, with its almonds and blossoms, and the chest which the Philistines had sent as a gift to the God of Israel.

In *The Vision of Baruch* is described the angel who came while the Temple was burning to rescue its holy vessels: "And I saw him descend into the holy of holies and take from thence the veil, and the holy ark, and the mercy seat, and the two tables, and the holy raiment of the priests, and the altar of incense, and the forty-eight precious stones, wherewith the priest was adorned, and all the holy vessels of the tabernacle. And he spoke to the earth with a loud voice: Earth! earth! earth! Hear the word of the mighty God,/And receive what I commit to thee,/And guard them until the last times,/So that, when thou art ordered, thou mayst restore them,/So that strangers may not get possession of them./For the time comes when Jerusalem also will be delivered for a time./Until it is said, that it is again restored forever. "And the earth opened its mouth and swallowed them up."

It is told that the holy ark and other vessels of the Temple are hidden in the sealed Well of the Souls, which is below the cavern of the Foundation Stone, in the Dome of the Rock.*[136]

* See legend II:10.

2 / THE HOLY CURTAIN

Josephus Flavius relates that after the destruction of the second Temple, many of its vessels were taken to Rome and placed in the palace of the emperor.°

The rabbis tell about Titus: "He entered the holy of holies, . . . then took a sword and slashed the curtain. Miraculously, blood spurted out, and he thought that he had slain himself. Titus further took the curtain and shaped it like a basket, and brought all the vessels of the sanctuary and put them in it, and then put them on board ship to go and triumph with them in his city [Rome]. . . . And a gale sprang up at sea which threatened to wreck him."

Rabbi Yossi, who visited Rome in the second century and saw the curtain, writes: "I saw it in Rome, and upon it were several drops of blood."[137]

3 / THE GOLDEN MENORAH

The Romans also removed from the Temple the beautiful menorah candelabrum and took it to Rome. On the Arch of Titus, which still stands today, this menorah appears among the booty taken by the Roman soldiers (fig. 37).

It is told that in Constantinople, formerly capital of the Byzantine Empire and Turkey, one candelabrum from the Temple was guarded. In the tenth century it was still kindled in processions on Christian holidays.

In the famous cathedral called "The Great Dome," in the city of Prague, stands a bronze candelabrum which a local legend ascribes to the Temple. It was brought as booty from a battle in Italy in 1158.[138]

° For a description of the curtain, see legend VII:9. It is also mentioned in the New Testament (Matthew 27:51): "And, behold, the vail of the temple was rent in twain from the top to the bottom."

FIG. 37. THE TEMPLE'S VESSELS BORNE BY ROMAN SOLDIERS
AFTER DESTRUCTION OF THE TEMPLE (1ST CENTURY)
Bas-relief on Arch of Titus in Rome. The Romans are crowned with
garlands of laurel, symbol of victory. They carry candelabrum,
trumpets, and other holy vessels.

4 / PILLARS FROM THE TEMPLE

Legend says that some of the pillars of the Temple were
taken to Rome. The famous traveler Rabbi Benjamin of
Tudela, who was in Rome in 1175, tells about his visits
to interesting sights of Rome: "Another remarkable object
is Saint Giovanni in Porta Latina, in which place of worship there are two copper pillars, constructed by King
Solomon of blessed memory, whose name 'Solomon son of
David' is engraved upon each. The Jews in Rome told
Benjamin that every year, about the time of the ninth day
of the month Ab [the memorial day of the destruction
of the Temple], these pillars sweat so much that the water
runs down from them. You see there also the cave in which
Titus the son of Vespasian hid the vessels of the Temple,
which he brought from Jerusalem."*[139]

* It is told about Rabbi Joshua son of Levi, who visited Rome in the
third century, "that he saw there pillars covered with tapestry, in winter
so that they should not contract, and in summer, that they should not
split." He does not mention where these pillars are from.

On the crown of the high priest was a golden plate, as described in the Torah: "And thou shalt make a plate of pure gold, and engrave upon it, like the engravings of a signet: HOLY TO THE LORD."

"And they made the plate of the holy crown of pure gold, and wrote upon it a writing, like the engravings of a signet: HOLY TO THE LORD."

This golden plate was taken to Rome with the Temple booty. Rabbi Eliezer son of Rabbi Yossi relates about the plate of the high priest: "I saw it in Rome, and on it was written 'Holiness to the Lord.' "[140]

6 / KING SOLOMON'S THRONE

King Solomon had a precious and beautiful throne.

"Moreover, the king had a great throne of ivory and overlaid it with the best gold. The throne had six steps, and the top of the throne was round behind: and there were stays on either side on the place of the seat, and two lions stood beside the stays. And twelve lions stood there on the one side and on the other upon the six steps; there was not the like made in any kingdom."

Rabbis tell: "When Nebuchadnezzar rose up and destroyed Jerusalem, he carried it off to Babylon."

And from Babylon to Persia.

And from Persia to Greece.

And from Greece to Rome.

Rabbi Eliezer son of Rabbi Yossi relates about Solomon's throne: "I saw its fragments in Rome."[141]

7 / VESSELS IN BABYLON

Many of the Temple's vessels were taken to Babylon, and hidden in the tower of Baghdad, in Barsif (Barsippa) in the wall of the city Babylon, in Tell Beruk, and in various other places there.

"One hundred thirty Levites were killed, and one hundred were saved and escaped with 500,000 plates of fine gold, and 1,200,000 plates of silver, and 36 golden trumpets. All these they secreted in a tower in the land of Babylon, in the walled city Baghdad. And they brought with them 100,000 candelbra of fine gold, each with seven candles . . . 77 gold tables, whose gold was from the walls of the Garden of Eden that was revealed unto Solomon the king, and whose glitter is as the brightness of the sun and the moon . . . all these were brought and hidden together with precious stones of which the Temple was built. Pearls, silver, and gold that King David had consecrated . . . all these were cached and hidden from the Chaldean soldiers in a place called Barsif [Barsippa], with treasures of silver and gold from the time of David, until the reign of Zedakiah, and until the exile of Israel to Babylon. All this was hidden in the wall of the city Babylon and in Tell Beruk, under the great willow tree."

"And Israel hid the vessels . . . until there shall arise a righteous king in Israel . . . and they swore never to reveal these vessels until David shall come—when the exiles of Israel shall be gathered from the four corners of the earth, and ascend in glory unto the land of Israel. In that time, a mighty river named Gihon shall stream forth from the holy of holies, and it shall flow through the great and awful desert, and mix with the waters of the Euphrates River. . . . And immediately, the vessels shall rise and be revealed."[142]

XIV
THE TEMPLE
OF HEAVEN

1 / THE TEMPLE OF HEAVEN AND OF EARTH

The Temple of earth is directed toward the Temple of heaven. Moses, the man of God, says in his song: "The place, O Lord, which Thou hast made for Thee to dwell in [machon],/The sanctuary, O Lord, which Thy hands have established." The ancients interpreted: "Do not read 'machon'—to dwell in—but 'mechuvan'—to direct toward." The sanctuary is directed toward His dwelling in heaven.

"Those who stand and pray on the Temple Mount, turn their countenance toward the house of the holy of holies. To which house is this? Toward the holy of holies of heaven."

A Jerusalemite rabbi, around 1835, gives advice to a Jew who visits the Temple courtyard: "And this is the short prayer which you shall recite when facing the Temple Mount at the Western Wall: 'Here am I directing my heart toward the land of Israel, toward the Holy Temple, and toward the Temple in heaven.' "[143]

2 / THE HEAVENLY TEMPLE

The Temple is built in the heights of firmament in a heavenly Jerusalem. In it are holy vessels, and priestly services are also performed there. The archangel Michael serves as high priest.

"Seven things preceded the creation of the world by two thousand years." One of them is the Temple of heaven.

To the psalmist's words, "Honor and majesty are before Him:/Strength and beauty are in His Sanctuary," the legend adds: "This is the Temple of God, which stands on the summit of firmament, whose brilliance illuminates all the rooms of heaven. One thousand and eighteen hosts stand before the divine Presence in the celestial Temple, and every day they invoke it, calling: 'Holy! Holy!' And every host is composed of many thousands of ministering angels."

The horses which surround the heavenly Temple are also described: "There are horses of darkness, horses of blood, horses of iron, and horses of mist. They stand next to troughs of fire, filled with coals of the broom-brush plants. And rivers of fire stream beside the troughs, and the horses drink of them an amount equal to the quantity of water which flows in the Brook of Kidron, and the quantity of rainwater which falls in the area of Jerusalem."[144]

3 / SERVICE IN THE CELESTIAL TEMPLE

"And God created the Temple on earth, and correspondingly He created the Temple in heaven, each facing the other . . . and at the time when the Temple stood, while the high priest sacrificed and burnt incense below, the archangel Michael sacrificed and burned incense up above.

"When the Almighty, blessed be He, destroyed His house, He said to Michael the archangel: 'Michael, whereas

I have wasted My house and burned My sanctuary, devastated My shrine, and demolished My altar—do not sacrifice to Me any more.'

"Said Michael: 'Master of the universe! How shall Thy people atone for their sins?'

"Said the Almighty: 'Bring unto Me the merits, the prayers, and the souls of the righteous who dwell under My seat of honor, and the purity of the innocent children, and I shall remit the sins of Israel. . . .

"The Almighty, blessed be He, said: 'From the day that I destroyed and laid waste My house below, I have never sat and rested in My house above, but I have dwelt in dew and rain.' "

Seven firmaments are spread out in the heavens; one of them is called Zebul. The prophet Isaiah calls to God: "Look down from heaven, and behold from the habitation [*zebul*] of Thy holiness and of Thy glory."

"In Zebul are heavenly Jerusalem, the Temple and its altar. And Michael, the high priest stands and brings sacrifices to it every day. What are his offerings?—The souls of the righteous.

"In Zebul, too, is the dwelling place of groups of ministering angels who sing at night, and contemplate by day, for the glory of Israel."[145]

4 / MOSES IN THE TEMPLE OF HEAVEN

When Moses, the man of God, ascended to heaven, straightaway the Lord cleaved the seven firmaments and showed him the Temple of heaven.

"On the same day when Moses was to die, the Almighty, blessed be He, lifted him up to the skies, and He showed him what reward awaited him therein, and He unfolded before him the mysteries of the days to come. . . . And Moses saw the Almighty, blessed be He, building the Temple of heaven out of precious stones and pearls, and between stone and stone there rested the splendor of the divine Presence. . . .

"The Messiah sat inside the Temple; and the brother of Moses, Aaron, wearing priestly raiments, stood beside him. . . . Aaron told Moses: 'No man may enter here until he forgets the taste of life and gives up his soul to the angel of death.'

"When he heard these words, at once Moses fell on his face before the Almighty, and said: 'Master of the universe! I beseech Thee, allow me to speak with the Messiah before death taketh me.' . . .

"Moses said to the Messiah: 'The Almighty, blessed be He, confided unto me and that He shall build His holy house on earth—the Temple of Israel . . . and yet I saw Him with my own eyes erecting His Temple in the heavens!'

"Said the Messiah: 'Moses, Jacob thy father saw the house that He would build on earth, and also the house that the Almighty shall erect with His own hands in the skies.'

"When Moses heard these words from the lips of the Messiah, he greatly rejoiced. He knew then from the depths of his soul that the house which the Lord buildeth with his own hands in the heavens, out of precious stones, and out of the glory of the divine Presence, shall be the house of Israel forever and ever until the end of time.

"Moses returned to the Presence of the Holy One, and asked: 'O Lord of the universe! When shall the earthly Jerusalem be humbled and degraded?'

"The Lord replied: 'The answer to this I have revealed to no creature. Shall I then tell you?'

"Moses pleaded: 'Master of the universe! Give me a hint of Thy deeds!'

"And the Almighty declared: 'In the beginning, I shall grant succor to Israel . . . then they shall be dispersed among all the nations of the earth . . . but I shall repent and gather again all those who were exiled.

"At that moment, Moses descended from heaven completely contented, and passed on his soul to God willingly."[146]

5 / DAVID IN THE TEMPLE OF HEAVEN

"When King David ascended unto the celestial Temple, a throne of fire, forty parasangs high, and doubly long and doubly wide, was prepared for him.

"When David arrived and sat in this throne, facing the throne of his Creator, with all the kings of the dynasty of David seated before him, and all the kings of the kingdom of Israel seated behind him, he immediately rose and sang songs of praise and thanksgiving, whose like have never been heard by mortal men."[147]

XV
ANCIENT JERUSALEM

1 / POSSESSION OF THE TRIBES

According to the Bible, the borders of two tribes of Israel passed within the area of Jerusalem: on the south —Judah, and on the north—Benjamin.

But legend tells that "Jerusalem was not apportioned to any of the tribes"; it is in the possession of all the tribes of Israel, as it is said in the Book of Kings: "For Jerusalem's sake, the city which I have chosen out of all the tribes of Israel."

To the words of the Torah, "For the Lord thy God hath chosen him out of all thy tribes," the sages add: "This is Jerusalem, which was built on the merits of the tribes."[148]

2 / HOW DID DAVID CONQUER?

When King David went out to fight against the Jebusites in Jerusalem, he said to his followers: "Whosoever smiteth the Jebusite first, shall be chief and captain."

What did David's commander, Joab, do? He brought a green cypress tree and fixed it by the side of the wall of

Jerusalem. Then he climbed on David's shoulders, bent down the flexible head of the cypress, and hung on to it. The tree straightened itself, lifting him up to the top of the wall, which he then scaled.

What did the Almighty do? He shortened the wall, and David climbed after Joab, for David said in his Book of Psalms: "In the day that the Lord delivered him from the hand of all his enemies. . . ./For by Thee I run upon a troop;/And by my God do I scale a wall."[149]

3 / CUSTOMS AND MANNERS

Certain customs and manners were peculiar to Jerusalem. A flag would be displayed at the door of a house where a feast was being held, and after it had been removed, no one might enter.

If a man commissioned his neighbor to prepare a dinner for him and the neighbor spoiled it, he was obliged to pay two fines: one for the shame he had caused to the master of the house and the other for the shame he had caused to the guests.[150]

4 / MARKETS IN JERUSALEM

The sages of Israel relate: "The markets of Jerusalem were swept daily."

There were several markets in Jerusalem, all built along the two sides of the main thoroughfares. Each, says legend, served a different section of the population. There was the market of Kings, the market of Prophets, the market of Priests (Cohanim), the market of Levites (Leviim), and the market of the rest of Israel. Those who came to them could be recognized by their garments, which were unique to each group.

"There were twenty-four thoroughfares in Jerusalem. Each thoroughfare had twenty-four side-turnings; each side-turning had twenty-four roads; each road had twenty-four streets; each street had twenty-four courts; each court had twenty-four houses; and each court—residents double the number of those who came out of Egypt."

The Torah tells the number of those who went out of Egypt: "From twenty years old and upward, all that were able to go forth to war in Israel were six hundred thousand and three thousand and five hundred and fifty."[151]

5 / THE SPICE MARKET

There was in Jerusalem a special market selling various spices: myrrh, nard, balsam, and others. It was similar to the spice market (in Arabic *Suk al-Attarin*) in the Old City of today. The men of the city used to buy fragrant spices for the women to perfume themselves with.

The rabbis said: "The bridegroom must undertake [to give his wife] ten denarii for her basket. Which basket is meant?—The perfume basket. . . . This ruling applies only in Jerusalem."

Legend says that it was unnecessary for the brides of Jerusalem to perfume themselves, for the fragrance of the incense burnt in the Holy Temple would spread about, infusing the air with the odor of frankincense and perfuming the women as well.

The prophet Isaiah describes the women of Jerusalem: "The daughters of Zion are haughty,/And walk with stretched-forth necks/And wanton eyes,/Walking and mincing as they go,/And making a tinkling with their feet."

" 'A tinkling with their feet'—they put myrrh and balsam in their shoes and strolled through the markets of Jerusalem."[152]

6 / REGULATIONS IN ANCIENT JERUSALEM

Our forefathers point out the regulations practiced in Jerusalem in the olden days for the benefit of the inhabitants and the pilgrims:

"That peddlers selling spicery be allowed to travel

about in the towns, for the purpose of providing toilet articles for the women so that they should not be repulsive in the eyes of their husbands. . . .

"That neither beams nor balconies should be allowed to project there [the commentator explains that this is so as not to harm the pilgrims visiting the Holy City].

"That no dunghill should be made there, on account of reptiles.

"That no kilns should be kept there, on account of the smoke [which would blacken the buildings of the town and its walls].

"That neither gardens nor orchards should be cultivated there, with the exception, however, of rose gardens that existed from the day of the former prophets.

"That no fowls should be reared there [on account of the smell].

"That no dead person be kept there overnight—this is known by tradition."

It had already been said: "Never did serpent or scorpion do harm in Jerusalem, and no man said to his fellow: The place is too strait for me that I should lodge in Jerusalem."[153]

7 / THE COIN OF JERUSALEM

The rabbis tell about coins which were minted in Jerusalem for the use of the inhabitants. On them were the names of the first two kings of Jerusalem, and the picture of the city—their residence. "What was the coin of Jerusalem?—David and Solomon—on one side. And Jerusalem, the Holy City—on the other."[154]

8 / THE GOLDEN CITY

In olden days Jewish women adorned themselves with an ornament called "the golden City" or "the golden Jerusalem," because the Holy City was pictured on it.

The rabbis prohibited carrying this ornament on the Sabbath: "A woman may not go out . . . with a 'golden city.'" But Rabbi Eliezer said: "A woman goes out [on the Sabbath] with the golden city."

"What is the golden city?—A golden Jerusalem."

It is told that Rabbi Akiba loved his wife but was too poor to buy an ornament for her. He said: "If only I could afford it, I would present you with a golden Jerusalem."

Later, when he acquired the means, Rabbi Akiba bought "the golden Jerusalem" for his wife, and when the wife of Rabban Gamaliel saw it she envied her, and asked her husband for the same.[155]

9 / WHAT SHALL BE SOLD?

In the end of days, the markets of Jerusalem shall sell the delicious meat remaining from the same Leviathan, the legendary whale, which will be served in paradise.

"The Holy One, blessed be He, will in time to come make a banquet for the righteous from the flesh of Leviathan . . . the rest will be distributed and sold out in the markets of Jerusalem."[156]

10 / STONE OF INQUIRY

There was a stone in Jerusalem known as the Stone of Inquiry (in Hebrew *Eben To'en*). All lost property was deposited there, so that those who lost anything knew where to go to inquire after their loss. On their giving proof of their identity, it was returned to them.

The Stone of Inquiry was high, and when the rains were strong and water covered it, it was a danger sign of approaching floods.

Rabbi Honi the circle-maker once prayed for rain, and the water descended in such torrents that the people beseeched him: "Just as you prayed for the rain to fall, pray now for the water to be removed."

He told them to go out and see if the Stone of Inquiry had been covered and disappeared "in the rainwater!"*[157]

11 / LODGE OF ACCOUNTANTS

Near Jerusalem stood the Lodge of Accountants, and all who had accounts to render or business to transact would repair to it.

This lodge was placed outside the city, because of the words in Psalms: "In the city of our God,/His holy mountain,/Fair in situation, the joy of the whole earth; even mount Zion."

And how could anyone whose heart is troubled with cares of business be regarded as joyous?[158]

12 / COURT AT BETH YAAZEK

There was a large courtyard in Jerusalem called Beth Yaazek, where all the witnesses who saw the new moon came and were examined by the sages of the court, who accordingly declared the first day of the new month and the holidays. The sages prepared large meals for the witnesses, so that they might make it their habit to come and testify.

"How do they examine the witnesses?—The pair which comes first, they examine first. They bring in the elder of the two and say to him: 'Tell us how thou sawest the moon —facing the sun or turned away from it?—to the north or to the south?—How high was it?—To which side was it leaning?—And how broad was it?'

"If he said: 'Facing the sun,' he has said naught. Afterward, they bring in the second witness, and examine him. If their words are found to agree, their evidence holds good.

* See legend XXIV:8.

"The other pairs of witnesses were asked only the main points, not because there was need of them, but that they should not go away disappointed, and that they might make it their habit to come.

"Thus did they announce the benediction of the new moon: The chief of the court says: 'It is hallowed!,' and all the people answer after him: 'It is hallowed! It is hallowed!' "

Following this proclamation, they went directly to the Mount of Olives (*Mish-ha*), and on its summit lit the first torch. From there torches were lit on all the other mountains, announcing the new moon to the dwellers of the Holy Land and the lands of the exile.*[159]

13 / THE ARMORY OF JERUSALEM

In the days of Nehemiah, there was in Jerusalem a place called "Going Up of the Armory"—in Hebrew *Aloth ha-Neshek*. Nehemiah tells of the rebuilding of the city: "And next to him repaired . . . another portion over against the ascent to the armory, at the Turning [of the wall]."

An ancient commentarian explains: "Aloth ha-Neshek—a place where are stored the weapons of war, for men did not enter Jerusalem armed with weapons, in order to fulfil the words of the Torah: 'And I will give peace in the land. . . . Neither shall the sword go through your land.' "[160]

14 / TOWER OF THE HUNDRED

On the wall of ancient Jerusalem stood the Tower of the Hundred (in Hebrew *Migdal ha-Meah*). In Nehemiah's description of the city, he tells of the families of priests who built part of the wall: "Even unto the tower of Hammeah they sanctified it."

A commentarian explains the origin of the name Tower of Ha-Meah (the Hundred): "This was the House of the

* See legend XXVIII:14.

Great Assembly in Jerusalem—where the members answered Amen, one hundred times each day."[161]

15 / TOWER OF THE OVENS

In the days of Nehemiah, in the wall of Jerusalem stood the Tower of Ovens. At the dedication of the wall, the procession of thanksgiving passed by this tower.

One commentator explains the name Tower of Ovens: "This is the place where were ovens for the baking of bread for the inhabitants of Jerusalem. For there were no ovens within Jerusalem because of the smoke."

Special regulations were applied to Jerusalem, and one of them was "that no kilns be kept there" because the smoke would blacken the buildings of the town.

Rashi adds: "And also the wall—because that is a disgrace."[162]

16 / PILGRIMS IN JERUSALEM

One of the ten restricting ordinances in Jerusalem was "that neither beams nor balconies should be allowed to project . . . so as not to cause harm to the pilgrims who come for the festivals."

"No man said to his fellow: 'The place is too strait for me that I should lodge in Jerusalem.'"

"Jerusalem was not apportioned to any of the tribes, as it has been taught.

"People cannot let out houses in Jerusalem, as they do not belong to them.

"They may not hire out beds either. Therefore the householder who took in pilgrims should seize the skins of the visitors' sacrifices."[163]

17 / OATH IN HOLY JERUSALEM

In ancient days it was a custom among the people of Israel to take oaths by Jerusalem the holy. They also used to swear by the Temple, the abode of the Lord.

Jesus of Nazareth, in his Sermon on the Mount, said to his followers: "But I tell you that you should not bind yourselves by any oath, nor by the earth—for the earth is the footstool of His feet; nor by Jerusalem, for it is the city of the great king."[164]

18 / WONDERS OF THE WALLS

The walls of Jerusalem had special qualities—whoever gazed upon them was cured of his ailments. "If one were hurt, and gazed upon her walls, he was healed. Never did serpent or scorpion do harm in Jerusalem."

In the Middle Ages a mosque stood in Jerusalem which was named after the serpents. In it were displayed two pillars, upon whose capitals were engraved poisonous snakes. The Arabs of Jerusalem believed that these images were a charm against snake bite. By their merit, a man bitten by a snake felt no pain as long as he remained within the walls of the city. But were he to leave Jerusalem within three hundred sixty days from the time when he was bitten, he would surely die immediately. After this period, however, there would be no danger even outside of Jerusalem's walls.[165]

19 / WATCHMEN ON THE WALLS

"Thou shalt call thy walls Salvation
And thy gates Praise."

Angels guarded the walls of ancient Jerusalem: "Come and see the love of the Holy One for His people Israel. For the ministering angels who are mighty in strength do the Lord make to watch over Israel."

Who are they? The archangels Michael and Gabriel.

As the prophet Isaiah says: "I have set watchmen/Upon thy walls, O Jerusalem,/. . . till He make Jerusalem/A praise in the earth."[166]

XVI
THE DESTRUCTION OF JERUSALEM

1 / KING OF BABYLON TO JERUSALEM

Nebuchadnezzar, king of Babylon, destroyed the first Temple of Jerusalem. It is said that before he approached the land of Israel on his way to Jerusalem he consulted sorcery and divination. The prophet Ezekiel describes this, and the rabbis expound on his words.

" 'For the king of Babylon standeth at the parting of the way'—at the head of two roads which divide off into two directions.

" 'At the head of two ways'—two roads were there, one leading to the wilderness and the other leading to an inhabited place [Jerusalem].

" 'To use divination'—he began to practice divination using the name of Rome, but without success, the name of Alexandria, but without success, then the name of Jerusalem and it succeeded.

" 'He made his arrows bright'—in the name of Rome, but without success, in the name of Alexandria, but without success, then in the name of Jerusalem, and it succeeded.

"He tried to kindle torches and lanterns in the name of Rome, but they would not light, in the name of Alexandria, but they would not light, then in the name of Jerusalem, and they lit up.

" 'He consulted with images'—they floated ships on the river Euphrates in the name of Rome, but they would not go, in the name of Alexandria, but they would not go, then in the name of Jerusalem and they went.

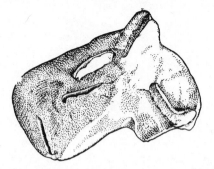

FIG. 38. MODEL OF A LIVER MADE OF CLAY (C. 1400 B.C.E.) Found at Megiddo excavations. Form of liver was used for divination and foretelling future. Another liver of clay of the same period was uncovered in the excavations of Hazor, upper Galilee.

" 'He looked in the liver'—like an Arab who slays a lamb and inspects its liver [for omens]."

In the excavations of historical sites in Palestine and in Babylon there were found models of the liver made of clay for divination and sorcery (figs. 38 and 39).[167]

2 / THE FATE OF THE DESTROYER OF JERUSALEM

Titus was the commander of the Roman army that destroyed Jerusalem and its Temple. The rabbis call him "the wicked Titus" because he blasphemed God and insulted heaven.

FIG. 39. JERUSALEM (1727)
In center, Mosque of Omar, Dome of the Rock, stands out as symbol of the Temple in olden days. Mountains are drawn behind Holy City; over them appear words of Psalms: "As the mountains are round about Jerusalem" (Psalms 125:2).

"What did he do?—He entered the holy of holies . . . took a sword and slashed the curtain. Miraculously, blood spurted out. . . . Titus further took the curtain and shaped it like a basket and brought all the vessels of the sanctuary and put them in it, and then put them on board ship to go and triumph with them in his city [Rome]. . . . A gale sprang up at sea which threatened to wreck him.

"He said: Apparently the power of the God of these people is only over water. . . . If He is really mighty, let Him come up on the dry land and fight with me.

"A voice went forth from heaven saying: Sinner! Son of Sinner! . . . I have a tiny creature in my world called a gnat. . . . Go up on the dry land and make war with it.

"When he [Titus] landed, the gnat came and entered his nose, and it knocked against his brain for seven years.

"One day as he was passing a blacksmith's it heard the noise of the hammer and stopped.

"He said: I see there is a remedy! So every day they brought a blacksmith who hammered before him. If he was a non-Jew they gave him four coins. If he was a Jew they said: It is enough that you see the suffering of your enemy.

"This went on for thirty days, but then the creature got used to it . . . and when he [Titus] died they split open his skull and found there something like a sparrow. . . .

"When he [Titus] died he said: Burn me and scatter my ashes over the seven seas so that the God of the Jews should not find me and bring me to trial!"[168]

3 / AN ANGEL BROKE THROUGH

When the enemy besieged Jerusalem, it was decreed from above that the Holy City should be delivered into his hands. At this time, the Almighty said to Jeremiah the prophet, who was in Jerusalem: "Rise, and go to Anathot" (his birthplace).

As Jeremiah came out of Jerusalem, an angel descended from heaven, set his feet on the walls surrounding the city, and broke through them.

And he called out: "Let the foe come and enter the house wherein its Lord does not dwell, and let him loot and destroy it. Let him come into the vineyards and cut off the vines which the watchman has left behind. That the foe should not boast that he has conquered her.

"A conquered city hast thou overcome!

"A murdered nation hast thou killed!" [169]

4 / FROM THE WALL TO THE TEMPLE

On the seventeenth of the month Tammuz, the enemies broke through the wall of Jerusalem and fighting continued within the city. After twenty-one days they penetrated into Mount Moriah, and on the ninth of the month of Ab they destroyed the Temple.

The sages interpret the words of Jeremiah: " 'We are

confounded, because we have heard reproach'—this refers to the seventeenth of Tammuz: 'Shame hath covered our faces'—this refers to the ninth of Ab: Four strangers are come into the sanctuary of the Lord's house."

"The fourth fast day of the year is on the seventeenth of Tammuz,—when the wall of the Holy City was pierced. The fifth fast is on the ninth of the month of Ab—the day of the destruction of both the first and the second Temple."

The time between the penetration into Jerusalem and the destruction of its Temple was compared by the ancients to the period of the blossoming of the almond tree till the ripening of its fruit.

"A sign thereof are the words of Jeremiah the prophet: I see a rod of an almond tree."

For twenty-one days after it first blossoms, the fruit of the almond tree ripens. Likewise, twenty-one days passed from the day the wall was broken down to the day when the Temple was destroyed.[170]

5 / WITHIN THE STRAITS

The Book of Lamentations describes the great tragedy which befell Jerusalem and Israel: "She findeth no rest,/All her pursuers overtook her/Within the straits."

"Within the straits" (in Hebrew *bein ha-metzarim*) is the period of time between the seventeenth of Tammuz and the ninth of Ab. Twenty-one days of troubles and dangers when the *ketteb meriri* prevails everywhere.

According to the Holy Scriptures, *ketteb meriri* is "bitter destruction," as is mentioned in the words of Moses about Israel, who "forgot God that bore him": "I will heap evils upon them;/I will spend Mine arrows upon them;/. . . And bitter destruction [*ketteb meriri*]."

The psalmist promises to him "that dwellest . . . in the shadow of the Almighty": "Thou shalt not be afraid of the terror . . ./Nor . . . of the pestilence that walketh in darkness,/Nor of the destruction [*ketteb*] that wasteth at noonday."

According to the legend, *Ketteb Meriri* is the name of a demon who "stalks through the greater part of the midday period, from the beginning of the sixth hour until the end of the ninth."

The demon is covered with eyes, scales, and hair. One big eye is on his heart. Everyone who sees him falls and dies.[171]

6 / WHY WAS JERUSALEM DESTROYED?

There is no sorrow in the life of Israel like that of the destruction of Jerusalem and the burning of the Holy Temple. On that day their national freedom was lost, and the people commenced to count the new era of exile and suffering.

Why was Jerusalem destroyed?

Jerusalem was destroyed only because of the desecration of the Sabbath.

Jerusalem was destroyed only because the morning and evening prayers were abolished.

Jerusalem was destroyed only because the children of the schools remained untaught.

Jerusalem was destroyed only because the people did not feel shame toward one another.

Jerusalem was destroyed only because no distinction was drawn between the young and the old.

Jerusalem was destroyed only because one did not warn or admonish the other.

Jerusalem was destroyed only because men of scholarship and learning were despised.

Jerusalem was destroyed only because there were no longer men of faith and hope in her midst.

Jerusalem was destroyed only because her laws were

founded upon the strict letter of the Torah and were not
~~interpreted in the ways of mercy and kindness.~~[172]

7 / RENDING THE GARMENTS

"He who mourns for Jerusalem
Will live to share in her joy."

The sages of Israel taught: "He who sees the cities of
Judah in their desolation should say with the prophet
Isaiah; 'Thy holy cities are a wilderness!'—and rend his
garments.

"He who sees the city of Jerusalem in its desolation
should say, 'Zion is a wilderness, Jerusalem a desolation!'
—and rend his garments.

"He who sees the Holy Temple in its desolation should
say: 'Our holy and beautiful house where our fathers
praised Thee, is burned up with fire, and all our pleasant
things are laid waste!'—and rend his garments."

Rabbi Joseph Caro, a well-known scholar in Safed in
the sixteenth century, said: "One rent should be made on
seeing the cities of Judah, a second on beholding Jerusalem, and a final one on catching the first glimpse of the
Temple site. The rending should be carried out standing;
it should be done with the hand; the rents should be ex-
tended until the heart is laid bare; and they must never
be sewed up again."

"Simeon asked Rabbi Hiyya: I am a donkey driver and
come to Jerusalem very often. Must I rend my garments
each time?—

"Rabbi Hiyya replied: You need rend your garments
only if you visit Jerusalem after thirty days' absence."[173]

8 / THE MOURNERS FOR JERUSALEM

"If I forget thee, O Jerusalem,
Let my right hand forget her cunning.
Let my tongue cleave to the roof of my mouth,
If I remember thee not;
If I set not Jerusalem
Above my chiefest joy."

The prophet Isaiah consoles the mourners in Jerusalem: "To appoint unto them that mourn in Zion, to give unto them beauty for ashes, the oil of joy for mourning, the garment of praise for the spirit of heaviness, that they might be called trees of righteousness, the planting of the Lord, that he might be glorified. And they shall build the old wastes; they shall raise up the former desolations, and they shall repair the waste cities, the desolations of many generations."

"Our rabbis taught: When the Temple was destroyed for the second time, large numbers in Israel became ascetics, binding themselves neither to eat meat nor to drink wine.

"Rabbi Joshua went into conversation with them and said to them: My sons, why do you not eat meat nor drink wine?—

"They replied: Shall we eat flesh which used to be brought as an offering on the altar, now that this altar is in abeyance?—

"Shall we drink wine which used to be poured as a libation on the altar, but now no longer?

"He said to them: If that is so, we should not eat bread either, because the meal offerings have ceased.

"They said: That is so, and we can manage with fruit.

"—We should not eat fruit either, because there is no longer an offering of first fruits.

"Then we can manage with other fruits.

"But we should not drink water, because there is no longer any ceremony of the pouring of water [on the Feast of Tabernacles].

"To this they could find no answer.

"So he [Rabbi Joshua] said to them: My sons, come and listen to me. Not to mourn at all is impossible, because the blow has fallen. To mourn overmuch is also impossible, because we do not impose on the community a hardship which the majority cannot endure."

The well-known Jewish traveler Benjamin of Tudela, who visited in the East around 1175, tells of Jewish ascetics in Arabia, called mourners of Zion and mourners of Jerusalem: "These eat no meat and abstain from wine, dress always in black and live in caves or in low houses, and keep fasts all their lives except on Sabbaths and holy days."[174]

9 / THE COMFORTING OF JERUSALEM

"The Lord will console thee, O Jerusalem,
Save in Peace."

The Lord said to the prophets of Israel, "Go forth and console My city Jerusalem." The prophet Hosea went to console her and said to her: "The Lord has sent me to console thee." Jerusalem asked him: "Wherewith wilt thou console me?"

He answered: "I will be as the dew unto Israel;/He shall blossom as the lily,/And cast forth his roots as Lebanon."

Then came the prophet Joel with his consolation: "Then shall Jerusalem be holy,/And there shall no strangers pass through her any more,/And it shall come to pass in that day,/That the mountains shall drop down sweet wine,/And the hills shall flow with milk."

Then came the prophet Amos, who said: "In that day I will raise up/The tabernacle of David that is fallen,/And close up the breaches thereof,/And I will raise up his ruins,/And I will build it as in the days of old.

Then the prophet Micah said: "Who is a God like unto Thee, that pardoneth the iniquity,/And passeth by the transgression of the remnant of His heritage?/He retaineth not His anger for ever,/Because He delighteth in mercy."

Then came the prophet Nahum, who said: "Behold upon the mountains the feet of him/That bringeth good tidings, that announceth peace!/Keep thy feasts, O Judah,/Perform thy vows;/For the wicked one shall no more pass through thee."

Then came the prophet Zephaniah:

"Sing, O daughter of Zion,/Shout, O Israel;/Be glad and rejoice with all thy heart,/O daughter of Jerusalem./The Lord hath taken away thy judgments./He hath cast out thine enemy."

FIG. 40. JERUSALEM AND ITS WALLS (17TH CENTURY) Atop mountain is the Temple.

And so all the prophets returned to the Lord with words of consolation upon their lips, and said: "Lo and behold, Thy city of Jerusalem refuseth to be consoled."

And the Lord answered them: "You and I will go forth together so that we may console her," with the words: "Comfort ye, comfort ye, My people,/Saith your God./Bid Jerusalem take heart,/And proclaim unto her,/That her time of service is accomplished,/That her guilt is paid off. . . ./O thou that tellest good tidings to Zion,/Get thee up into the high mountain;/O thou that tellest good tidings to Jerusalem,/Lift up thy voice with strength;/Lift it up, be not afraid;/Say unto the cities of Judah:/'Behold your God!' "175

XVII

JERUSALEM IN THE END OF TIME

"Eternity—they name Jerusalem."

1 / WHEN WILL JERUSALEM BE RESTORED?

The rabbis relate: "Jerusalem will not be rebuilt in its entirety till all the children of Israel will be gathered from exile. . . . As it is written [in Psalms]: 'The Lord doth build up Jerusalem, He gathereth together the dispersed of Israel.'"

"When does God build Jerusalem?—When he gathereth the dispersed of Israel."

In the end of time, Jerusalem, the tent of God, will spread forth in all directions. All the children of Israel will return from exile and find rest and peace within her border, as it is prophesied by Isaiah: "Enlarge the place of thy tent,/And let them stretch forth the curtain of thy habitations, spare not;/Lengthen thy cords, and strengthen thy stakes./For thou shalt spread abroad on the right hand and on the left."

"God will gather the outcast of Israel in peace!"

FIG. 41. JERUSALEM AND ARRIVAL OF THE MESSIAH
The Messiah rides on a donkey, and before him strides Elijah the prophet, blowing shofar. They are nearing East Gate. Drawing is from Hebrew manuscript of sixteenth century.

"In the end of time, Jerusalem will become the metropolis for all lands."

"In the end of time, Jerusalem will be a shining light to all the nations of the earth, who will walk in its brightness" (figs. 41 and 42).[176]

FIG. 42. MESSIAH AND ELIJAH ADVANCING TOWARD JERUSALEM (1753)

2 / JERUSALEM IN THE FUTURE

The prophet Isaiah describes Jerusalem's restoration: "Behold, I will set thy stones in fair colours,/And lay thy foundations with sapphires./And I will make thy pinnacles of rubies,/And thy gates of carbuncles,/And all thy borders of precious stones."

"The Holy One, blessed be He, will in time to come add to Jerusalem a thousand gardens, a thousand towers, a thousand palaces, and a thousand mansions."

The Almighty will surround Jerusalem with seven walls: a wall of silver and a wall of gold; a wall of precious stones and a wall of lazulite; a wall of sapphire, a wall of emerald, and a wall of fire; and its brilliant splendor will radiate to the four corners of the globe.

The borders of Jerusalem in the future will be full of precious stones and pearls, and all Israel will come and take what they please.

In this world Israel marks its boundaries with common

stones, but in the world to come it will mark them with
precious stones and pearls.

"In the end of time, the Almighty will build a great
tabernacle for the righteous from the skin of the Leviathan
[whale], and that which remains will adorn the walls of
Jerusalem so that its brilliant splendor will radiate to the
four corners of the globe."[177]

3 / THE CELESTIAL JERUSALEM

Not only on the face of this earth is there a Jerusalem,
called in Hebrew *Yerushalaim Shel Matta* (the Lower),
but also in heaven is there such a city: *Yerushalaim Shel
Maalah*—Jerusalem the Upper.

Rabbi Yohanan said: "The Holy One, blessed be He,
said: I will not enter Jerusalem the Upper, until I can
enter Jerusalem the Lower."

In the upper Jerusalem there is also a Temple, and
when the high priest of Israel entered the Temple on
Mount Moriah and offered sacrifices and incense, the
archangel Michael entered the heavenly Temple and
offered sacrifices and incense.

Everyone who wishes can go to Jerusalem on earth, but
not to Jerusalem in heaven. Here only those who are invited can enter. When Moses was taken by the angel, God
opened before him the seven heavens and showed him
Jerusalem with its Temple.

Jeremiah prophesied: "Behold, I will turn the captivity
of Jacob's tents,/And have compassion on his dwelling-
places;/And the city shall be builded upon her own
mound,/And the palace shall be inhabited upon its wonted
place."

The legend interprets the words of the prophet: "And
the city shall be builded upon her own heap" refers to
Jerusalem the Lower. "And the palace shall remain after
the manner thereof" refers to Jerusalem the Upper.

In the second century the church father Tertullian

writes about the divinely built city of Jerusalem which is in heaven: "It is evident from the testimony of even heathen witnesses that in Judea there was a city suspended in the sky early every morning. . . . As the day advanced, the entire figure of the walls would wane gradually, and sometimes it would vanish instantly."*[178]

4 / LIVING WATERS IN JERUSALEM

*"A river, the streams whereof
make glad the city of God."*

The prophet Zechariah foretells: "And it shall come to pass that day,/That living waters shall go out from Jerusalem."

The living water will stream from the Temple, as the prophet Joel describes: "And it shall come to pass in that day/. . . And a fountain shall come forth of the house of the Lord."

The prophet Ezekiel describes in his vision how he was taken to Jerusalem and to the house of the Lord: "And he brought me unto the door of the house; and behold, waters issued out from under the threshold of the house eastward . . ./and it was a river that I could not pass through./. . . Now when I had been brought back, behold, upon the bank of the river were very many trees on the one side and on the other."

The rabbis describe this river, and the streams which branch from it: "The spring that issues forth from the holy of holies in its beginning resembles the antennae of the grasshopper.

"As it reaches the entrance of the sanctuary—it becomes as the thread of the warp.

"As it reaches the hall—it becomes as the thread of the woof.

* See legends XIV:1–5.

"As it reaches the entrance of the court—it becomes
as large as the mouth of a small flask."

"The water will bubble forth from under the threshold
of the sanctuary. From there onward it becomes bigger,
rising higher and higher, or until it reaches the entrance
to the house of David.

"As soon as it reaches the entrance to the House of
David, it becomes even as a swiftly running river."

The waters of Jerusalem shall stream eastward to the
Dead Sea and westward to the Mediterranean Sea.

This stream which will flow from Jerusalem will be
called Gihon, and its waters will withdraw and reveal, in
the end of time, the hidden vessels of the Temple.[179]

5 / THE PILGRIMAGE IN THE FUTURE

"In the end of time, Jerusalem will spread over the
whole of the land of Israel. And the land of Israel will
spread over the whole world."

How shall the people come from all corners of the
earth and pray in Jerusalem? The clouds of the heavens
will carry them to Jerusalem the first day of every month
and every Sabbath, and bring them back to the place from
which they came.

The prophet Isaiah praises them and says: "Who are
these that fly as a cloud?"

The prophet Nahum describes the redemption in the
future: "Behold upon the mountains the feet of him/That
bringeth good tidings, that announceth peace!/. . . the
chariots rush madly in the streets. . . ./The appearance
of them is like torches,/They run to and fro like the
lightnings."

The words of the prophet refer to the children of Israel
in the end of time: "The lightning spread from one end
of the world to another in a very short time. So the children of Israel run to Jerusalem, from the ends of the
world, and sacrifice and return to their places swiftly."[180]

XVIII
KOTEL HA-MAARAVI
—THE WAILING WALL

The Wailing Wall of the Jews is the only remains of the
wall which surrounded the Temple court on Mount
Moriah. The Jews call it *ha-Kotel ha-Maaravi (Maarabi)*—
the Western Wall—because it was a part of the Western
Wall. For many generations Jews from all the corners of
the world have come here, to this sad relic of departed
glory, to mourn for the destruction of Jerusalem and its
Temple and to pray for their restoration. The Wailing
Wall is also called the Wall of Weeping and the Wall
of Tears (fig. 43).

1 / THE EVERLASTING WALL

*"And it was decreed in Heaven:
The Wailing Wall may never be destroyed."*

At the siege of Jerusalem by the Romans, four com-
manders were each assigned one wall of the Temple to
destroy. Three of the walls were destroyed, but the fourth

FIG. 43. THE WESTERN WALL (C. 1743)
Upon the layers of stones is written (in Hebrew): "This is the form of the Western Wall" and the words of the Lord to King Solomon at the consecration of the Temple: "Mine eyes and My heart shall be there perpetually" (1 Kings 9:3). It is oldest known picture of Western Wall.

commander failed to carry out the instructions to destroy his part.

When the Roman caesar reproved him, the commander replied, "Had I destroyed my wall as the others did, none of the nations coming after you could have known how glorious was the work that you have destroyed, O Caesar; but as this wall is left standing, succeeding generations will be able to gaze upon it and say, 'see what a glorious thing Caesar conquered and destroyed!' "

Legend says that this wall which was not destroyed is the Western Wall—*ha-Kotel ha-Maaravi.*[181]

2 / THE WALL AND THE SULTAN

The Turkish sultan Salim conquered Jerusalem and all the land of Israel in 1517. It is said that when the Turks entered Jerusalem, the Wailing Wall was buried beneath piles of rubbish, and no one knew its location. Only by chance was it discovered and restored to its sacred place in the lives of the Jews.

Moses Hagiz, a famous rabbi in Jerusalem in the seventeenth century, tells an interesting story about the Turkish conquest of Jerusalem and the discovery of the Wailing Wall. He heard it from the Moslems, "who are familiar with the history of the Ottoman Turks."

One day when Sultan Salim was in Jerusalem, he saw an old Christian woman who brought a mass of ordure and cast it upon a spot near his palace. Growing exceedingly wroth, he sent one of his men to bring the woman before him. The woman excused herself, saying that she lived two days' journey from Jerusalem and had come in obedience to the bishops, who had ordained that a mass of ordure be brought once in thirty days and cast on the

FIG. 44. WESTERN WALL AND SURROUNDING BUILDINGS (1850)

Below, center: layers of stones of wall; left: Gate of the Chain (*Bab es-Silsila*); above: Dome of the Rock (Mosque of Omar); right: al-Aksa mosque (King Solomon's Study House). On eastern side of Temple court is eastern wall; beyond it, Mount of Olives. On its summit is building wherein lies grave of Hulda the prophetess.

spot where the house of the God of Israel had formerly stood. If they could not destroy it in its entirety, they wished it to be swamped and forgotten.

The sultan, on inquiry, found that she spoke the truth. So he took many coins of gold and silver and, with basket and shovel in hand, issued the following proclamation to all his people: "Whosoever loveth the king and desireth to give him pleasure, let him see his actions and do likewise."

Going to the dunghill, the sultan threw into different parts of it many purses of coins so that the poor might dig away the rubbish in order to find the treasure. And the Sultan himself stood by them, urging them on. Finally more than ten thousand men worked for thirty days till the dunghill was completely removed, and the *Kotel ha-Maaravi*, the Western Wall, stood revealed as it is seen today (fig. 44).[182]

3 / UNCOVERING THE WAILING WALL

Sultan Suleiman reigned in Turkey after his father, Sultan Salim, who had conquered Jerusalem. Because his reign was successful and glorious, he was called "Suleiman the magnificent." In 1538 he completed building Jerusalem's wall, the same wall which stands today.

Rabbi Eliezer Nahman Puah, about the year 1540, relates how the Wailing Wall was discovered while Suleiman the magnificent visited in Jerusalem.

This tale, similar to the preceding one, is narrated in connection with the words of the psalmist, attributed to King David: "Who raiseth up the poor out of the dust,/ And lifteth up the needy out of the dunghill."

And these are the words of Rabbi Eliezer: "David, inspired by the Holy Spirit, foresaw how disgracefully the nations of the world would treat the site of the Holy

Temple, where is the Western Wall on which the divine Presence ever rests.

"I have been told that in the day of Sultan Suleiman, the site of the Temple was not known, and the sultan had every corner of Jerusalem searched for it. One day the man in charge of the work, despairing after much searching and inquiring in vain, saw a woman coming with a basket of garbage and filth on her head. He asked her: 'What are you carrying on your head?'—And she replied: 'Garbage.'

" 'And whither are you carrying it?'

" 'To such and such a place.'

" 'Where do you live?'

" 'In Bethlehem.'

" 'Is there no dunghill between Bethlehem and this place?'

" 'It is a tradition among us that whoever takes a little garbage to that place performs a meritorious act.'

"The curiosity of the officer was aroused and he commanded a great number of men to remove the garbage from that place, which lower down had molded to dust with age; and the holy site was revealed to his gaze.

"And when the sultan learned of this, he rejoiced greatly and ordered the place to be swept and sprinkled and the Wailing Wall washed with rose-water."[183]

4 / THE RING AND THE DIVINE PRESENCE

*"The divine Presence
has never departed from the Wailing Wall!"*

The divine Presence rests eternally upon the Wailing Wall, hovering in hidden and mysterious waves.

Once Rabbi Nathan entered into the Temple precincts and found the whole Temple destroyed except for one wall, which was still standing. He asked what that wall was, and someone said to him: "It is the Western Wall, where the divine Presence still rests. I will prove it to you if you like."

The man took a ring and fixed it on the wall, and the ring started to sway to and fro.

And Rabbi Nathan saw the Almighty, blessed be His Name, bowing down and mourning for the desolation of the Temple and for Israel exiled.[184]

FIG. 45. JEWISH PILGRIMS PRAYING AT WESTERN WALL (C. 1880)

5 / WHO SAW THE DIVINE PRESENCE?

Whoever desires to see the face of the divine Presence in this world must devote his life to the study of the law in Eretz Israel.

Very few people have been found worthy to see the divine Presence hovering over the Wailing Wall. It is told that one of them was Rabbi David son of Zimra (Radbaz), a famous scholar who lived in Safed in the sixteenth century.

Rabbi Abraham Halevy, too, a resident of Safed and a famous disciple of Ha-Ari the holy, the great teacher of the mystics, deserved to see the divine Presence at the wall. Once the holy Ha-Ari said to Rabbi Abraham: "Know that your days are numbered and that you will soon die if you will not do what I tell you; but if you do, you will live yet another twenty-two years. This is what I bid you do: go to Jerusalem and pour out your prayers before the Wailing Wall and you will prove yourself worthy by seeing the divine Presence there."

Rabbi Abraham went home, shut himself in his house for three days and three nights, clothed himself in sackcloth and ashes, and fasted the whole time. Then he went forth to Jerusalem; he stood before the Wailing Wall in prayer, deep meditation, and weeping. The image of a woman, clad in black, appeared to him on the face of the wall. Immediately he fell upon the ground in great fear. Tearing his hair, he cried in a loud voice: "Woe is me, what have I seen?"

Finally he fell in a deep slumber and in a dream the divine Presence appeared to him, clad in fine raiment, and said to him: "Console thyself, My son Abraham; there is yet hope for thee, and the children of Israel will return to their inheritance, and I will have mercy upon them."

He arose and returned to Safed, and when Ha-Ari the

holy saw him, he said to him at once: "Now I know that you have seen the divine Presence and you can rest assured that you will live another twenty-two years."

Rabbi Menahem Mendel describes his visit to the Wailing Wall about 1835: "And the cantor stands by a certain stone, where the divine Presence was revealed to a righteous man . . . and let it be known to you, that prayer at this spot flows from the very heart of the worshiper."

Another pilgrim tells us: "The northern corner of the Wailing Wall is where it is believed the divine Presence reveals itself."

Not far from the Wailing Wall is the main entrance to the Temple area. The Arabs call it *Bab es-Silsila*—the Gate of the Chain. In the Middle Ages it was known to them as *Bab es-Sekinah*—the Gate of the Divine Presence—in Hebrew *Shechinah* (fig. 46).[185]

6 / GOD IS BEHIND THE WALL

To the words of the Song of Songs, "Behold, he standeth behind our wall," the legends add: "behind the Wailing Wall of the Great Temple."

Why is this so? Because the Almighty, blessed be He, pledged Himself that the Wailing Wall would never be destroyed.

Another tradition pictures the Almighty "standing behind the wall wherefrom He keeps vigil and watches the sons of men."

The Holy One, blessed be His Name, stands as it were behind the wall and peeps through the crevices. He sees but is not seen.

"And every man in Israel must believe in this."[186]

7 / THE HILL OF GOD

Rabbi Moshe the Jerusalemite, about the year 1769, develops an interesting interpretation of the Hebrew name *ha-Kotel ha-Maaravi*—the Western Wall.

FIG. 46. WORSHIPER AT WESTERN WALL
Drawn by J. Levi in Jerusalem.

He divides the word *kotel*—wall—into *ko* and *tel*. The two letters *ko* in Hebrew are equal to twenty-six. And the four letters of YaHaVeH, the Name of God, are also equal to twenty-six. Consequently, *ko* equals Yahaveh, Jehovah.

Tel in Hebrew means hill. *Kotel* then means "Hill of Yahaveh," of God.

Rabbi Moshe concludes that the Wailing Wall is the hill of God, toward which all Jews direct their prayers.[187]

FIG. 47. PRAYER AT WESTERN WALL (1845)

8 / "MY HOUSE" ENGRAVED ON THE WALL

The English traveler John Sanderson, who went to the Holy Land in 1601, accompanied by Jews from Syria, also visited Jerusalem and toured its holy places. He tells about the Temple Mount and of the Moslem buildings situated upon it, and says that no Christian or Jew is permitted to enter them. Thus he describes the Wailing Wall without mentioning it by name: "Outside of that site [the Temple Mount] there is seen a fragment of a wall. According to what I was told by the Jews, this is part of the wall of King Solomon. On one of its stones is engraved in Hebrew the word *bayti*—my house."[188]

9 / THE WALL SHEDS TEARS

*"Though the gates of prayer are closed,
The gates of weeping are not closed."*

The Wailing Wall is also called the Wall of Weeping or the Wall of Tears, for in front of this last remnant of the Great Temple, Jews from all parts of the world came to lament and shed tears over their past glory and present desolation.

On the night of the destruction of the Temple, the ninth of the month of Ab, as on most summer evenings, the stones of the wall are covered with small drops of dew. The simple folk say that the wall participates in the sorrow of the people, and cries bitter tears with them.

It is told that once in the month of Elul in 1940, when the worshipers stood in front of the wall pouring out their sorrowful hearts, they suddenly discovered small rushes of water oozing out between the cracks. They cried out: "The wall is weeping! The wall is crying!"

When the news spread among the people, hordes

streamed to behold the "tears of the wall"; women endeavored to collect these "tears" to treasure as a valuable
remedy for various ailments."*[189]

FIG. 48. JEWS PRAYING AT WESTERN WALL (1940)

10 / A LAMENTATION

This is one of the lamentations recited by the Jews on
the ninth day of the month of Ab, the memorial day of

* See legend XIII:4, about the pillars in Rome brought from the Temple
in Jerusalem, from which tears descend on the eve of Tisha be-Av.

the destruction of the Temple, as they fast and pray before the Wailing Wall: "On account of the palace which
is laid waste/We sit solitary and weep./For the sake of
the Temple which is destroyed/We sit solitary and weep./
For the walls that are thrown down/We sit solitary and
weep./For our glory which hath departed from us/We sit
solitary and weep./For our wise men who have perished/
We sit solitary and weep./For the precious stones which
are burnt/We sit solitary and weep./For our priests who
have fallen/We sit solitary and weep./We implore Thee
to have mercy on Zion,/Reassemble the children of Jerusalem./

"Haste! Haste! O Redeemer of Zion,/Speak in favor of
Jerusalem./May beauty and majesty surround Zion./Turn
with Thy clemency toward Jerusalem./Grant soon that
royal power may shine upon Zion/Console us who weep
over Jerusalem./May peace and happiness enter Zion,/
May the scepter of power turn toward Jerusalem!"[190]

11 / A PRAYER AT THE WAILING WALL

"May it be Thy will, O Lord God of hosts, dwelling
with cherubim in the heavens, to accept with mercy and
desire our prayers; and open unto us the Gates of Will and
the Gates of Repentance, the Gates of Paradise and the
Gates of Justice, the Gates of Blessing and the Gates of
Prayer.

"As Thou hast hearkened unto the prayers of our Father
Abraham on Mount Moriah, of Isaac, his son, upon the
altar, and of Jacob at Bethel; and the prayers of our forefathers at the Red Sea, of Moses at Horeb, and Aaron at
his service; the prayers of Pinchas when he rose up from
the congregation, Joshua at Gilgal, and Samuel at Mizpeh;
the prayers of David and Solomon in Jerusalem, of Elijah
on Mount Carmel, of Elisha at Jericho, of Jonah in the
belly of the whale, and of Hannaniah Mishael and Azariah

in the midst of the burning stove; the prayers of Daniel in the lion's den, and of Mordecai and Esther in Shushan ha-Bira, and of Ezra in exile; and the prayers of all the righteous and innocent and just; thus hearken unto the voice of Thy servant.

"Remove from among us wickedness of heart and evil inclination; set in our hearts awe of Thee, and may we merit the Torah and good deeds. Let us, this day and every day, find grace and kindness and mercy in Thine eyes, and in the eyes of all our beholders. Spare us from harsh judgment, and from the trial of hell [Gehenna]; from whipping at the grave and from the bonds of the Messiah, and favor us with Thy loving-kindness. Amen, Selah."[191]

12 / THE MOURNING DOVE

"Over the Wailing Wall flies a flock of doves,
one white and fine.
To me whispered the ancient, faithful believers:
the Presence divine.
"A dove among the doves, since the break of
dawn she flies about on high,
But at the Wall of Sorrows stands alone and coos
as the sun goes down the sky."
—J. D. Kamzon

It used to be said that on the eve of the ninth of the month of Ab (Tisha be-Av), when the Jews lamented at the Wailing Wall for the destruction of the Temple, the sound of their weeping would cleave the heavens, and a white dove would appear in the darkness of the night and join the people of Israel in their mourning.

The dove is the symbol of the congregation of Israel. One of Jerusalem's inhabitants writes: "On the eve of every Tisha be-Av, with the fall of day a dove appears and stands at the corner of the Wailing Wall. All the night it will wail and moan, and all the next day too, till night comes."

This legend is based on the tale of Rabbi Yossi, about a century after the destruction of the Temple: "Once while on the road I entered a ruin in Jerusalem to pray. Thither came Elijah the prophet, and waited at the door till I ended my prayers. Then he said, 'Peace be with thee, my master rabbi!' I answered, 'Peace be with thee, my master and my teacher!' And he said, 'My son, why didst thou enter this ruin?' 'To pray,' was my reply; whereupon he asked, 'My son, what voice didst thou hear in this ruin?' And I answered, 'I heard a holy voice like unto that of a dove, which said: "Woe is Me that I have destroyed My house/And have burned My holy palace,/And have scattered My children/Amid the nations!" ' "[192]

13 / RABBI SHALOM AT THE WAILING WALL

Rabbi Shalom Sharabi, who lived in the seventeenth century, was the head of the mystic cabalists in Jerusalem. He was wont to go to the Wailing Wall alone every night and there repeat the prayer of mourning for the destruction of the Temple and the desolation of Israel.

One night as Rabbi Shalom wept bitterly and raised his voice loud in prayer, he awoke his neighbors, who in their anger threatened to fall upon and destroy him. But they had scarcely lifted up their hands against him when the fear of the Lord came upon them, and they became like pillars of stone, without being able to move hand or foot.

The rabbi continued his prayer, completed it, and then passed by them as he returned to his home. When the friends and relatives of the stricken men saw this, they went to Rabbi Shalom, prostrated themselves before him, and said, "Grant pardon unto them, thou holy man of God."

Rabbi Shalom forgave them, and their strength and vigor were restored to them.[193]

14 / THE WALL AND THE NAILS

Since olden times Jews from all the corners of the globe have gathered at the Wailing Wall to bemoan the destruction of the Temple and to pray for the rebuilding of their ancient homeland. The Jews were wont to fix nails in the crevices of the wall, in order to fulfill the words of the prophet Isaiah: "And I will fasten him as a peg in a sure place!"

And Ezra, who returned with the exiles from Babylon to restore Jerusalem, said before the Lord, "And now for a little moment grace hath been shown by the Lord our God, to leave us a remnant to escape, and to give us a nail in His holy place, that our God may lighten our eyes."

To the words of Isaiah, who said to the man Shabna, who was "over the house": "What hast thou here? and whom hast thou here?"—the sages of Israel added these words: "Exiled one, son of an exiled one! Which wall did you build here, which pillar did you erect here and which nail did you fix here?"

Rabbi Eliezer said: "A man should have a fixed nail or peg in the synagogue!"[194]

15 / A MISSIVE TO THE WALL

Jews were wont to write down their wishes and prayers on small pieces of paper, folding them carefully and inserting them in the crevices between the stones of the Wailing Wall. They fully believed that these notes would come unto the Almighty, blessed be He, and that He would answer them, bestowing peace, happiness, and health on the suppliants.

In the eighteenth century there lived in Jerusalem
Rabbi Haim ben Attar, better known by his title "Or ha-
Haim"—the Light of Life, which is the name of his com-
mentary on the Torah.

"There was once a man, a disciple and intimate of Rabbi
Haim ben Attar, who lived by the sweat of his brow; and
it happened that the wheel of fortune turned against him,
and he came in distress to his master Rabbi Haim the
holy (may his merits defend us) and poured out to him
the bitterness of his heart, and told how his house was
poverty-stricken and his family starving for bread. . . .

"The holy Rabbi Haim was filled with pity for the poor
man, and wishing to answer his cry for mercy, he wrote
a small note, folded it with care and handed it to the
pauper, saying: 'Hold well this missive and repair forthwith to the Wailing Wall; search for an empty space between the holy stones and there place this note; then go
back to your home and salvation shall come to you!'

"The man did thus, holding fast to the missive. And
while on his way, a stormy wind suddenly arose from the
ground and tossed his hat away from his head, but he
did not pay heed, and proceeded on his way holding fast
to his skullcap with his left hand while his right hand
grasped the epistle. The wind raged and circled him
around till it lifted aloft his skullcap, and the poor man
was bareheaded; when he tried desperately to save his
cap from the clutches of the powerful wind, the missive
dropped from his hand and flew away. With a sorrowful
heart, the unfortunate man returned to the house of
Rabbi Haim and told him of his adventure. The rabbi
answered, 'What can I do for you, if heaven does not
stand by you?'

"And afterward the message was found in the streets of
Jerusalem. It was returned to the holy rabbi, and they
saw that it was addressed to the divine Providence in these

terms: 'My Sister, my Beloved, my innocent Dove, I entreat thee to have pity and bestow upon So-and-so son of So-and-so a good livelihood.' And he signed his holy name in full."[195]

16 / THE MERITS OF A MISSIVE

Before he went to the Holy Land, Rabbi Haim ben Attar (Or ha-Haim) lived in North Africa. The Jerusalemite Rabbi Haim Yosef David Azulai (Hida) met him in his travels in the lands of exile, and told him of Jerusalem and her holy sites. When Rabbi Azulai left for Jerusalem, Rabbi Haim ben Attar gave into his hands a letter to be placed on the Wailing Wall. Azulai took the letter and fixed it to his coat; then the matter passed out of his mind.

When Rabbi Azulai got to the Holy Land, he made a vow to enjoy only the fruits of his own manual work, and he bought a donkey and cart and carried clay. This lasted for about two years. Then suddenly the donkey died, and the rabbi was left without a livelihood. The suspicion grew in his heart that he was being punished for not delivering his master's letter to the Wailing Wall. Forthwith he went and cleansed and purified himself and proceeded to the holy wall. There he placed the letter and prayed for its delivery and fulfillment.

When he returned to the house of study, a powerful awe fell upon the people who beheld him, and all greeted him with dread and reverence. Azulai asked them, "Why do you treat me today differently from yesterday?" And they answered: "We ourselves do not know why today is different. Pray tell us!"

He told them of the letter that his master had entrusted to him to place at the Wailing Wall, and how he had left this duty unfulfilled until that very day, and how he had been punished for his negligence. The rabbi then told him that he was most eager to see the letter, and asked him to point out the place where he had set it. They both went together to the Wailing Wall, found the letter, and read its contents. And these were its words:

"My Sister, my Bride, I beseech Thee to come to the aid of my dear pupil in his time of need."

When they saw the letter, they knew that Rabbi Azulai was destined to be a great and learned man, and they appointed him as teacher of the law in the Holy City.[196]

17 / THE WALL OF THE POOR

When Solomon wished to build the Temple in the Holy City, Jerusalem, an angel of God appeared to him and said: "Solomon son of David, king of Israel, since thou dost know that the Temple which thou wilt build Me will be the holy place of the people, the portion of all Israel, summon all Israel and let each man take part in the work, each one according to his capacity."

So King Solomon sent forth and summoned assemblies of his people Israel, and not one man was missing. There came the princes and the rulers, the priests and the nobles, as well as the needy and the poor. And Solomon cast lots for the labor, for everything was apportioned by lot. And the lots fell in this manner: to the princes and rulers, the cupolas of the pillars and the steps; to the priests of Aaron's seed and to the Levites, the ark of the testimony and the curtain which is upon it; to those mighty in wealth, the eastern side; and to the poor and the needy, the Western Wall. Thus were the lots cast, and since it came from the Lord, may it be forever a wonder in our eyes!

Then began the labor for the House of God.

The princes and rulers and all the rich men of Israel took the golden earrings from the ears of their wives and their daughters, as well as all their jewels, which were very precious; and they bought cedar wood wherewith to cover both the ground and the walls, cypress wood for the doors, and olive wood for the lintels. They hired day laborers from the Sidonians and the Tyrians and others of the heathens who dwelt in the land; and over them they appointed foremen to urge them and press them on, saying, "Ye slackers, finish your work!" Thus was speedily ended and completed the work of the princes and rulers and the mighty in wealth; also that of the priests of Aaron's seed and of the Levites, according to their families.

Only the work of the poor was delayed exceedingly, for they could not bring fine things from afar; and the men, the women, and the children hewed stone, until by the toil of their hands they completed their portion, the Western Wall.

Now, when the holy work was ended and the Temple stood upon its height, perfect in its beauty, the divine Presence descended and rested upon it; and the Lord chose the Western Wall, for he said, "The toil of the needy and poor is precious in My eyes, and My blessing shall be upon it." And an echo went forth, saying, "The holy Presence shall never be removed from the Western Wall."

So when the enemy destroyed our house of glory— speedily may it be builded and established in our days, Amen—the angels of the Most High descended and spread their wings over the Western Wall; and an echo went forth, and proclaimed, "Never shall the Western Wall be destroyed."

In the narrow alley leading to the Wailing Wall, poor Jews used to sit asking for alms; and they would call out with pride, "Truly the Western Wall is the fruit of the toil of the needy, and only through their merit does it exist!" (fig. 49).[197]

FIG. 49. BEGGING ALMS IN ALLEYWAY BY WESTERN WALL (1936)

18 / THE STONE OF IDOLATRY

The rabbis of Safed sent a letter in 1625 to one of the Jewish communities in France, telling about a young man, twenty-eight years old, who had come to the Holy Land. His name was David of the tribe of Reuben, and he spoke three languages: Hebrew, Indian, and Arabic.

King Hannanel sent this young man to remove a stone from the Wailing Wall, a stone which had an image of idolatry upon it. This stone had been inset by Manasseh, king of Judah, and it delays the day of the redemption of Israel. It was impossible to remove the stone except with the help of the ineffable Name.

And David the messenger went to the Wailing Wall, uttered the secret incantation revealed to him by King Hannanel, and the stone with its engraving of idol-worship —fell and vanished.[198]

19 / THE STONE WHICH HINDERS REDEMPTION

It was believed that among the stones of the Wailing Wall there is set a stone which hinders the redemption of Israel; and as long as it shall remain in the wall, salvation will not come. This stone was fixed through sorcery by Jeroboam son of Nebat, the wicked king of Israel—and no one knows which stone it is.

In 1528 an inhabitant of Jerusalem, Rabbi Raphael, tells of a man who came from afar with the purpose of detecting this stone and withdrawing it from the wall, thus hastening the day of redemption. Perhaps he refers to David ha-Reubeni, the well-known false Messiah who went to the Holy Land in 1523 and succeeded in entering the Temple area, which was then forbidden to Jews.*

FIG. 50. SEAL OF JEWISH CONGREGATIONS (1900)
This is seal of a Jewish congregation in Holy Land. In center is picture of Western Wall and buildings of Temple court.

* See legend II:9.

"There came a youth from the ten tribes, his father belonging to the tribe of Reuben, and his mother to that of Dan. And he brought us great news, and he told us wonderful things of approaching redemption and how soon the twelve tribes would come to the land, and the tribe of Reuben first. He said that he was sent by the king of Reuben's tribe to Jerusalem to remove one stone from the Western Wall of our house of glory.

"And this youth boasted that he found it and took it out."[199]

XIX

PRAYERS
AND SYNAGOGUES

1 / GOD PRAYS IN JERUSALEM

"In the beginning, God the Almighty, blessed be He, set up in Jerusalem a tabernacle, so to speak, wherein He prayed; therefore it is said in the Book of Psalms: In Salem also is His tabernacle, And His dwelling-place in Zion. Salem is the old name for Jerusalem, which is also called by God Ohaliba—My Tabernacle is in her!

"What were the words of the prayer of the Holy One? 'May it be that My children shall do My will, so that I need not destroy My house and My sanctuary.'

"And after it was destroyed, he prayed: 'May it be that My children shall repent, so that I may hasten the rebuilding of My house and my sanctuary.'

"How do we know that the Holy One, blessed be He, prays? It is said in the words of Isaiah the prophet: 'Even them will I bring to My holy mountain,/And make them joyful in My house of prayer.' It is not written 'their . . . prayer,' but 'My . . . prayer'—from this do we learn that the Lord prays."[200]

2 / ALL HEARTS TOWARD JERUSALEM

After the consecration of the Temple, King Solomon uttered thanksgiving to God, and spoke in the name of the people of Israel: "And they pray unto the Lord toward the city which Thou hast chosen, and toward the house which I have built for Thy name. . . . And pray unto Thee toward their land, which Thou gavest unto their fathers."

Jews when praying turn toward Jerusalem. The rabbis said that worshipers in the lands of the dispersion should pray facing the land of Israel; worshipers in the land of Israel should pray facing Jerusalem; worshipers on the Temple Mount should pray facing the house of the holy of holies. Those standing at the north turn toward the south; those at the south face northward. Those standing at the east turn toward the west; those at the west face eastward.

Thus it is that all of Israel prays toward one place.*[201]

3 / HOW MANY SYNAGOGUES?

The prophet Isaiah calls Jerusalem "the faithful city . . . that was full of justice,/Righteousness lodged in her." The legend finds in the phrase "that was full"—in Hebrew *mileti*—the number of synagogues that stood in ancient Jerusalem. *Mileti* is equal to the number 481.† Four hundred eighty synagogues stood in the biblical Jerusalem, not including the Temple.

It is said that there were 480 synagogues in Jerusalem, and in each of them was a school and a seminary. The school was for the study of the Bible, and the seminary, for the Talmud.[202]

4 / THE IMPORTANCE OF PRAYER IN JERUSALEM

Jerusalem lies under the Gate of Heaven; therefore prayers offered within her limits have special significance,

* See legend XI:6.
† M=40, L=30, E=1, T=400, +I=10; total: 481.

as they ascend directly to the throne of glory of the Almighty.

"When one prays in Jerusalem, it is as if he prays before the Lord's throne, for the Gate of Heaven is there, and it is open to the voices of worshipers."

In the name of Saadia Gaon, an outstanding sage of the tenth century, it was told: "Whoever desires to be certain of complete forgiveness, and wishes his supplications to be heard, let him dwell in Jerusalem and pray there."

The mystics in Israel particularly valued prayers said in Jerusalem. According to their belief, this world is wrapped in several spheres which envelop it completely. But over the Holy Land and Jerusalem there is a gap in these spheres which forms a sacred opening toward the Gate of Heaven.[203]

5 / THE MERITS OF PRAYER IN JERUSALEM

Moslem tradition, too, attributes great significance to prayers offered in Jerusalem. In the beginning of Islam, Muhammad the prophet commanded his Moslem believers to face toward Jerusalem during their prayers, as is the custom among the Jews. After some time he changed the direction and had them face toward Mecca, the holy city of Moslems, in Arabia.

A tradition attributed to Muhammad himself claims that one of the three wishes of King Solomon was that he who came to perform his devotions at the Temple in Jerusalem might go forth from there as innocent as on the day of his birth.

He who worships in Jerusalem is likened to him who worships in heaven.

One prayer in Jerusalem outweighs a thousand prayers elsewhere.

What shall a man do who is unable to visit Jerusalem?

He shall donate olive oil for the lamps. He who makes a donation for Jerusalem is like him who worships there.

A certain woman was admitted to paradise because she had donated a skein of wool for Jerusalem.[204]

6 / JERUSALEM OPPOSITE THE "HOLY OPENING"

The famous cabalist Rabbi Abraham Azulai, who lived in Hebron in the seventeenth century and spent some time in Jerusalem, writes: "And by the merits of our ancestors and the mercy of the Almighty, blessed be He, and through the rights of our holy fathers, a gap was opened in heaven, and all the spheres were pierced, that the holiness might pass through the opening . . . and this opening hovered over the tents of Israel's tribes while they wandered in the desert, and it followed them from above until it reached the land of Israel, where it rested, covering the whole land. . . . Thus it is said that the land of Israel is holy, and its air is holy . . . as the Holy Land is the dominion of God, outside it is the dominion of 'exterior forces.'

"Let it be known to you that when it is said that the land of Israel is placed under the gate of heaven, that means under the opening in the 'window' which is in the firmament . . . of the size of the Holy City of Jerusalem, and the divine Emanation came from above through the 'royal channel' . . . and descended on the Temple and from its own strength spread over all the Holy Land."

Rabbi Azulai drew a design of the world and its five spheres (fig. 51). On the left side of the spheres, he wrote down words taken from the Book of Genesis: "In the beginning God created the heaven and the earth. Now the earth was *unformed* and *void,* and *darkness* was upon the face of the *deep.*"

On the right side, he wrote words taken from the prophecy of Ezekiel: "Behold, a *stormy wind* came out

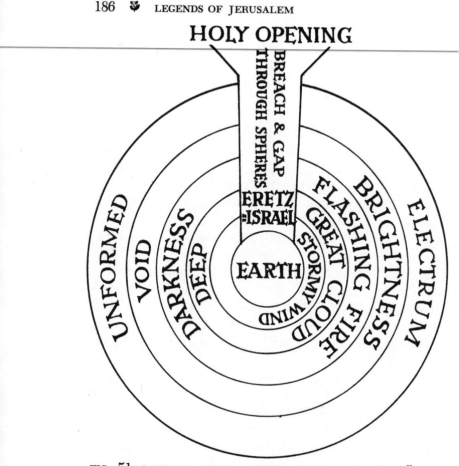

FIG. 51. LAND OF ISRAEL—ERETZ ISRAEL—OPPOSITE "HOLY OPENING" (1685)

of a *great cloud* with a *fire flashing* up, so that a *brightness* was round about it; and out of the midst thereof as the color of *electrum*, out of the midst of the fire."[205]

7 / THE WINDS WORSHIP IN JERUSALEM

It is said that the source of all the winds of the world is hidden beneath the holy Rock of Jerusalem, which lies on the top of Mount Moriah.

Rabbi Obadiah of Bertinoro, the well-known commentarian, writes in 1489 from Jerusalem: "All possible winds blow in Jerusalem. It is said that every wind, before going where it listeth, comes to Jerusalem to prostrate itself before the Lord, Blessed be He, who knoweth the truth."[206]

FIG. 52. SYNAGOGUE OF YOHANAN BEN ZAKKAI IN JERUSALEM, OLD CITY (1945)

Above double holy ark at right is picture of Western Wall; on left, building above Machpelah cave in Hebron. At right, on upper part of wall (not shown) is lattice which holds shofar and pitcher of oil (see fig. 53). This synagogue was destroyed by Arabs in Israel's War of Liberation in 1948 and restored in 1972.

In the Old City of Jerusalem is the synagogue of Rabbi Yohanan ben Zakkai. According to tradition, this learned rabbi, who lived in the last years of the second Temple, used to pray on this site. The synagogue is almost completely buried underground; this is evidence of its antiquity. A few steps lead down to the prayer hall. Pious men willingly came here to pray, for the sages advised: "Man should not stand on heights to pray—but go ye unto a low place, for the Lord dislikes haughtiness." As the psalmist sang: "Out of the depths have I called Thee, O Lord" (fig. 52).

In the southern wall of the synagogue, below the ceiling, there is a tall lattice on which lies a big ram's horn (shofar) and a vessel containing olive oil (fig. 53). Tradition

FIG. 53. LATTICE IN SYNAGOGUE OF YOHANAN BEN ZAKKAI
In it were placed a pitcher and a shofar.

says that both the horn and the oil come from the Temple, and woe betide the man who dares to lay hands on them, for he will not live out the year. When the building is cleaned and whitewashed, the sacred vessels, the shofar and the oil, have to be moved. The movers must first dip themselves in running water to be ritually clean.

And when Elijah the prophet shall appear in the later days—may they come speedily and in our time, Amen—he will take this horn to proclaim the redemption of Israel, and he will use the oil for the everlasting light of the Almighty in the restored Temple.[207]

9 / THE SYNAGOGUE OF ELIJAH THE PROPHET

"Happy is he who has greeted Elijah and the salutation was returned."

In the Jewish quarter of Old Jerusalem there are four synagogues built together under one roof. One of them is the synagogue of Eliyahu. In a small, dark cave at the side of the wall stands an old chair (fig. 54).

Elijah the prophet sat on this chair; thus it is holy to the Jews, and a perpetual light shines in front of it. Sickly persons come here hoping to find relief from their ailments; barren women, or those desiring a male child, prostrate themselves before it, assured that henceforth their womb will bear the desired fruit.

Many centuries ago there was a very small Jewish community in Jerusalem, consisting of only nine men all told. Once when they assembled together on the eve of the Day of Atonement, there was no person to complete the minyan (required quorum of ten for prayer). The day was already late when suddenly an old man entered, weary and covered with dust, looking as if he came from a great distance.

The men rejoiced upon seeing him, gave him the seat of honor, and began the service. The next day when they completed the service, each turned to the old man to invite him home for supper, but he was nowhere to be

FIG. 54. SYNAGOGUE OF ELIJAH THE PROPHET IN JERUSALEM, OLD CITY (1945)
This synagogue was destroyed in Israel's War of Liberation in 1948 and restored in 1972.

found. Then they understood that it was Elijah the prophet who had come to complete their minyan. They called the synagogue by his name and preserved the chair he sat on for many generations.

Rabbi Jacob, who visited the Holy Land in the thirteenth century, relates: "Within Jerusalem is a synagogue of Elijah the prophet, may his memory be blessed. And there is hewn into the wall a place for the scroll of the law . . . and a Name of four letters [YaHaVaH—Jehovah] is engraved on the stone."

An inhabitant of Jerusalem tells in 1835 of the four adjoining synagogues: "In the holy congregation is a synagogue named 'Talmud Torah,' where, according to a tradition, Elijah the prophet revealed himself." The famous wonder-working Rabbi Haim ben Attar, when he went to Jerusalem, the goodly mountain, said that in this same spot he experienced a great illumination.[208]

10 / THE MIRACLE IN ELIJAH'S SYNAGOGUE

*"And I will place salvation in Zion
for Israel My glory."*

In the synagogue of Elijah the prophet, in old Jerusalem, in the southern wall there is a closet where Holy Bibles and prayer books for the use of the worshipers are kept. Here a great miracle was wrought by the saintly Rabbi Kelonimus, who saved the Jewish community of his city from a terrible danger.

One Sabbath eve, a short while before Passover, a Christian priest stole into the synagogue of Elijah and placed within the book closet the body of a slain boy. Next day, on the morning of the holy Sabbath, angry crowds led by their priests broke into the Jewish quarter and streamed to the synagogue, shouting menacingly, "You have murdered our child! Your hands have shed this innocent blood! We shall avenge ourselves sevenfold! Now your bitter end has come!"

At this moment Rabbi Kelonimus entered the synagogue and saw the unruly mob pointing to the body of the dead child in the closet. Before the threatening multitude, although it was the holy day of Sabbath, he wrote on a piece of paper the ineffable Name in full and placed it on the dead child's forehead. Immediately, to the astonishment of the people, the boy stood up, and in answer to the questions of the rabbi he designated a man in the crowd and said, "This is the priest who tormented me, then killed me and brought me here under the dark cloak of night."

People looked at each other in amazement. The chief of the priests rose and ascended the platform, where he confessed his grievous error and craved the pardon of the rabbi and all his congregation.

Thus, through the merit of Rabbi Kelonimus, the Jews of Jerusalem were delivered from dire distress, and they finished the Sabbath day in rejoicing, singing psalms to the glory of the Guardian of Israel. Since then, they called their rabbi "Kelonimus *baal ha-ness*—the miracle-maker."

Nevertheless, the righteous rabbi suffered greatly in his heart for having desecrated the holiness of the Sabbath. Before his death he ordered his body to be buried, not on the Mount of Olives, as was befitting his prominence, but at the lowest end of the Jewish cemetery in the Valley of Kidron. According to his wish, no tombstone was erected on his grave; instead, a heap of stones marked his sepulcher, and each man who passed by it cast a stone thereon, that the Almighty, blessed be He, should forgive his threefold sin—the profanation of the Sabbath in a synagogue in the Holy City.

Until a few years ago, the heap of stones over Rabbi Kelonimus was shown in the Valley of Kidron. And whoever passed by added a stone to the mass. It was customary, too, to pick a stone out of the heap as an amulet of special virtues. People who departed for a trip in foreign lands carried with them a pebble from the tomb, promising to return it after their safe arrival home. It is told that whoever took this precaution succeeded in his travels and came

back safely to his family, through the merits of the righteous Rabbi Kelonimus the miracle-maker, peace be upon
him.

FIG. 55. THE FORM OF THE "SKULL"
In wall of synagogue of Elijah the prophet; underneath it is frame
surrounding Hebrew inscription.

In the holy ark of Elijah's synagogue lies a stone, engraved in Hebrew with the ineffable Name—Jehovah—and
the picture of a menorah, the symbol of Israel. This stone
is kept as a witness for the coming generations of the
miracle which was wrought in this place. Over the closet
a round shape protrudes from the wall; it is held to be a
reminder of the head of the child whom Rabbi Kelonimus
brought back to life (figs. 55 and 56).[209]

FIG. 56. STONE WITH DIVINE NAME, JEHOVAH, IN HEBREW
This stone was preserved in holy ark of synagogue of Elijah the
prophet. On sides of the candelabrum are Hebrew words *Lenegdi
Tamid*: "Always before me," from Books of Psalms: "I have set the
Lord always before me" (Psalms 16:8).

By the side of the synagogues of Yohanan and Elijah stands the synagogue of Istanbuli. It is so called because its worshipers were Sephardic Jews, emigrants from Istanbul (Constantinople), once the capital of Turkey.

In a corner of the Istanbuli synagogue there is a small dark room which is used as a storage chamber (genizah) for disused sacred books. In it were gathered defective scrolls of the law, torn pages, and outworn Bibles and prayer books.

In ancient generations it was customary to remove the papers from the genizah at certain times and convey them to a grave in the Jewish cemetery. This interment was carried out as a great festival—generally once in seven years. The timeworn books and pages were heaped into large sacks and taken to the outskirts of the city, escorted by throngs of citizens, including Arabs and Christians, to the accompaniment of singing and merrymaking. The people believed that this procession assured them of a year of blessed rains and plentiful crops.

A Jerusalemite in 1877 described such a procession: "First marched the bearers of the sacks—some thirty in all, surrounded by a company of men singing and shouting in triumph and rejoicing greatly. At the very end was carried the scroll of the law under a silken canopy. In front of it walked the attendants of the chief rabbi, may the Lord watch over him and cause him to prosper, and staffs with knobs of gold were in their hands . . . and among them went an officer of high rank, which the imperial Turkish government sent to honor the assembly. Many men bore lanterns and large, burning wax candles upon which were written words from the Book of Proverbs: 'For the commandment is a lamp, and the Law is a great light.'

"On the roofs, too, and on the wall of the city, people stood, and among them were Ishmaelites and Christians. The joy reached its highest peak . . . and the shofar [ram's horn] was blown, and afterward all recited in unison the prayer for rain. . . . At the sounding of the shofar, from every eye tears fell. Some sang hymns; some wept and their faces streamed with tears.

"Afterward they stored the sacks and the scroll of the law within a cave, and they sealed it with soil. May the Lord grant that we shall soon hear the call of the great shofar, heralding the time when the sons shall return to their land. Amen!"

The holy books were generally buried in the Jewish cemetery on the slope of Mount Zion, in a cave hewn out of rock which faces the Mount of Olives.[210]

12 / BETHEL—CENTER OF THE MYSTICS

In the Jewish quarter of old Jerusalem, there stands a small synagogue known as Bethel—the House of God. Here the cabalists of Jerusalem come together and devote themselves to the study of the mystic secrets of the law. Once the place used to be crowded with the great among the cabalists, and the cry was repeated: Oh, how great and fearful is this holy place, where the lions of learning dwelt in all their glory!" (fig. 57).

The synagogue Bethel was once the abode of Shalom Sharabi, the great Yemenite rabbi who lived in Jerusalem in the beginning of the seventeenth century. It is told that Elijah the prophet would sit next to Rabbi Shalom in Bethel and unfold to him the secrets of the holy law and the hidden mysteries.

Legend relates that when our pious master Rabbi Shalom, the memory of the righteous and holy be blessed, may his merits defend us, sat in Bethel, there was a woman who tended to him. From time to time she used to serve

FIG. 57. SYNAGOGUE OF BETHEL (C. 1895)
Picture is decorated with parts of biblical verses which mention
Bethel; under cupola, in large characters, the name Bethel—House
of God; below, on both sides of building: "And this is the gate of
heaven"; at top, on right: "How awesome is this place!" (Genesis
28:17); on left: "Belonging to the Sepharadi community, may its
light shine."

him a cup of coffee. On one occasion, she brought him two
cups at one time. He asked her, "Why did you bring two
cups?" The woman replied, "I brought one for Your Reverence, and one for the man who sits with you."

He said to her, "May it be known to you that this is
Elijah, his memory be blessed; but do not disclose this
to anyone."

She said, "I shall not reveal this secret if you pledge
yourself that I shall be found worthy of paradise and have
there a seat next to you."

And Rabbi Shalom promised, "So it shall be!" [211]

13 / THE FIG TREE IN THE COURTYARD

In old Jerusalem there is a house of study known as *Or
ha-Haim*—the Light of Life. It is named after the famous
Rabbi Haim ben Attar, who composed the commentary *Or ha-Haim* on the Torah (fig. 58).

Rabbi Haim settled in Jerusalem in 1742. He relates:

FIG. 58. SYNAGOGUE OF OR HA-HAIM—LIGHT OF LIFE—IN
JERUSALEM, OLD CITY (1945)
This was destroyed in Israel's War of Liberation in 1948.

"The Almighty enlightened me, and I arose to ascend unto
the place where the divine Presence rests, unto God's beloved city. I girded my loins and wandered from town to
town, encountering great dangers, until the Lord brought
me to the land of my desire . . . for there is no rejoicing
but in the life of the Holy Land."

Rabbi Haim spent many hours studying within the walls
of this house of learning. "And he used to sit wrapped in
a prayer shawl, the phylacteries on his arm and forehead; and whoever beheld his radiant face thought him to
be an angel of the Lord of hosts, for the divine Presence
hovered over him all day long."

In the courtyard of the house of study a fig tree grew. Unruly children used to climb its branches to pick the fruits, and their noisy shouting interrupted the work of the holy rabbi. Then Rabbi Haim arose and decreed that the fig tree should no longer bear fruit. And the tree ceased to put forth its fruit.[212]

14 / THE BIRTHPLACE OF HA-ARI THE HOLY

Beside a narrow lane in the Jewish quarter of old Jerusalem there is a small, humble courtyard. In a corner of this yard stands a tiny dark room where, according to tradition, ha-Ari the holy, head of the Safed mystics, was born in 1534. For many years this place served as a synagogue; but when the Jewish community in the Old City dwindled, the house was occupied by its Arab owners, who put it to secular use. They were soon punished for their sacrilegious behavior: the head of the family died, and since then the consecrated little room has remained shut.

The father of Ha-Ari, blessed be his name, was a pious and righteous man, who was often rewarded by the prophet Elijah's company and teaching. When Ha-Ari was born, Elijah, his memory be blessed, revealed himself to his father and said, "On the day of thy son's circumcision, make sure not to start the ceremony until thou shalt see me standing by thy side!"

On the eighth day, as is the custom, the child was taken to the synagogue, and his father looked right and left seeking Elijah the prophet, his memory be blessed; but he was nowhere to be seen. All the people standing around were astonished at the delay and rebuked him, but he paid them no heed. Meanwhile, Elijah appeared and said to the father, "Sit on the chair!" And he sat with the child in his arms. Then Elijah took the infant from his father and put him in his bosom, holding him with both hands.

And he said to him, "Keep this child well, for a great light shall shine forth from him to Israel and to the whole world!"[213]

15 / THE KING AND THE DOME

Among the houses in the Old City of Jerusalem stands the beautiful domed building of the synagogoue *Tifereth Israel*—the Glory of Israel (figs. 59 and 60). It was founded

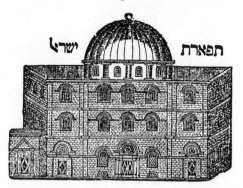

FIG. 59. SYNAGOGUE TIFERETH ISRAEL—GLORY OF ISRAEL (FOLK DRAWING, C. 1900)
This synagogue was also known by the name of its founder, Nissan Bak. It was destroyed during Israel's War of Liberation in 1948.

some hundred years ago by Nissan Bak, whose father, Israel Bak, was the founder of the first Hebrew publishing house in Jerusalem.

In 1870 the king of Austria, Franz Joseph, famous for his kindness to the Jews, passed through Jerusalem. Some of his subjects who were then in the city went out to receive him with much honor. They invited him to see the work of their hands and accompanied him to their synagogue, *Tifereth Israel*, whose dome had not yet been added.

The king turned to his retinue and asked, "And where is the dome of the synagogue?"

FIG. 60. SYNAGOGUE TIFERETH ISRAEL—GLORY OF ISRAEL (1945)
In alley on left is courtyard of Karaites, within which is their old synagogue (see fig. 61).

They answered, "The king appears to wonder! Even the synagogue rejoiced in the coming of His Royal Highness to the Holy City, and therefore removed its dome, as a man removes his hat in honor of his master."

The king understood the hint and contributed a sum of money toward the building of this dome.[214]

16 / THE SYNAGOGUE OF THE KARAITES

In the Jewish quarter of old Jerusalem is the synagogue of the Karaites. A narrow stairway leads down into the house of worship, which resembles a cellar. In the court-yard dwell the few remaining Karaites who live in Jeru-salem. Their number is extremely small, and their males number less than the ten required for congregational prayer (fig. 61).

In the eighteenth century the Jews of Jerusalem suffered great poverty and distress because of the oppression of the Moslem rulers of the city. In 1755 the Turkish governor

FIG. 61. SYNAGOGUE OF KARAITES IN JERUSALEM, OLD CITY (1932)

demanded a vast sum of money from the leaders of the Jewish community, and threatened that if the sum was not forthcoming, they would be expelled from the Holy City.

The notables decided to take counsel and seek some plan to ward off this abominable decree. But they feared to meet in one of their own synagogues, and therefore requested the Karaites who lived in their neighborhood to permit them to assemble in their house of prayer, which was hidden in the earth in a closed and secret courtyard.

The Karaites acquiesced. The worthy men assembled in the courtyard of the Karaites and started to descend the narrow steps into the synagogue—the chief rabbi at the head. Suddenly, as the rabbi took his first step on the stairway, his foot slipped and he fell, rolling down the stone stairs—and after him, all his followers. The startled notables could not understand the reason for this and decided to examine the stone slabs of the stairs. Suppose some evil spirits had penetrated into them! They searched, and to their great consternation they found under the steps of the stairway the books of the famous Rabbi Maimonides (Rambam)—soiled and damaged. The Karaites, despising the rabbi's teachings, had banned his books and as a means of desecrating them had placed them under the stairs so that every passerby would trample upon them.

When the Jews saw this, they were very angry at the Karaites. They left the courtyard and marched directly to their synagogue. There they gathered all the members of the congregation and told them of the shameful deed of the Karaites. They declared a ban against them and cursed them with these words: "Never shall the number of their males reach the 'required ten' [minyan for the congregational prayer]."[215]

17 / SOIL FROM JERUSALEM

In the land of Babylon (today Iraq) stood a synagogue called *Shaf ve-Yathib*. It was situated in the city of Nehardeah, famous as a center of Jewish learning and inhabited by noted scholars of the Talmud for several generations.

Legend explains the derivation of the Aramaic name *Shaf ve-Yathib*, which contains the words *shaf*—erased—and *ve-yathib*—and was set. The synagogue was erased from the land of Israel and set in the land of Babylon.

A tradition tells that this synagogue was built of soil and stones brought from the Temple in Jerusalem by the exiles of Zion, who were expelled along with Jehoiachin, king of Judah, and led to Babylon.

The sages of Israel said: "Come and see how beloved are Israel in the sight of God—so that to every place where they were exiled, the divine Presence went with them.

"Where? In Babylon, in the synagogue of *Shaf ve-Yathib*."

And the sages add: "The synagogues and houses of learning in Babylon will in time to come be planted in the land of Israel."[216]

18 / STONE FROM JERUSALEM

Nesibis (in Hebrew *Nezibin*) was an important city on the northern border of Babylon. Today it is located within the boundaries of Turkey. In ancient times there was a large Jewish community in Nesibis. One of its members was Rabbi Yehudah son of Bathira, the famous scholar of the third century.

The words of the Torah, "Justice, justice shalt thou follow," were explained by the sages: "This means 'Follow the scholars to their academies . . . follow Rabbi Yehudah the son of Bathira to Nesibis.'" His influence was great in the land of Israel, too, and it was said of him: "Yehudah son of Bathira dwells in Nesibis, yet his net is spread in Jerusalem."

In the Middle Ages the rabbi's grave was shown in Nesibis and also the synagogue that was named after him. A traveler who visited the city around 1180 tells of this synagogue: "And there is a house of prayer which was built by Ezra the scribe. In its wall is set a red stone, which Ezra brought with him from the Temple in Jerusalem."[217]

19 / THE SYNAGOGUE "ALTNEU-SHUL"

In the city of Prague, the capital of Czechoslovakia, there is a synagogue which dates back to the most ancient days of the exile. According to tradition, its foundation contains stones taken from the Great Temple in Jerusalem (fig. 62).

After the destruction of the Temple, angels carried on their wings a number of its stones, and said to the Holy One, blessed be He: "Lord of the universe, we take these holy stones on the condition that when the Temple is rebuilt, we are to return them to their place."

Then the angels took the stones to Prague and left them in the Jewish quarter; over them a synagogue was built. Therefore the Jews named the synagogue "On Condition"—in Hebrew *Al Tenai*. With the passing of generations, the name *Al Tenai* was corrupted into Altneu-Shul, which in Yiddish means Old-New Synagogue.

It is reported by Rabbi Yitzhak of Moskovera: "The old synagogue in the city of Prague was built from the stones of the Temple, because as the children of Israel went forth into exile, they carried with them stones from the Temple in the abundance of their love for its holiness, to fulfill the words of the psalmist: 'Because Your servants desired her stones.'

"And when they came to the city of Prague, they built there a synagogue, and they placed there these stones."

When the Temple was destroyed, the Holy One, blessed

FIG. 62. AL TENAI SYNAGOGUE (ALTNEU-SHUL) IN PRAGUE
This is one of oldest synagogues in Europe.*

be He, scattered its stones over all the world. And on every place where a stone fell, a synagogue was erected. Therefore, each synagogue is called "a little Temple" (*Mikdash Me'att*) because it contains within it a little of the Great Temple of Jerusalem.[218]

* Inspired by the name Altneu-Shul, Herzl entitled his book on a proposed Jewish state *Altneu-land*. The Hebrew translation of this work was entitled *Tel Aviv*—Hill of Spring, from *tel*, a mound covered with the remains of an old city, and *aviv*, spring, the symbol of renewed life. This name was later given to the first city established by Zionist efforts in the land of Israel.

XX
JERUSALEM
—THE OLD CITY

The Turkish sultan Salim conquered Jerusalem in 1517, laying the foundation for Turkish rule in the Holy Land during the next four hundred years, until the British conquest in 1917 in the First World War (fig. 63).

The Jewish historian Joseph Sambari, who lived in Egypt, writes in the seventeenth century: "Two years before the Turkish Sultan Salim conquered Palestine and Egypt, he was told by a Jewish scholar, Solomon Dil-Midrash, that he would succeed in conquering these countries."

Rabbi Solomon referred the sultan to the prophecy of Micah: "And this shall be peace . . . shall come into our land." The word peace, in Hebrew *shalom*, is a hint to Salim.

When the rabbi was asked the date of the successful conquest of Salim, he referred to the words of Isaiah: "And I will give over the Egyptians/Into the hand of a

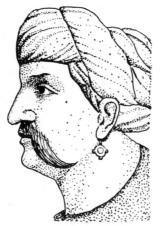

FIG. 63. SULTAN SALIM OF TURKEY

cruel lord;/And a *fierce* king *shall rule* over them, saith the Lord."

The Hebrew word for fierce is *az*, which is equal to the number 77. This is the short form of the year 5277, which, according to the Jewish calendar as dated from the creation of the world, is the same as 1517 C.E., the year of the conquest of Egypt and Palestine by the Turks.

The Hebrew word for shall rule is *imshol—shalim—* Salim, the name of the Turkish sultan.[219]

2 / ENTRANCE INTO JERUSALEM

Moses Hagiz, a famous rabbi in Jerusalem in the seventeenth century, tells a story about the Turkish conquest of his city.

"Three years before the sultan Salim captured Jerusalem, there came an astrologer who predicted this conquest in the following words: 'When the letter S will be inserted into another letter S, then the first S will conquer a double S.'

"The people did not understand him then, and only

after three years, when Sultan Salim conquered Palestine, did the prophecy of the astrologer become clear.

"When the letter S, that is Salim, is inserted into another letter S, that is, after three years [in Hebrew *shalosh*], the first S, that is Salim, will conquer a double S; namely, he will capture the cities of Damascus and Jerusalem."[220]

3 / FATE OF THE ARCHITECTS

The Turkish sultan Suleiman the magnificent was the son of Salim, conqueror of Palestine. In 1538 Suleiman built the wall which still surrounds the Old City of Jerusalem today.

After the wall was completed, the sultan visited the city to survey the work and to see if everything had been done according to his command. During the tour of inspection he noticed that the holy tomb of David was beyond the wall, on Mount Zion.

He summoned his two architects in anger and said: "Why was this holy tomb not included within the circuit of the wall?"

The architects answered: "Lord sultan, we knew not that the tomb of David was sacred to Moslems, and therefore we left it out."

The sultan, very wroth at these two ignorant architects, ordered them to be hanged at the side of the Jaffa Gate, in view of all the populace. After their deaths they were buried in a small yard near the Jaffa Gate, and their names were forgotten. And theirs are the two anonymous tombstones which still stand today, in the shade of cypress trees.[221]

4 / HANNAH'S LANE

In the Jewish quarter of the Old City there is a narrow winding alley, ascending a few steps, on the way from Jaffa Gate to the Street of the Jews. Among the old Jews of Jerusalem this lane is named for Hannah and her seven sons, who were ordered killed by the Greek king for refusing to bow down to false gods.

Hannah and her martyred sons are buried somewhere under the steps of the lane, and therefore all who climb them quickly tire and become weary.[222]

5 / ZELA—THE KARAITE QUARTER

The portion of the tribe of Benjamin is described in the Bible: "And Zela . . . and the Jebusite—the same is Jerusalem. . . . This is the inheritance of the children of Benjamin according to their families."

According to the legend, Zela was a part of ancient Jerusalem. And in the end of days the remnant of the Jews shall gather together in Zela, led by Nehemiah and Elijah the prophet. "Three battles shall take place in the land of Israel . . . and the third will be waged by Nehemiah in Zela . . . and to the Lord shall be the kingdom."

A tradition of the Middle Ages tells that the Karaite section of the Jewish quarter of Jerusalem is located in the same spot as the ancient Zela. Therefore the Jews call the Karaites in the city "the sect of Zela."

The name Zela has a double meaning in Hebrew. It is the word for rib and slope of a mountain; it also means limping. Therefore, the Jew scornfully referred to the Karaites as "the limping sect," or *ha-Zoleah*—the limping.[223]

6 / DROUGHT IN JERUSALEM

In the past many Jews of the Old City of Jerusalem used to engage in wine-making, and they sold their product to the inhabitants of the city. The Moslem Arabs do not drink wine because it is forbidden by their religion, and therefore the extremists among them looked with hatred upon the Jews for drinking wine during their holidays.

A student of the well-known commentator Rabbi

Obadiah of Bertinoro, who visited the Holy Land in 1495, tells of Jerusalem: "At times the Ishmaelites gather and descend upon us, trying to spill the wine and break the vessels. For they say that is because of the sins of the Jews, who drink wine, that the rain does not fall."[224]

7 / THE PROTRUDING STONE

At the end of the Jewish quarter, near the Dung Gate, there is a stone which sticks out of the wall surrounding the al-Aksa mosque. This stone is shaped like the section of an arch. It is the remnant of an ancient bridge that connected the Temple Mount with the upper city. It is now called "Robinson's Arch" in honor of an American scholar, Edward Robinson, who discovered it in 1838 (fig. 64).

Legend relates that once Jewish scholars sat in King Solomon's Study House (on the site of the al-Aksa mosque) discussing the Torah. An argument broke out over a certain rule. Finally, one scholar rose and said angrily: "Your words are as nothing; my interpretation is correct! If you don't believe me, the walls of the study house shall prove it!"

Immediately the stones of the walls moved from their places and almost crumbled. The protruding stone, Robinson's Arch, was one of the stones that moved during the argument of the scholars.*[225]

8 / IN THE SHOPS

In the Old City there is a dark alleyway leading to the Temple court and to its beautiful gate, called in Arabic *Bab al-Kattanin*—the Gate of the Cotton Workers. Today the rows of shops in this street are deserted, but in past

---

* This story is told in the Talmud about an argument between the sages which took place in the city of Yavneh, in the coastal plain.

FIG. 64. PROTRUDING STONE—ROBINSON'S ARCH (1900)
This stone projects from wall surrounding the Temple courtyard, near Western Wall.

generations they were occupied by weavers and clothiers; therefore it was called *Suk al-Kattanin*—Market of the Cotton Workers.

The Jewish residents called this street "The Shops." They believed that the shops once used as the meeting place of the Sanhedrin, the Supreme Court of ancient Israel, were here.

Sages tell: "Forty years before the destruction of the Temple, the Sanhedrin went out [from the Temple courtyard] into exile, and took its seat in the shops."

"The Sanhedrin was exiled from the Chamber of Hewn Stone [*Lishkat ha-Gazith*] to the shops, from the shops to

Jerusalem, and from Jerusalem to Yavneh." Yavneh is a
town near the Mediterranean coast of the Holy Land.[226]

9 / THE BATH OF HEALING

Near the Temple Mount, in the marketplace of "The
Shops," there is the most famous Moslem bath in Jerusalem, called in Arabic *Hammam esh-Shifa*—the Bath of
Healing. They believe that its waters come from the Well
of Zamzam in Mecca, the holy city of Arabia. Should you
appear unconvinced, they will tell you the following story,
which you must admit is conclusive proof.

A few years ago a Moslem from India went on his
pilgrimage to Mecca. As he was bathing in the holy waters
of the Well of Zamzam, a unique and valuable bowl which
he had brought with him was carried away by the stream.
This bowl was made of copper, and engraved thereon
were many artistic and distinctive pictures and designs.

The pilgrim was much grieved over his loss and consoled himself by visiting sacred sites. From Arabia he
traveled to Jerusalem, and there he went to the Bath of
Healing. When he was bathing, he suddenly saw in the
flowing waters the very bowl he had lost. Only the water
which flows underground from the Well of Zamzam in
Mecca to Jerusalem could have carried it thither![227]

10 / GOLGOLTHA—GOLGOTHA

One of the mountains upon which the Old City of
Jerusalem is built was called Golgoltha, which means "the
Skull." On top of this mountain stands the Church of
the Holy Sepulchre. The name Golgoltha has entered the
Christian tradition as "Golgotha," and the site has become
sacred. The word was translated into Latin, and it is now
known as Calvary.

Why was the mountain called Golgoltha—the Skull?
According to an ancient legend, cited by early Christian

sources as a Jewish tradition, the skull of Adam, the first man, lies hidden in this mountain. It is also told that Shem, son of Noah the righteous, hid this skull here after he left the ark, at the end of the flood on the earth.

Christian lore relates that when Jesus was crucified on Mount Golgotha, a drop of his blood fell to the earth, touched the skull of Adam and revived in it a breath of life for a fleeting moment.[228]

11 / GOLGOTHA—CENTER OF THE WORLD

In the Church of the Holy Sepulchre on Mount Golgotha there is a large hall in the possession of the Greeks. They call it Catholicon. On the floor of the Catholicon stands a large stone bowl, which marks the central point of the world. Therefore it is called in Greek *Amphalos,* and in Latin *Umbilicus Terra*—Navel of the

FIG. 65. NAVEL OF WORLD IN HOLY SEPULCHRE, JERUSALEM

Earth. Its Arabic name is *Nafs ed-Dunya*—Soul of the World (fig. 65).

Many Christian pilgrims mention this "navel of the world' and refer to it as "the Compass." Saewulf, who came to Jerusalem in 1102 says: "Not far from the place called Calvary, is the place called Compass, which our Lord Jesus Christ himself signified and measured with his own hand as the middle of the world, according to the words of the psalmist: 'Yet God is my king of old,/Working salvation in the midst of the earth.'" John Mandeville writes in 1322: "In myddes of that chircle is a compass . . . and that compass, seye men, is the myddes of the world."

George Sandys writes in 1610: "There is a little pit in the pavement; it is the navel of the world . . . which they fill with holy water."

This legend is parallel to the Hebrew tradition which tells that the navel of the earth is in the Foundation Stone, on nearby Mount Moriah, the site of the Temple in ancient days.[229]

12 / MELCHIZEDEK AND ABRAHAM

After defeating his enemies, the patriarch Abraham returned to his habitation. In the Torah is written: "And Melchizedek king of Salem brought forth bread and wine; and he was priest of God the Most High. And he blessed him, and said: 'Blessed be Abram of God Most High, Maker of heaven and earth.'"

Salem is an ancient name for Jerusalem. A Christian tradition tells that the meeting between Abraham and Melchizedek took place on Mount Golgotha, where the Church of the Holy Sepulchre stands today. There is a room in the church named after Melchizedek, king of Salem. According to an Eastern Christian legend, the grave of Melchizedek is also hidden on Mount Golgotha.[230]

XXI
GATES
AND TOWERS

1 / WHY WERE THE GATES CLOSED?

Around 1850 Rabbi Moshe Reisher, a Jerusalemite, writes of the gates of Jerusalem and of the Turkish soldiers who kept guard over them: "The gates are locked at night, from two o'clock after midnight till the light of dawn. And on the gates, armed guards keep vigil all day and all night long.

"On the eve of Sabbath [Friday] at midday, all the gates are closed, as Friday is the Moslem day of rest. And the Turks gather to pray on the site of the Temple in the mosque which is built there. The Turkish governor [pasha], too, repairs to the mosque with his escorts. And for that reason, the gates are kept closed [for two hours].

"The simple folk say that this is done to prevent the Messiah of Israel from coming to Jerusalem, for they hold that the Messiah shall appear on the eve of Sabbath at noontime.

"But this is obviously nonsense, for the sages, blessed be

their memory, have already stated that the son of David shall not come on the eve of Sabbath."[*][231]

2 / THE GATE OF LIONS

The Gate of Lions, in the wall of Jerusalem, faces the Valley of Kidron, opposite the Mount of Olives. Two pairs of lions are carved on its lintels, and the gate receives its name from them (fig. 66).

FIG. 66. GATE OF LIONS IN EASTERN WALL
On both sides of gate is engraved a pair of lions.

* The sages say: "It has already been promised to Israel that Elijah shall not come on the eve of Sabbath, nor on the eve of a holiday." A Christian traveler who visited the Holy Land in 1682 tells of the closing

The Turkish sultan Suleiman oppressed the Holy City and set grievous taxes upon it. The ruined and diminished city became very much impoverished. Finally, the unfortunate dwellers could pay no longer. But the harsh king decided to punish them for not fulfilling his commands and sought various plans in order to make them pay.

One night the sultan dreamt that four fierce lions leapt upon him from the Jordan thickets and, seizing him in their jaws, were tearing him to pieces. The sultan grew faint and cried aloud in fear and mortal anguish. Finally, he woke in great trembling, his soul terrified.

When day dawned he summoned all his wise men and interpreters of dreams and told them of his vision by night, asking them to explain the lions of his dream.

Fear of the king fell upon the wise men, and they became so terrified that words failed them; they could say nothing. The king sat before them with angry face and gloomy eyes, awaiting their interpretation and threatening to slay them if they failed.

Then an old sheikh came forward and, kneeling before the king, said: "Let me summon courage enough to address my lord the king. If it seems good to the king, let him tell us of what he thought yesterday ere he slept, and by Allah's aid we shall interpret the dream."

The sultan told them that he had been considering an order to his officers for them to punish severely the men of Jerusalem who did not pay their taxes.

Then the old sheikh said: "In the name of Allah the compassionate and merciful, know you that Jerusalem is sacred to Allah from all time; there did dwell His glory

---

of the gates of Jerusalem from Friday at noon till the completion of the Moslems' prayers in the mosques: "For there is a widespread belief among the people that on Friday, while the Moslems are engaged in prayer, the Christians will suddenly attack and capture Jerusalem."

and there His chosen and anointed sat on the throne, ~~David and Solomon and their descendants after them.~~ Lions were engraved on their signet rings, and lions guarded their thrones as long as they held sway. And now, as you planned evil against this Holy City, Allah sent the lions to destroy you! Therefore, treat this Holy City with goodness and mercy, that Allah's blessing may find you; for if not, evil must befall the king."

The sultan decided to go to Jerusalem himself, in order to view it and learn how to atone for his evil intents. He went to Jerusalem and found its walls destroyed and its forts burnt, so he decided to build a new wall surrounding the city. He summoned two wise architects, together with a great number of slaves and stone-hewers and masons; and he set the architects over all, commanding them to beautify and adorn the wall.

The architects divided the work between them, and parted. One went north and built the wall opposite Mount Scopus, whence he passed to the Shechem (Damascus) Gate and beyond. And the other turned south and built opposite the Mount of Olives, across Mount Zion. The work took seven years before the two parties met by the Jaffa Gate, where the wall was completed. This is the wall which still surrounds the Old City today.

Then the sultan with all his court came to view the wall. He made a circuit of it, counting the towers and battlements and gazing upon its wonderful magnificence. When he came to the spot where the work began, he ordered a great gate to be made there with two pairs of lions upon it like the lions of his dream, as a memorial to later generations of how Allah changed the king's heart regarding the Holy City, and caused him to raise it from ruin and destruction.[232]

3 / THE DUNG GATE

One of the gates of Jerusalem is called the Dung Gate —in Hebrew *Shaar ha-Ashpoth*. It leads to the Brook of Kidron and to the Pool of Siloam.

The Dung Gate was known in the days of Nehemiah, who rebuilt the wall of the city. He tells: "The dung gate [was] repaired [by] Malchijah . . . he built it, and set up the doors thereof, the bolts thereof, and the bars thereof." After the work was completed, the ceremony of the dedication of the wall was held, and the center of festivities was the Dung Gate. Nehemiah describes it: "With gladness, both with thanksgivings, and with singing, with cymbals, psalteries, and with harps . . . and . . . purified the people, and the gates, and the wall. Then I brought up the princes of Judah upon the wall, and appointed two great companies that gave thanks and went in procession: on the right hand upon the wall toward the dung gate."

It is told that the gate received its name because of the dung that was brought through it to be deposited outside Jerusalem, for it was forbidden to leave it within the Holy City. Therefore the rabbis said: "There is no part of Jerusalem more detestable than the Dung Gate."

One of the special regulations applied to Jerusalem was "That no dunghills be made there—on account of reptiles"; they are a source of defilement.[233]

4 / THE GATE OF FLOWERS

In the northern wall of Jerusalem is the Gate of Herod, which is also known as the Gate of Flowers. What is the origin of this name?

In the Middle Ages the Arabs called it by the name *Bab es-Sahira*. The nearby Moslem graveyard is still called *es-Sahira*.

Es-Sahira means in Arabic "the awake at night" or "the wakefulness." This is the name mentioned in the Koran as the place where the dead shall come to life again at the end of time, when they shall forever remain awake through the days and the nights. Because the resurrection of the dead shall take place first in the Holy Land, Moslem tradition also designates Palestine as *es-Sahira*.

The Moslem geographer al-Mukaddasi, in the tenth century, describes *es-Sahira*, an area on the heights of the Mount of Olives, where "the earth is white, for never has blood been shed upon it." A Persian traveler, Nasir Khosrau, who visited the Holy Land in 1047, tells about *es-Sahira* spreading north of the Temple court and says that to it "come people from all the world."

People have corrupted the word *es-sahira* into *ez-zahra*—the flowers. They call the gate *Bab ez-Zahra*—the Gate of Flowers. The name seems quite appropriate, too, for the outside of its entrance is decorated with carvings of flowers.[234]

5 / THE TOWER AND THE POOL

In the wall of Jerusalem, dominating the surrounding area, stands the Tower of David, once an important fortress for the city's defense. Jewish folk tradition says that this is the tower mentioned in the Song of Songs: "Thy neck is like the tower of David,/Builded with turrets" (fig. 67).

The Arabs in the Middle Ages believed that in the Tower of David was the place of prayer of King David, on the very spot where a Moslem mosque now stands, with a minaret overlooking it. They called the tower *Mihrab Daud*—the Prayer Cell of David. The nearby Jaffa Gate was also called this.

Christian pilgrims in the late Middle Ages said that the Tower of David was King David's home, and was therefore named after him.

FIG. 67. TOWER OF DAVID (1850)

In the narrow valley below the Tower of David, between Mount Zion and the New City, is a pool called the Pool of the Sultan. From the Tower of David there is a fine view of it.

Pilgrims named this pool for Bathsheba, the wife of Uriah the Hittite. They said that here she was bathing when David saw her from the tower, as it is written in the Bible: "And it came to pass at eventide that David arose from off his bed, and walked upon the roof of the king's house; and from the roof he saw a woman bathing;

and the woman was very beautiful to look upon. And
David sent and inquired after the woman. And one said:
'Is this not Bath-sheba . . . the wife of Uriah the Hittite?' "

David sent Uriah into the battle at Rabbath Ammon,
and there he was killed. "David sent and took her [Bath-
sheba] home to his house, and she became his wife. . . .
But the thing that David had done displeased the Lord."

An Arab traveler in the tenth century describes the
grave of Uriah the Hittite in Rabbath Ammon, today
Amman, capital of Jordan (fig. 68).[235]

FIG. 68. TOWER OF DAVID AND POOL OF BATHSHEBA (C. 1610)
Above, on mountain, is Tower of David. Below it is Pool of Bathsheba. To left of tower is Jaffa Gate. To right of tower is building
over grave of David on Mount Zion. Along the side lies Valley of
Hinnom.

6 / GOLIATH'S FORTRESS

Near the present wall of Jerusalem, by the New Gate, are the remains of an ancient tower. Today they lie in the basement of the French college École des Frères, which is built over them. Some scholars believe that these are the remnants of a tower known by its Greek name: *Psephinos*, famed since the time of the Jewish rebellion against the Romans and the siege of Jerusalem in 70 C.E.

The Arabs call this tower by the name *Kalaat Jalud*—Goliath's Fortress, after Goliath the Philistine who was slain by the shepherd David. The houses close to this ruin were called in Arabic *ed-Jawaldiye*—the Goliathians.*

It is told in the Scriptures that after his victory "David took the head of the Philistine, and brought it to Jerusalem; but he put his armour in his tent."

The battle between David and Goliath took place in the Valley of Elah, in the mountains of Judah, southwest of Jerusalem. A medieval legend places this encounter close to Jerusalem and also asserts that David collected the stones for his slingshot in the Brook of Kidron. Other pilgrims believed that this fight took place in the Valley of Moza, west of Jerusalem.[236]

* The Roman citadel in Amman (Rabbath Ammon) in Jordan is also known by the name *Kalaat Jalud*—Goliath's Fortress.

XXII
JERUSALEM
—THE NEW CITY

The New City of Jerusalem lies outside the wall built by the Turks about four hundred years ago. The New City was started about 1860 by Jewish settlers.

1 / WHERE EZRA WROTE THE TORAH

"And when the Torah was forgotten in Israel, Ezra arose and established it."

Outside the northern wall of Jerusalem grows an old pine tree. It is inside the courtyard of the Rockefeller Museum in the New City and is one of the most ancient pines in the country.

Arab legend relates that on the site of this pine tree Ezra the scribe sat and wrote the Torah for Israel.

In the fourth Book of Ezra it is told that when the scribe went to Jerusalem, he went out into a field, and there he wrote the Torah. But the location of this field is not mentioned.* [237]

---

* In northern Syria there is a village named Tadif, in the vicinity of the city of Aleppo. In Tadif is a synagogue named after Ezra the scribe. Rabbi Isaac ben Alfara relates around 1441: "There is a synagogue, and

2 / THE STONING PLACE

Near the Damascus Gate, within the New City, a small hill rises, upon which is an Arab cemetery. Jewish tradition tells that in ancient days this site was the stoning place, in Hebrew *Beth ha-Sekila*. Here criminals sentenced by the court were brought to be stoned.

The rabbis said: "When the sentence [of stoning] has been passed, they take him forth to stone him. The place of stoning was outside the court. . . . One man stands at the door of the court with a towel in his hand, and another, mounted on a horse, far away from him [but near enough] to see him.

"If one said: 'I have somewhat to argue in favor of his acquittal!'—that man waves the towel, and the horse runs and stops him [that was going forth to be stoned]. . . .

"If then they found him innocent, they set him free; otherwise he goes forth to be stoned.

"A herald goes out before him calling: 'Such-a-one, the son of such-a-one, is going forth to be stoned. . . . If any man knoweth aught in favor of his acquittal, let him come and plead it!'

"When he was about ten cubits from the place of stoning, they used to say to him: Make thy confession! For everyone that makes his confession has a share in the world to come. . . .

"The place of stoning was twice the height of a man. One of the witnesses knocked him down. . . . If he straight way died that sufficed. But if not, the second [witness] took the stone and dropped it on his heart. If he straight way died, that sufficed, but if not, he was stoned by all Israel."[238]

within it is a stone that Ezra the scribe sat upon and wrote the scroll of the Torah. And there still remains the impression of the oil of the candle by whose light Ezra wrote." Rabbi Meshullam of Volterra describes a book of Ezra in Alexandria, Egypt, "and in it is his signature."

The prophet Jeremiah mentions a place near ancient Jerusalem called "the Ashes," which in the end of time shall be part of the Holy City. He says: "Behold, the days come . . . that the city shall be built to the Lord . . . the ashes, and all the fields."

Rashi interprets: " 'The ashes'—the place where the ashes of the sacrifices were poured, which was outside of Jerusalem. It shall be added to the city and included within her walls."

North of the New City, at the side of the road going up to Mount Scopus, between the suburb of Meah Shearim and the Tombs of the Kings, until about thirty-five years ago there were little mounds of ashes. They were called in Arabic *Telul al-Massabin*, which means Mounds of the Soap Works. It is told that here the ashes from the soap factories in Jerusalem were dumped. With the building of houses and the paving of roads, the mounds of ashes disappeared.

Jews called the mounds *Beth ha-Deshen*—House of Ashes—or *Shefech ha-Deshen*—Pouring of the Ashes. They believed that here was where their ancestors used to pour out the ashes of the burnt offerings from the Temple. A rabbi who lived in the country in the fourteenth century mentions the House of Ashes north of Jerusalem: "It is a very small and low mound."

The Torah instructed the priest who burnt the sacrifices: "Even the whole bullock shall he carry forth without the camp unto a clean place, where the ashes are poured out, and burn it on wood with fire; where the ashes are poured out shall it be burnt."

The sages of Israel explain: " 'Without the camp'—to the north of Jerusalem. . . . They were burnt in the place where the ashes of the sacrifices were deposited."[239]

4 / MONASTERY OF THE CROSS

In the New City of Jerusalem, set in a small vale between the suburb of Rehavia and the Israel Museum, stands the ancient Monastery of the Cross. Erected in the fifth century, it was built like a fortress to protect its monks from the attacks of the surrounding bedouins.

Why was the monastery built on this site and why is it named for the cross?

Some Christian commentators tell that in this spot grew the tree from which the cross of Jesus Christ was made. Others say that Lot had already planted the tree and that he used to sprinkle it with holy waters brought from the Jordan. There is a dissention as to the nature of the tree. Some say it was a cypress, others, a cedar.

To this day, in the ancient church of the monastery there is an opening in the floor that marks the place where the tree of the cross grew, a spot most holy to the Christian visitors.[240]

5 / WHY WAS IT CALLED MEAH SHEARIM?

One of the first suburbs to be founded by Jews outside the wall of the Old City of Jerusalem was Meah Shearim. It was built in 1875, during the week when the Toldoth portion of the Torah was read in the synagogue. The name Meah Shearim was based on a narration in this portion concerning the patriarch Isaac: "And Isaac sowed in that land, and found in the same year a hundredfold [in Hebrew *meah shearim*]; and the Lord blessed him." From each grain of wheat that Isaac sowed, he reaped one hundred more. One hundredfold is a symbol of plenty, and this was the aspiration of the first settlers of Meah Shearim—to see their number increase rapidly.

Meah Shearim also means "hundred gates" in Hebrew. When the settlement was constructed, great danger threatened from the entire surroundings. Therefore Meah Shearim was built in the form of a huge courtyard, with gates whose doors were of iron. At sunset the gates were closed, and at sunrise they were opened. Legend tells us that there were one hundred gates, and the suburb received its name from them.

Residents of Meah Shearim interpreted a verse in the prophecy of Isaiah as referring to them. The prophet says: "And all thy children shall be taught of the Lord;/And great shall be the peace of thy children [*verab shalom banaich*]."

Hebrew letters also stand for numbers: A=1, B=2, and so on. The letters of the three Hebrew words above add up to 666 and so do the letters of the name Meah Shearim.[241]

6 / AGRIPPAS STREET—BEILEH PATH

Agrippas Street, one of the main thoroughfares of the New City of Jerusalem, is named after the last king of the Jews during the revolt against Rome.

For some time after the street was first traced it was known as Beileh Path, and this is the reason why: At the end of the nineteenth century, when Palestine was under Turkish rule, two new suburbs were established in this area: Even (Stone of) Israel and Mishkenot (Dwellings of) Israel. They were separated by a plot of land owned by an Arab who stubbornly refused to give the settlers the right of passage over his land. This was the cause of much hardship. Under the cover of darkness one night the inhabitants collected together, hurriedly removed the stones which hindered the way, and traced the first track connecting the two suburbs. Since according to Turkish law an established fact which benefited the people could not be abolished, the path once made remained open.

The Jews nicknamed it Beileh, the acronym for the Hebrew *bin leilah haya*—it was (made) overnight. Beileh is also the Yiddish corruption of the biblical name Bilha, one of Jacob's wives.[242]

7 / THE ASSYRIAN CAMP

During the reign of Hezekiah, king of Judah, the armies of Assyria, led by their king, Sennacherib, penetrated into the Holy Land. They approached Jerusalem and encamped nearby, planning to capture the city.

The Book of Kings relates: "And it came to pass that night, that the angel of the Lord went forth, and smote in the camp of the Assyrians a hundred fourscore and five thousand; and when men arose early in the morning, behold, they were all dead corpses." The Book of Chronicles tells of this same incident: "And the Lord sent an angel, who cut off all the mighty men of valour, and the leaders and captains in the camp of the king of Assyria. So he returned with shame of face to his own land." (fig. 69).

FIG. 69. THE ANGEL SMITES THE ASSYRIANS IN JERUSALEM (C. 1743)

The rabbis relate: "When the angel smote the Assyrian soldiers, their bodies were burnt, but their clothes were untouched."

In the following generations, the Jews still knew the location of the campsite of the Assyrians. And when the Roman forces went to Jerusalem to suppress the Jewish rebellion, they camped on this same spot.

It is probable that the Assyrian camp was on the spot where the French monastery Nôtre Dame de France stands today, overlooking the Old City and the Temple Mount. On this same spot Israeli fighters inflicted heavy damage on the Arab armies which attempted to burst into the heart of the New City in Jerusalem during the War of Liberation in 1948.[243]

8 / THE FINGER OF OG

In the middle of the New City of Jerusalem, in the Russian compound, lies a stone pillar over twelve meters long (fig. 70).

Formerly there was a quarry on the site where pillars were hewn for buildings. It seems that this pillar was prepared for Herod's temple but broke before its completion, and so was left by the masons where it now lies.

The children of Jerusalem say that this pillar is the petrified finger of Og, the giant king of Bashan, who was defeated by the tribes of Israel, when they conquered the land of Canaan.

In olden times the stone which King Og wanted to throw upon Israel when they came to fight with him was also shown, and the sages said: "He who beholds this stone should give praise and glory unto his Creator."[*][244]

---

[*] Abba Saul related: "I was a gravedigger; once I chased a deer which had entered the thighbone of a skeleton. Along this thighbone I ran for a distance of three parasangs, but did not reach the deer nor the far end of the thighbone. I understood the reason when I returned and was told that this was the skeleton of Og, king of Bashan."

FIG. 70. PILLAR CALLED "FINGER OF OG, KING OF BASHAN"
This pillar is found in Russian compound in Jerusalem, New City.

9 / WHY THE NAME MAMILLA?

One of the streets in the New City is called Mamilla Road. Nearby is a large pool which is filled with water during the rainy season. Around the pool is a Moslem cemetery.

The Arabs call this cemetery by the fitting name *ma-aman-Allah*—With the Security of God; in short, Mamilla. Some say that Mamilla is a contraction of the Arab words *ma-min-Allah*—Water from God.[245]

10 / WHY IS IT CALLED ABU-TOR?

In the southern part of Jerusalem there is a suburb on a high mountain, opposite Mount Zion and the Old City. It is called by the Arabic name *Abu-Tor*, which means Father of the Ox.

Father of the Ox is the nickname of an Arab, Ahmad

al-Kudsi, a Jerusalemite who was a warrior in the army of Moslems commanded by Saladin, which captured Jerusalem from the hands of the Crusaders in the twelfth century.

It is told that Ahmad used to ride into battle on a brave ox (in Arabic *tor*) and thus acquired his nickname, *Abu-Tor*—Father of the Ox. His ox was a very sagacious beast; he was accustomed to go by himself to the market to bring supplies for his master.

When Saladin conquered Jerusalem, he divided it among his faithful fighters, and *Abu-Tor* received as his portion the mountain where he was later buried and which has been called by his name ever since. The same name is given to the suburb which was built on it about forty years ago.[246]

11 / MOUNT OF ABRAHAM

In the midst of a beautiful grove, high upon a mountain peak south of Jerusalem, stands a splendid edifice—formerly the residence of the British high commissioner for Palestine. Today the building is occupied by officials of the United Nations.

The peak of the mountain, called in Arabic *Ras al-Mukkaber*—the Mighty (Mount)—rises 820 meters above sea level. From it one may view a magnificent panorama of ancient Jerusalem and its surroundings. In the distance can be seen Mount Moriah, the Mount of God, to which the patriarch Abraham journeyed to sacrifice Isaac, his son. The Torah narrates: "Abraham lifted up his eyes, and saw the place afar off. And Abraham said unto his young men: 'Abide ye here with the ass, and I and the lad will go yonder; and we will worship, and come back to you.' "

Legend praises the ass of Abraham: "This is the ass, son of the ass which was created in twilight. . . . This is the ass which Moses rode upon when he came from Egypt. And on this ass, the Messiah son of David is destined to ride."

In the Middle Ages people said that from the Mighty Mount, Abraham stood and gazed upon Mount Moriah.

In a Hebrew booklet describing the shrines of the Holy Land, written in 1537, it is told: "And opposite Jerusalem is a high mountain, and there are two trees. It is said that from here our Father Abraham viewed Mount Moriah. And people come here to meditate and to pray."[247]

12 / VALLEY OF REPHAIM

South of Jerusalem lies the Valley of Rephaim. Within its limits are several suburbs: Katamon, Mekor-Haim, and Bakaa—called after the Arabic name for this valley.

The valley received its name, Rephaim, from the early peoples who dwelt in the land. The Rephaim were one of the giant races, whose terror spread over the neighboring tribes. The Torah tells: "A people great [gigantic] . . . these are also accounted Rephaim."

In the name Rephaim legend finds the Hebrew word *rapha*—feeble and soft. "Rephaim—whoever saw them, their hearts softened like wax." Others said: "Whoever saw them, their hands became feeble."

In days of old, the valley was covered with fields and plantations. At the harvest season the peasants gathered their crops, and following them came the poor people, who picked the remaining grain which had escaped the sickle of the reapers. Isaiah foretold the bitter future of Israel: "That the glory of Jacob shall be made thin/. . . And it shall be as when the harvestman gathereth ears . . ./In the valley of Rephaim."

"Like a harvestman in the valley of Rephaim" is a Hebrew simile for a poor man who ekes out here and there his scant livelihood.[248]

One of the vales of Jerusalem is known as the Valley of Baca or Bechaim. Pilgrims in bygone days passed it on their way to the Holy City. The psalmist expressed his longings for Jerusalem and its Temple, and sang: "My soul yearneth, yea, even pineth for the courts of the Lord/. . . Passing through the valley of Baca, they make it a place of springs;/Yea, the early rain [in Hebrew *moreh*] clotheth it with blessings./They go from strength to strength,/Every one of them appeareth before God in Zion."

The Hebrew word *moreh* which has been translated "the early rain" is most likely the poetical form of the name Moriah—the Mount of God.

It seems that the Valley of Baca is the same as Bechaim, where King David and his army ambushed the Philistines who came up against Jerusalem. *Bechaim* is the plural of *baca*, which according to some scholars is the ancient Hebrew name for the mulberry tree. The English translation does not use Bechaim as a place-name, but renders it "mulberry trees."

In the Scriptures is told: "And when the Philistines heard that David was anointed king over Israel, all the Philistines went up to seek David . . . And when David inquired of the Lord, He said: 'Thou shalt not go up; make a circuit behind them, and come upon them over against the mulberry-trees [*bechaim*]. And it shall be, when thou hearest the sound of marching in the tops of the mulberry-trees [*bechaim*], that then thou shalt bestir thyself; for then is the Lord gone out before thee to smite the host of the Philistines."

Popular folklore finds in the name Baca the Hebrew word *bacha*—to weep. The sages of Israel said: "Baca signifies that they weep and shed tears," whence the

Hebrew appellation *Emek ha-Baca*—the Valley of Weeping—for anyplace where Jews are persecuted. This is also the title of a well-known book which describes the sufferings of the Jews in Europe in the Middle Ages.[249]

14 / HOSTEL FOR THE ONE HUNDRED AND FORTY-FOUR THOUSAND

Until recently the ruins of a large building stood near the Pool of Mamilla, on the border of Independence Park. This ruin and the house nearby, which has since given way to Heikhal Shelomo, were named by the local Arabs *el-Amira*, "the princess."

Who was "the princess"?

In the middle of the nineteenth century, when Jerusalem was under Turkish rule, a Dutch lady named Jean Marx bought this plot of land and started to erect a hostel for the hordes of Israelites expected to return to Zion at the end of time, as the author of the Book of Revelation relates: "I also observed another angel ascending from the sunrise, holding a seal from the living God. . . . I then heard the number of those sealed out of every tribe of Israel's sons one hundred and forty-four thousand."

The Dutch benefactoress first prepared a large cistern for collecting rainwater in ever-thirsty Jerusalem; then the lower story was begun. She squandered all her wealth on this venture, and the unfinished mansion soon crumbled into ruin.

The many-storied Plaza Hotel stands today on this site.[250]

15 / TENT OF THE MESSIAH

About ninety years ago there arose among American Presbyterians the belief that the time for the coming of the Messiah was fast approaching. He would appear suddenly in Jerusalem, in all his glory, as the prophet Malachi tells: "Behold I send My messenger,/And he shall clear the way before Me;/And the Lord whom ye seek,/Will suddenly come to His temple;/And the messenger of the covenant,/Whom ye delight in,/Behold, he cometh,/Saith the Lord of hosts."

Large sums of money were collected among the enthusiastic congregations, and a large tent was purchased to be the first dwelling of the Messiah, his retinue, and the favored few who would be first to welcome him.

The tent, large enough to provide shelter for five thousand people—ropes, beams, wedges, and all—was sent to the Holy City, its sides marked with the seals of the various communities which had contributed. The believers intended to come to Jerusalem to raise the tent on the summit of the Mount of Olives and be among the first to meet the Messiah.

The tent and all its accessories were handed over to the keeping of Sir Gray Hill, an English nobleman who had a mansion on top of the Mount of Olives, on a site now occupied by the Hebrew University.

At the outbreak of the First World War, Sir Gray Hill, an alien in Turkish territory, had to leave the Holy Land. He deposited the tent in the cellars of the Rothschild hospital, which stood in the Street of the Prophets (today a part of the Seligsberg Vocational School, established by the Hadassah Women's Organization of America).

The hospital fell upon difficult days during the war. There was no linen, no covering for the suffering patients; and in the cellars the large flaps of the Messiah's tent were slowly rotting away. The doctors decided to prevent such waste. Sheets and cloths for the ailing were cut out of the tent, and on cold winter nights the beams and wedges were used to heat the hospital.

And thus the tent of the Messiah came to an end.[251]

16 / ROD OF THE MESSIAH

In Jerusalem is hidden the rod which will be brought to light and given into the hands of the Messiah, as the psalmist sings: "The rod of thy strength the Lord will send out of Zion."

Our sages explain that the rod which is hidden in Zion, the Holy City, is the rod of Jacob the patriarch—and that this is the rod which was in the hand of Moses the law-giver, may peace be upon him, the same rod which was held by Aaron the priest, by David King of Israel, and by all the kings of Israel up to the destruction; and since then it has been hidden. When the Messiah comes, God the Almighty will deliver it into his hands, may it be speedily, in our days. Amen.[252]

XXIII
CAVES
IN JERUSALEM

1 / THE CAVE OF ZEDEKIAH

Below the wall of Jerusalem, near the Damascus Gate, there is an entrance to a large cavern, which is called by the Jews "The Cave of Zedekiah," the last king of Judah (fig. 71).

Jeremiah the prophet tells of the flight of the king from Jerusalem and of the fate that befell him and his followers: "And it came to pass, that when Zedekiah the king of Judah saw them, and all the men of war saw them, then they fled, and went forth out of the city by night, by the way of the king's garden by the gate betwixt the two walls; and he went out the way of the Arabah. But the army of the Chaldeans pursued after them, and overtook Zedekiah in the plains of Jericho."

When King Nebuchadnezzar and his army entered the land of Judah and conquered Jerusalem, all the princes and priests fled the city; and Zedekiah, the king of Judah, in great fear, likewise wished to escape the foe. But how could he flee when Nebuchadnezzar held all the roads?

FIG. 71. CAVE OF ZEDEKIAH THE KING (SOLOMON'S QUAR-
RIES), JERUSALEM
Interior view.

His men told him: "Beneath Jerusalem is a great cave;
there is a passage leading to the plains of Jericho. Let
our lord the king flee that way." And Zedekiah entered
the cave and pursued his path in dread almost to the
plains of Jericho.

At the very time that Zedekiah entered the cave, several soldiers of Nebuchadnezzar went hunting on the
plains of Jericho, and their quarry led them among the
bushes near the caves. At a certain passage they heard
the sound of footsteps, and thinking to themselves that
some fine game was approaching, they held themselves in
readiness. But to their astonishment there stood before
them Zedekiah, the king of Judah! They seized him immediately, and took him to the king of Babylon.

At the far end of the Cave of Zedekiah there is a small spring whose waters trickle down, drop by drop. Children of Jerusalem call these drops "the tears of King Zedekiah," and they say: "When the king fled into the cave, tears fell from his eyes, and these teardrops have been falling ever since."[253]

2 / THOSE WHO DARED ENTER THE CAVE

It is told that when the inhabitants of Jerusalem discovered the Cave of Zedekiah, some of them decided to explore it.

"Rabbi Eliezar and a group of friends, about ten men in all, armed themselves with weapons against wild beasts, snakes, and scorpions, which they feared they might encounter on their expedition. They also took with them one hundred ells of rope to measure how far they penetrated into the depths of the cave. Thus prepared they entered the grotto, carrying torches to light their way. They climbed up huge and fearful mountains and descended into deep and grim valleys—until they came to the end of the rope.

"Suddenly they heard the rumbling of great masses of water, and they almost fell into a rushing stream. And they were seized with a great fear, and stood bewildered. Then hurriedly they retraced their steps and ran out of the cave.

"At that time the sultan of Turkey and the king of England were at war with the czar of Russia; when the sentry posted at the Gate of Damascus saw the men walking about carrying firearms, he suspected them of being spies. He arrested them on the spot and haled them in front of the Pasha [the Turkish governor of Jerusalem]. The Pasha had them escorted to their consul at the Austrian Consulate.

"The consul admonished them severely saying: 'Indeed,

you know there is a war on! How were you foolhardy enough to undertake such a dangerous enterprise? You have made yourselves liable to a death sentence!'

"He kept them in custody for half a day; then he called them before him. They justified themselves to him, and swore that they were only honest citizens. The chief rabbi vouched for them, and they were finally released and set free."[254]

3 / KING SOLOMON'S QUARRIES

The cave of King Zedekiah is known among the English as King Solomon's Quarries. It is told that from this cave, King Solomon hewed out stones to build the Temple. Today the Arabs call it *Magharath Suleiman*—Cave of Solomon.

The Freemasons look upon the builders of the Temple as the forerunners of their association. Therefore, they adopted the word mason as a name for their brotherhood.

Since the masons of the Temple worked in this quarry, it became famous among the Freemasons. They occasionally held secret meetings in the dark recesses of King Solomon's Quarries.[255]

4 / WHERE DOES THE CAVE LEAD?

An Arab legend of the Middle Ages relates that the cavern of King Zedekiah penetrates far into the bowels of the earth. It reaches the places where are hidden away Korah and his companions, the followers of Moses, who were swallowed up by the earth while Israel wandered in the desert of Sinai, as is written in the Torah: "And the earth opened her mouth, and swallowed them up together with Korah . . . two hundred and fifty men . . . nothwithstanding the children of Korah died not."

The Jerusalemite geographer al-Mukaddasi, in 985, describes the Cave of Zedekiah as one of the wonders of

Palestine: "In Jerusalem, outside the walls, there is a sizable cavern, and I have heard learned men tell, and I have read in books, that it reaches down to the men of Moses."

There were times when people were afraid to enter the Cave of Zedekiah; many lost their way in its tortuous galleries and never returned to tell of their experiences. But one man managed to find a way out of the maze. He took with him a ball of string, and tying one end to the entrance, he allowed the string to trail on the ground as he proceeded on his way. In this manner, he explored the cave thoroughly, and when he decided to return, he wound up the string, and followed its trail till he reached the entrance in safety.[256]

5 / JEREMIAH'S COURT OF THE GUARD

Close to the northern wall of Jerusalem, by the Damascus Gate and the Cave of Zedekiah, lies a cavern hewn out of a hill covered with Moslem tombs. The Jews call this cave *Hazar ha-Mattara*—the Court of the Guard. It is known as Jeremiah's Grotto. They believe that here Jeremiah the prophet was held prisoner by King Zedekiah of Judah, and that it was here that he composed the lamentations on the destruction of the Temple (fig. 72).

It is told in the Scriptures: "Then took they Jeremiah, and cast him into the pit . . . that was in the court of the guard, and they let down Jeremiah with cords. And in the pit there was no water, but mire; and Jeremiah sank in the mire. . . . Then the king commanded . . . saying: 'Take from hence thirty men with thee, and take up Jeremiah the prophet out of the pit, before he die.' . . . So they drew up Jeremiah with the cords, and took him up out of the pit; and Jeremiah remained in the court of the guard."

It is told of Ha-Ari the holy, head of the Safed cabalists

FIG. 72. COURT OF GUARD OF JEREMIAH THE PROPHET, JERUSALEM
Interior view.

in the sixteenth century, that he discovered the Court of the Guard and its pit into which Jeremiah was cast: "And the mouth of the pit is narrow and its bottom large and round, about two ells in diameter. And there are places cut out of the mountain rock, which were used as jails by the kings of Judah. And it is told that Jeremiah the prophet is buried in the Court of the Guard."[257]

6 / THE CAVE OF HA-RAMBAN

At the north of Jerusalem, on the side of the road to Mount Scopus, there is a cavern hewn out of the rock, close to the grave of Simon the just. The Jews tell that Ha-Ramban—Rabbi Moshe son of Nahman (Nahmanides) —was wont to pray in it, and therefore they named it after him (figs. 73 and 74).

FIG. 73. CAVE OF HA-RAMBAN (NAHMANIDES), JERUSALEM
Near entrance is a shepherd with his flock.

When Ha-Ramban arrived in Jerusalem he found there
only two Jews; they earned their livelihood from dyeing
cloth. Ha-Ramban wrote to his family in Spain: "The
blessing of God upon you, my son, and may you live to
see the favor of Jerusalem and to behold your children's
children. May your table be as full of blessing as was the
table of our forefather Abraham.

"From Jerusalem, the Holy City, I am writing this letter
to you. Praise and glory be to God my Creator that I was
able to come here in peace. . . . Great is the desolation
of the land. . . . Jerusalem is the most desolate of all. . . .
But with all her desolation, she finds favor in my eyes.
There are two Jews here, brother. . . . On the Sabbath,
about ten Jews used to gather together in their house to
pray, but now we have found a ruined building with

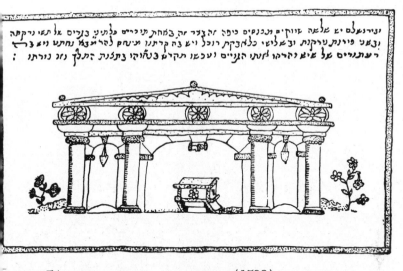

ונירושלם יש שלשה שווקים ונכנסים כיפה זה צדר זה במחת עי כריס גלתים בעדיס אל תשי נרקתה
ונשי פירינת ערקתת ובשלושי כלאבקת רוכל יש זה קרתנו תישים להר אנצא נחתש ויא ב ר
 דעתנריים של איא דהרהו לשתי הגויים ועכשו תקירש בשחיהי בתבנת זתלך נזו נורתנו   :

FIG. 74. SYNAGOGUE OF HA-RAMBAN (1598)
Hebrew inscription at top tells of various markets in Jerusalem and
adds: "And there is an ancient synagogue attributed to Ha-Ramban
with four marble columns in it, and it had been destroyed by the
gentiles, and now it has been built anew by the king's grace." From
illustrated manuscript describing holy places in Israel, written in
village of Casale Monferrato, Italy.

pillars of marble and a beautiful dome, which we have
made into a synagogue. For the city is no man's property
and whoever wishes to take possession of the ruins may
do so.

"And as the Almighty, blessed be He, has allowed me
to see Jerusalem in her destruction, so may He deem us
worthy to see the Holy City restored and rebuilt, when
the divine Presence rests again upon her."

In Jerusalem there once lived a rich Jew who gave a
great deal of charity to the poor. On the Feast of Purim
he gathered the needy and showered them with many
gifts. Once when he came to pray at the cave of Ha-
Ramban, part of the roof fell in and the Jew was buried

beneath it. It is told that every night of Purim, there appears from out of the debris of the cave a purse of gold from the treasures of this unfortunate benefactor.[258]

7 / THE CAVE OF THE LION

In the midst of a Moslem cemetery in the New City in Jerusalem is the Pool of Mamilla.* In medieval days it was known as the Pool of the Patriarch. Near this pool there was a small cave, called the Cave of the Lion, in Latin *Caverna Leonis*.

In a tract called "The City of Jerusalem," from about the year 1187 C.E. it is written: "Outside the gate of David [the Jaffa Gate] toward the west, there was a pool called the Pool of the Patriarch, where they collected the waters from round about to water the horses. Near to this was a charnel ground called the Cemetery of the Lion. Now I will tell you why they called it so. It happened, as they say, that one day, long ago, a battle was fought here, between this burying-place and Jerusalem, in which a great number of Christians were killed, and those of the city were going to burn them all next day on account of the stench. A lion, however, came by night, and conveyed them all to this ditch. And there was a church here, where they prayed daily."

Sir John Mandeville writes in 1322: "Also on the other side, two hundred paces from Jerusalem, is a church, where was formerly the Cave of the Lion: and under that church, at thirty steps deep, were interred twelve thousand martyrs in the time of King Chosroes, that the lion met in a night, by the will of God."

Rabbi Jacob the messenger, who visited the Holy Land in the thirteenth century, also tells about this cave: "There are found the bones of the righteous who were killed, in sanctification of the [Lord's] Name by the king of Greece, who planned to burn them on the following day. That

* See legend XXII:9.

night a lion came, and he took the bones of the righteous from the lower pool which was filled with them, and he brought them to this cave. In the morning, the king's men came and saw the lion crouching at the entrance to the cave, guarding the remains of the dead. Then the king and all his people knew that these were holy martyrs, and they did not desecrate their bones. Since that time, the cave has been called the Cave of the Lions."[259]

8 / THE CAVE OF THE AMORITES

The Amorites dwelt in the land of Canaan at the time of its conquest by the tribes of Israel. At one time the land was named after them, as it is written in the Scriptures: "And led you . . . to possess the land of the Amorites."

"Among all the peoples, there is none so moderate as the Amorite, for we find that they believe in the Almighty, blessed be He. They were exiled to Africa, and there the Lord gave them a beautiful country for their own."

It is told that the Roman emperor "the Wicked, who conquered Jerusalem, used to boast, saying: 'I took Jerusalem by my might!' "

"Answered Rabbi Yohanan ben Zakkai: 'Do not boast. Had it not been ordained from above, you would not have conquered.'

"And what did Rabbi Yohanan do?—He took the emperor and led him into a cave, where he showed him Amorites buried—one of them eighteen cubits tall.

"Rabbi Yohanan said: 'When Israel merited it, all these fell before us. And now, because of our sins, we have been given into your hands.' "[260]

9 / THE WONDROUS CAVERN

The Moslem writer Zakaria Kazwini, in 1280, narrates in his book *Wonders of Creation*: "In the mountains of Jerusalem, there is a cavern which is like a room built of well-hewn stones. Pilgrims are wont to come there. When the earth is shrouded in darkness, a bright light shines in this cave, although it contains no lamp, and there is no crevice whereby any rays could penetrate from outside."

The Moslem writer probably refers to a cave situated to the north of Jerusalem, in the vicinity of the Jewish suburb of Sanhedria. At its entrance layers of well-cut stones are hewn out of the rock. Today it serves only as a shelter for wandering shepherds roaming over the hills (fig. 75).[261]

FIG. 75. CAVE IN VICINITY OF JERUSALEM (RESTORATION)
Cave was hewn for burial at beginning of first century B.C.E.

XXIV
ALONG THE BROOK OF KIDRON

The Brook of Kidron flows along the eastern boundary of Jerusalem, passing between Mount Moriah, where the Temple stood in days of old, and the Mount of Olives, where the eternal resurrection shall take place in the end of time.

1 / THE MONUMENT OF ABSALOM

By the side of the Kidron, at the foot of the Mount of Olives, a beautiful stone monument rises, known as the Pillar of Absalom, in Hebrew *Yad Avshalom*—Hand of Absalom. He was the rebellious son of King David (figs. 76 and 77).

It is written in the Book of Samuel: "Now Absalom in his life-time had taken and reared up for himself the pillar, which is in the king's dale; for he said: 'I have no son to keep my name in remembrance'; and he called the pillar after his own name; and it is called Absalom's monument unto this day."

On top of the pillar is a carving of a half-opened flower

FIG. 76. MONUMENT OF ABSALOM (1848)

This monument stands in Brook of Kidron, at foot of Mount of Olives, opposite Mount Moriah. Beyond monument on east is Jewish cemetery.

FIG. 77. UPPER PORTION OF MONUMENT OF ABSALOM
In distance is wall which surrounds the Temple site on Mount
Moriah.

which is slightly chipped. The Jews say that once a hand
was carved above, and for that reason the monument was
called the Hand of Absalom (fig. 78).

Once a king came—some say it was Napoleon Bonaparte—who passed in front of the Pillar of Absalom and
aimed his pistol at the hand, saying: "The hand of a son
which was raised against his father the king—let it be
cut off forever!" After many failures, he at last succeeded

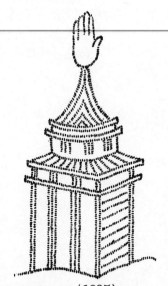

FIG. 78. HAND OF ABSALOM (1895)
This folk drawing is part of picture of Jerusalem and its holy
sites drawn by Shemuel Shulman. Preserved in Bezalel Museum in
Jerusalem.

in striking down the hand, which fell and disappeared.

Menahem Mendel, a Jerusalemite, writes in 1835 about
the Pillar of Absalom: "At the top is a handlike form,
called the Hand of Absalom. When Napoleon, king of
France, waged war on the Mount of Olives, the fingers
of the monument were shattered by his cannon fire."[*262]

2 / THE FATE OF ABSALOM'S MONUMENT

In the Middle Ages the Jews used to throw stones at the
monument named for Absalom, the accursed. The traveler
Samuel son of David, who visited Jerusalem in 1644,
describes the Pillar of Absalom. In front of it were "many
heaps of small stone. The Ishmaelites say whoever passes

---

[*] Napoleon Bonaparte actually did lead his armies in the Holy Land,
in 1799, but he was never in Jerusalem. His chief battles were fought
at Jaffa and at Acre, where he suffered a great defeat.

there throws a stone at it, because he rebelled against his father King David, peace be upon him." Another traveler, in 1824, also mentions that "the Moslems are wont to throw stones at it in anger, crying: 'This is the son who rebelled against his father'" (fig. 79).

FIG. 79. MONUMENT OF ABSALOM (1677)
Drawn from imagination. Pilgrims are casting stones at monument because Absalom rebelled against his father, King David.

The Jews of Jerusalem practiced yet another custom. Parents whose sons did not obey them would take them to the Pillar of Absalom and stand them alongside it. There they would remove the children's clothes and give their naughty offspring a sound beating, along with the following warning: "See what becomes of a son who rebels against his father, and mocks his mother! Look! Everyone despises and reviles him, and throws stones at his accursed tomb." It is said that this lesson helped.

In the course of generations so many stones were piled around the Monument of Absalom that they concealed a great part of it. In 1925 the Jewish Exploration Society removed the stones and cleared the monument.[*][263]

3 / THE SHELTER OF KING AZARIAH (UZZIAH)

By the Brook of Kidron at the side of the Pillar of Absalom there is a cave hewn out of the rock, at whose entrance stand two columns cut out of the stone (figs. 80

FIG. 80. BETH HA-HOFSHIT IN BROOK OF KIDRON
Hewn at base of Mount of Olives, facing Mount Moriah.

* The sages of Israel tell about worshiping the deity Merkolis, Mercurius (in Greek, Hermes), the patron of tradesmen and wayfarers: "He that throws a stone at Merkolis—this is how he [Mercurius] is worshiped."

and 81). The cave lies at the foot of the Mount of Olives and faces Mount Moriah. According to the Hebrew inscription carved over the entrance, this is the burial place of the sons of Hezir, a family of priests who served in the Temple. "The seventeenth to Hezir . . . these were the orderings to their service, to come into the house of the Lord."

The Jews called the cave *Beth ha-Hofshit* and believe that it was the shelter of Azariah (Uzziah), king of Judah, who was afflicted with leprosy. It is written in the Book of Kings: "And the Lord smote the king, so that he was

FIG. 81. ENTRANCE TO BETH HA-HOFSHIT

a leper unto the day of his death, and dwelt in a house set apart [*beth ha-hofshit*]."

Why was it called *Beth ha-Hofshit,* which means in Hebrew "the House of Freedom"? Because here King Azariah became free from his kingdom.

To the fate of Azariah are attributed the words of the psalmist: "I am counted with them that go down into the pit; I am become as a man that hath no help;/Set apart [*hofshi*] among the dead, Like the slain that lie in the grave,/Whom Thou rememberest no more."[264]

4 / THE WELL OF THE MAIDS

Next to the Pillar of Absalom, by the bed of the Brook of Kidron, is a cistern for rainwater. The Arab women of the vicinity come occasionally to draw from its waters.

Rabbi Moses Bassola of Italy, who visited Jerusalem in 1522, describes the "cistern which is called the Well of Bagtan[?]. It is held that the maids of Jerusalem threw themselves into it at the time of the Temple's destruction."[265]

5 / KING PHARAOH IN KIDRON

The Arab legend holds that Pharaoh, the king of Egypt, tarried awhile by the Brook of Kidron. Several monuments along its course are called after Pharaoh (in Arabic *Pharon*) and after members of his family.

The Arabs call the Pillar of Absalom *Tanturat Pharon*—the Hood of Pharaoh. The nearby *Beth ha-Hofshit* is known to them as *Diwan Pharon*—the Reception Room of Pharaoh. (fig. 82).

The tomb of Zechariah, also in this area, is named by Arabs *Jozat Pharon*—Pharaoh's Wife (fig. 77). The stone monument which stands in the neighboring Arab village Silwan is called by them *Bint Pharon*—the Daughter of Pharaoh (fig. 83). They believe that the daughter of the

FIG. 82. MONUMENT NAMED FOR ZECHARIAH THE PROPHET
Arabs call this monument "Pharaoh's Wife."

Pharaoh erected it to perpetuate her own memory while she lived in Jerusalem as the wife of King Solomon. As it is written: "And Solomon brought up the daughter of Pharaoh out of the city of David into the house that he had built for her."[266]

6 / KING SOLOMON'S MINT

In the Middle Ages a house was shown in the Brook of Kidron, where, according to tradition, King Solomon minted coins for his vast kingdom.

Rabbi Moses Bassola describes his visit at the Brook of Kidron and at the Pool of Siloam: "And it flows from the Mount of Jerusalem, but it is not known where it springs from. Some say that it comes from the Temple area.

"And on top of the mountain, there stands a building . . . with cupolas. It is believed that here King Solomon, peace be upon him, minted his coins."[267]

7 / KIDRON—PLACE OF REFUSE

Biblical Jerusalem, the city of David, was built on the heights of the mountain that rises above the Brook of

FIG. 83. MONUMENT NAMED FOR DAUGHTER OF PHARAOH
This monument stands on outskirts of village of Silwan.

Kidron. The refuse and rubbish of the city and of the Temple were cast into Kidron, as is the case today.

The Book of Chronicles describes the purification of the Temple, during the reign of Hezekiah, king of Judah. "And the priests went in unto the inner part of the house of the Lord, to cleanse it, and brought out all the uncleanness that they found in the temple of the Lord. . . . And the Levites took it, to carry it out abroad into the brook Kidron." It is also written: "And they arose and took away the altars that were in Jerusalem, and all the altars for incense took they away, and cast them into the brook Kidron."

The rabbis tell that the blood from the sacrifices in the Temple was taken out in a channel to the Brook of Kidron and sold to the gardeners as manure.[268]

8 / OPHEL AND KIDRON

" 'I will give you rain in due season'
—not flood, and not drought, but middling."

On the mountain ridge rising above the Brook of Kidron is the most ancient section of Jerusalem—the city of David. The upper part of the city of David, close to the Temple area, was called Ophel, which means in Hebrew "tower, stronghold, or acropolis."

The prophet Micah calls to Jerusalem: "In the end of days it shall come to pass,/That the mountain of the Lord's house shall be established as the top of the mountains. . . ./And thou, Migdal-eder [Tower of the flock], the hill [ophel] of the daughter of Zion . . ./The kingdom of the daughter of Jerusalem."

The steep mount of Ophel overlooks the Brook of Kidron, which runs along its base. In the rainy season, waters of the brook flow over the slopes of Ophel, southward. Apparently in days of old there was a projection in the shape of a horn on the slope of Ophel above Kidron. It was called *Keren ha-Ophel*—the Horn of Ophel. In years of very heavy rainfall, the Brook of Kidron overflowed its banks and approached the Horn of Ophel. If the waters rose too much, it was a sign of an overabundance of rain, which endangered the crops and the habitations of the people. "As long as the rain is heavy . . . the soil is washed away, and the land does not yield her fruit."

The rabbis relate: "Once there was a righteous man, and the people asked him to pray for rain. He did so, and the rains descended.

"Then they said to him: Just as you prayed for the rain to fall, now pray for it to stop!

"He replied: Go and see. . . . If a man standing on the Horn of Ophel can wet his feet in the water of Kidron, we shall pray that the rain may cease."

Rabbi Eliezer was asked: "When do we begin to pray for the rains to cease? He answered: When a man stands on the Horn of Ophel and wets his feet in the waters of Kidron." The rabbis add: "Not only his feet, but his hands, too."

Rabba the son of Bar-Hanna tells that he saw the Horn of Ophel, and a wandering bedouin was in front of it, riding a camel and grasping a spear in his hands. And next to the Horn of Ophel, he appeared as a very small worm.[269]

XXV
VALLEY OF
JEHOSHAPHAT

1 / THE JUDGMENT IN THE END OF TIME

The Valley of Jehoshaphat is part of the Brook of Kidron; it spreads east of Jerusalem, between the Mount of Olives on the east and Mount Moriah on the west. Tradition holds that the great Judgment of the Nations will be held in this valley after resurrection on the nearby Mount of Olives (fig. 84).

The name Jehoshaphat is composed of the Hebrew words: *Jeho*—God—and *shaphat*—to judge. For here God shall judge the nations and the people.

The prophet Joel describes that great event: "For behold, in those days, and in that time,/When I shall bring back the captivity of Judah and Jerusalem,/I will gather all nations/And will bring them down into the Valley of Jehoshaphat;/And I will enter into judgment with them there. . . ./Let the nations be stirred up, and come up/To the valley of Jehoshaphat;/For there will I sit to judge/ All the nations round about."[270]

FIG. 84. MOUNT OF OLIVES AND MOUNT MORIAH
Between them lies Valley of Jehoshaphat. Atop Mount Moriah, left, is al-Aksa mosque, in the Temple area. On slope of Mount of Olives, right, is Arab village of Silwan.

2 / THE JUDGMENT OF THE NATIONS

"At the end of two thousand years, the Almighty, blessed be He, shall sit on the seat of judgment in the Valley of Jehoshaphat. . . .

"And the Almighty brings forth every people and nation and asks: 'What did you worship in the world which has gone, and before whom did you prostrate yourselves?'

"They answer: 'Before gods of silver and gods of gold.'

"The Almighty commands: 'Cross here into the fire, and let your gods rescue you if they have the power.'

"Forthwith they pass and are devoured by the flames. . . .

"Afterwards, Israel stands before the Almighty and He says: 'And you, whom did you worship?'

"Straightaway they answer [the words of Isaiah]: 'For Thou are our Father, our Redeemer, for everlasting is Thy name!'

"At once the Almighty, blessed be He, preserves them from Gehenna, and they dwell in the Garden of Eden, and rejoice in its fruits. . . . And they live forever and ever in all the worlds to come."[271]

3 / ISRAEL IN THE VALLEY OF JEHOSHAPHAT

"The Almighty, blessed be He, shall say to Zion [in the words of Isaiah]: 'Arise, shine, for thy light is come,/And the glory of the Lord is risen upon thee.'

"Zion shall then answer: 'Lord of the Universe, stand Thou in front and I shall stand after Thee!'

"And the Almighty says: 'Thou has spoken well! For it is said [in the Psalms]: "Now will I arise," saith the Lord.' And in what does He rejoice?—In the joyful gathering of his children into Zion, as it is said in the prophecy of Isaiah: 'Lift up thine eyes round about and see:/They all are gathered together and come to thee.'

"At the same time the Almighty, blessed be He, calls to Elijah the prophet and the Messiah of Israel, and both come holding bowls of oil and their rods are in their hands. And all Israel gathers around them, the divine Presence rests in front of them and their prophets stand behind them, and the Torah is to their right, and the angels to their left, and they lead them to the Valley of Jehoshaphat. And all the nations are assembled there. . . .

"At the same time, the Almighty, blessed be He, brings forth the idols [of the heathens] and breathes life into them and says: 'Let every people and nation, each one with its own idol in its midst, pass over the bridge of Gehenna.'

"And they start to cross, and the bridge in front of them is as thin and frail as a thread, and they fall into hell—Gehenna.

"Then the children of Israel appear. Says the Almighty to them: 'Who are you?'—And they answer: 'We are Thy nation and Thy inheritance, the people of Israel.'

"He asks: 'Who will witness for you?'—They say: 'Abraham . . . Isaac . . . Jacob.'

"Then the Almighty, blessed be He, stands in front of them and they follow Him. And the Almighty brings forth the Torah and rests it on His bosom; and the splendor and glory of Israel illuminates the world from one end to the other."[272]

4 / THE TWO BRIDGES

On the day of resurrection, all human beings will be gathered together on the Mount of Olives, and the Judgment Seat will be on Mount Moriah, which is opposite.

Over the Valley of Jehoshaphat, which is between these two mountains, two bridges will appear for the passing of the resurrected ones to their judgment.

One bridge will be completely of massive iron and stone, and the second bridge, parallel to the first, will be of paper and will be light and frail.

All the heathens will cross over the iron bridge, which will collapse under them; they will fall into the depths of the abyss beneath, and none will remain.

All the Jews will pass over the bridge of paper in peace and safety and will live eternal life.[273]

5 / FROM THE SEA TO THE VALLEY

At the end of time, before the advent of the Messiah of Israel, there shall appear Menahem son of Amiel, Nehemiah son of Hushiel, and Elijah the prophet: "And they shall stand on the shores of the Great Sea, and shall pull out from its depths onto the dry land all the bodies of those who fell in the ocean struck by the enemy or sunk by its waves.

"And they shall draw them onto the Valley of Jehoshaphat, because there shall be the judgment of the wicked and the bliss of the righteous.

"And on the twenty-first day of the first month . . . shall come God's deliverance to Israel, and Menahem and Nehemiah and the prophet Elijah shall stand by the Great Sea, and they shall contemplate the vision of God. And all the bodies of the people of Israel who cast themselves into the sea to escape the enemy, shall come out of the water, and the sea shall rise over its banks and reject them alive in the Valley of Jehoshaphat, and on the Brook of Shittim, for there shall be the judgment of the nations."

The Brook of Shittim flows in the Jordan valley.[274]

6 / WITNESSES IN THE VALLEY OF JEHOSHAPHAT

The Christian monk Felix Fabri, who visited Jerusalem in the fifteenth century, wrote a detailed description of the city's holy shrines. He tells about the Valley of Jehoshaphat and the pilgrims who come there. They gather stones and pile them in heaps as a memorial; they believe this will assure them of a place on the great Judgment Day, which will be held in this valley at the end of time. People who do not have the opportunity to visit the Holy Land themselves pay pilgrims setting forth for Jerusalem to mark with stones a place in their memory in the Valley of Jehoshaphat. Thus they too hope to have a place at the Great Judgment when they stand before the Lord of the universe.

Among the Arabs there is a popular custom. When they near a holy site, they set up piles of stones as witnesses that they fulfilled the commandment of visiting at the shrine. The pile of stones is called in Arabic *mashad*—witness.

The Torah describes an ancient custom similar to this: "And Jacob said unto his brethren, 'Gather stones'; and they took stones, and made a heap. . . . And Laban called it: Jegar-sahadutha; but Jacob called it Galeed. And Laban said: 'This heap is a witness between me and thee this day.' Therefore was the name of it called Galeed."

The name Galeed is composed of the Hebrew words *gal* —heap—and *ed*—witness. Jegar-sahadutha is the Aramaic name and it also means "Heap of Witness."[275]

7 / THE PILLAR OF MUHAMMAD

> *"O Jerusalem . . . to thee*
> *will I run at the resurrection,*
> *as a bride to her groom."*
> —from the sayings of Muhammad

In the east wall of Jerusalem, which encompasses Mount Moriah and the Temple site, a round pillar is set, overlooking the Valley of Jehoshaphat, opposite the Mount of Olives. This pillar faces the Moslem cemetery which covers the slope of Mount Moriah. It is named after Muhammad, the prophet of Islam (fig. 85).

According to an Arab legend, when the Arab dead are resurrected at the end of days, Muhammad will sit on top of this pillar, and the Moslems will pass before him.*

On the day of resurrection, a bridge will appear between Mount Moriah and the Mount of Olives, spanning the Valley of Jehoshaphat. This bridge, called in Arabic *A-Sirat*, will be as thin as a hair and as sharp as a sword. The righteous Moslems will cross the bridge safely; the wicked will fall into the depths of the valley and be shattered to pieces.[276]

8 / VALLEY OF JEHOSHAPHAT-GEHENNA

During the Middle Ages, Moslems called the Valley of Jehoshaphat by the Arabic name: *Wadi Jehenam*—Valley

---

* Christian pilgrims of the Middle Ages told the same legend, substituting Jesus for Muhammad. A Christian traveler in 1566 says that Muhammad will sit on this pillar, and opposite him Jesus will sit. If Jesus sees that Muhammad is judging the Moslems justly and righteously, he will give him his sister in marriage, and perpetual friendship will reign between them.

FIG. 85. EASTERN WALL OF JERUSALEM AND PILLAR OF
MUHAMMAD
Pillar projects over Valley of Jehoshaphat, opposite Mount of Olives.

of Gehenna or Hell. The biblical valley Gehinnom is actually farther south.

The Persian pilgrim Nasir Khosrau, who visited Jerusalem in 1047, relates about his visit in the Valley of
Jehoshaphat, *Wadi Jehenam:* "The common folk say that
when you stand at the brink of the valley you may hear
the cries of those in Gehenna, which come up from below.
I myself went there to listen, but heard nothing."

Rabbi Moses Bassola, in 1522, tells of his visit in the
Valley of Jehoshaphat: "I descended into it—and there
at one end is a large hole from which I saw a kind of

cave. It is said that this is the mouth of hell, which shall be opened in days to come."[277]

The Valley of Decision, in Hebrew *Emek he-Harutz,* was in the area of biblical Jerusalem. Joel the prophet foresees the end of days: "Multitudes, multitudes in the valley of decision!/For the day of the Lord is near in the valley of decision./. . .And the Lord shall roar from Zion,/ And utter His voice from Jerusalem."

A legend tells of Armilius, a great foe of Israel: "Wicked and bold . . . and these are his sign: He is bald, his forehead is with leprosy . . . one eye is small, one is large. . . . His right ear is sealed, his left is open. . . . And he shall come up to Jerusalem and gather all the armies of the nations in the Valley of Decision to wage battle against Israel!"[278]

XXVI
GEHINNOM
—PLACE OF THE WICKED

1 / THE GATE OF HELL

South of ancient Jerusalem a steep, precipitous ravine stretches down and joins the Valley of Kidron. It was called by the Hebrews *Gei Ben-Hinnom*—Ravine of the Son of Hinnom, probably named after a man called Hinnom. To this valley came the wicked inhabitants of Jerusalem, to worship idols and to sacrifice their sons and their daughters. The Torah forbade this practice: "There shall not be found among you any one that maketh his son or his daughter to pass through the fire."

The Israelites contracted the name *Gei Ben-Hinnom* into Gehinnom. Because it was a valley of depravity and abomination, the same name Gehinnom (Gehenna) was given to the place prepared for the wicked in the world to come—the opposite of the Garden of Eden, where the just and righteous will dwell in everlasting happiness.

The sages of Israel said: "There are three entrances to Gehenna—hell: one in the wilderness, one in the sea, and one in Jerusalem." They established this interpretation on the following verse of Isaiah: "Saith the Lord, whose fire is in Zion, and His furnace in Jerusalem." Fire and furnace are Gehenna. They also said: "There are two palm trees in the Valley of Hinnom, and smoke rises from between them; here is the entrance to Gehenna."

The prophet Zechariah declared: "For I will gather all nations against Jerusalem to battle." Why shall they come to Jerusalem? Because Gehenna is set in Jerusalem, and the Almighty shall sit and pass judgment and shall cast the wicked forthwith into Gehenna.[279]

2 / VALLEY OF HINNOM—TOPHET

The Valley of Hinnon was a center of idolatry in ancient times. Here the wicked Jerusalemites erected altars to various heathen gods, and especially to the bloodthirsty Moloch (Molech), for whom small children were immolated. The prophets of Israel lifted their voices angrily against these abominable practices. A part of the Valley of Hinnom was called Tophet (Topheth).

The prophet Jeremiah says about the inhabitants of Jerusalem: "And they have built the high places of Topheth, which is in the valley of the son of Hinnom, to burn their sons and their daughters in the fire, which I commanded not, neither came it into My mind. Therefore, behold, the days come, saith the Lord, that it shall no more be called Topheth nor the valley of the son of Hinnom, but the valley of slaughter, for they shall bury in Topheth for lack of room. And the carcasses of this people shall be food for the fowls of the heaven, and for the beasts of the earth; and none shall frighten them away."

It is told that Manasseh, king of Judah, "made his children to pass through the fire in the valley of the son of Hinnom."

The sages ordered that all the places where idols are

worshiped must be designated by infamous names. "What is called: the face of Moloch—call it: the face of the dog."[280]

3 / IDOLATRY IN THE VALLEY OF HINNOM

The ancients described idol-worship in the Valley of Hinnom, the figure of Moloch, and the fences which surrounded it: "Although they made altars to all the heathen gods in Jerusalem, Moloch stood outside the walls of the town—in a separate place."

He was represented by a figure surrounded by seven fences. His face was shaped like a calf, and his hands were stretched out ready to receive whatever was offered to him. His body was hollow, and a fire was kindled within it. When the people brought him offerings, they approached him according to the nature of their sacrifice.

Whoever brought a fowl was only allowed to pass through the first fence and sacrifice. The man who brought a goat entered through the second fence; if he brought a sheep he entered the third. A calf allowed a man to enter through the fourth fence; a cow, through the fifth; and an ox, through the sixth.

But whoever brought his son as an offering entered through the seventh fence, close to Moloch. The man would kiss his son and then lay him in the arms of Moloch, which were red hot from the fire burning within him. The people used to bring drums and beat them vigorously, so that the cries of the child should not be heard and grieve the father's heart.

The sages explain why this valley was called Hinnom. Because the child groaned (in Hebrew *nohem*) in its agony.

Others say because the spectators groaned (in Hebrew *nohamim*) and exclaimed to Moloch: "Let his offering be sweet, pleasing, and fragrant to you!"[281]

4 / WHY IS IT CALLED TOPHET?

The prophet Jeremiah says: "And they shall bury in Topheth, for want of room to bury, . . . even making this city as Topheth; . . . and the houses of the kings of Judah . . . shall be as the place of Topheth."

Where did the word Tophet to designate a place whose people are sinners and evildoers come from? In the Book of Lamentations it is said of Jerusalem, destroyed by the enemy: "Her filthiness was in her skirts,/She was not mindful of her end."

Instead of "in her skirts" (in Hebrew *beshuleah*) the legend gives "in her low places" (*beshipuleah*)—and it adds: "There was a place below Jerusalem—and Tophet is its name . . . because of the 'tophta'—the place of burning, which is there."

Some believe that the name Tophet is one with the word *tophta*—stake or hearth, as it is used in Isaiah's prophecy:

"For a hearth is ordered of old;/. . . Deep and large;/ The pile thereof is fire and much wood."

Others derive the name Tophet from *pitui*—persuasion and enticement. And why was it called Tophet? Because all who entered there were enticed by the evil spirit.

Tophet is related by others to *toph*, the Hebrew word meaning drum. When the heathens immolated a child to Moloch, they beat the drums loudly so that the cries of the child would not reach his father's ear and arouse his pity.[282]

5 / VALLEY OF SLAUGHTER

A long time ago, when Palestine was under Egyptian rule, the caves in the Valley of Hinnom were inhabited by monks and holy men who spent their time in fasting and prayer.

Now, it happened that the ruler in Egypt needed money, and therefore he sent orders to the governor of Jerusalem to make everybody pay a tax. The governor wrote back to say that it was impossible to do so, because there were large numbers of poor and holy men who lived in caves and, since they earned nothing, could not pay the sum demanded of them.

On receiving this news, the ruler of Egypt ordered his secretary to write back the following order: "Number the men" (in Arabic *Ihsu al-Rijal*)—but through carelessness, the secretary wrote *Ikhsu al-Rijal*—"castrate the men."*

This cruelty was carried out literally. The sufferers all died in consequence and were buried in the caves where they had lived. The bones now found in the caves of the Valley of Hinnom are said to have belonged to these monks and holy men.[283]

* The difference 'kh' and 'h' in Arabic writing is only that of a dot above a letter.

XXVII
SPRINGS
AND FOUNTAINS

1 / ADAM IN THE WATERS OF GIHON

In the Brook of Kidron flows the Fountain of Gihon, the
most important source of water for ancient Jerusalem. Its
name derives from the Hebrew: *giah*—to gush and burst
forth, because its waters burst forth from the bowels of
the earth. One of the rivers in the Garden of Eden is also
called Gihon (fig. 86).

After Adam was expelled from the Garden of Eden, he
lived on adjoining Mount Moriah and used to descend
and dip himself in the waters of Gihon. "On the Sabbath
Adam immersed his body in the waters of upper Gihon
until they reached his neck. And he fasted for seven
weeks. . . .

"Then Adam prayed to the Almighty, blessed be He:
'Lord of the universe! Acknowledge my repentence and
clear me of my sins.' . . .

"And God heard his supplication and absolved him."[284]

2 / SOLOMON BY THE FOUNTAIN OF GIHON

Solomon was anointed king of Israel by the Fountain
of Gihon, as it is told in the Book of Kings: "Zadok the

FIG. 86. STAIRS TO FOUNTAIN OF GIHON

priest and Nathan the prophet . . . have caused [Solomon] to ride upon [David's] mule. And Zadok the priest and Nathan the prophet have anointed him king in Gihon; and they are come up from thence rejoicing, so that the city is in an uproar. This is the noise that ye have heard."

And because Solomon was anointed by the Fountain of Gihon, the rabbis said: "The kings are anointed only at a fountain, that their sovereignty may endure."[285]

3 / WHO SEALED UP THE GIHON?

A short time before the king of Assyria came to besiege Jerusalem, King Hezekiah sealed up the Fountain of Gihon and directed its waters through a tunnel into the Pool of Siloam. It is written in the Book of Chronicles: "This same Hezekiah also stopped the upper spring of the waters of Gihon, and brought them straight down on the west side of the city of David. And Hezekiah prospered in all his works."

It is told that King Hezekiah sealed the waters of Gihon without the consent of the sages. "Six things did Hezekiah the king, but the sages praised him for three only. . . . And for the other three the sages blamed him.' One of these was sealing up the waters of Gihon. This was not commanded because Hezekiah ought to have trusted in God, who had said: "I will defend this city!"[286]

4 / WHO UNSEALED THE GIHON?

In the sixteenth century Jerusalem was ruled by a tyrannical Turkish governor called Abu-Seifen—Father of Two Swords. Knowing that a king of Judah had sealed up the Fountain of Gihon, he asked whether there was anyone who could open it.

His friends advised him: "There is a wise Jew in this city, a man of God, and his name is Rabbi Haim Vital. He will surely know how to open it."

The governor sent for him on Friday, the Moslem day of rest, and said: "I command you to open the fountain, which was sealed by your king, during the time that I am at prayer in the mosque. If you obey not, your blood be on your head."

Then a miracle occurred, and there appeared to Rabbi Vital in a vision his teacher, Ha-Ari the holy, head of the mystics. He said: "The soul of King Sennacherib, the enemy of King Hezekiah, has been transmitted into the body of this governor, and in your body there is a spark of the soul of King Hezekiah, peace be upon him! And now is the time to open the Fountain of Gihon, for it was without the consent of the sages that Hezekiah sealed its waters.

"And now," continued Ha-Ari, "if you are able to open the sealed Gihon, you will bring great blessing upon the people!

Rabbi Vital answered: "I shall open the fountain!"[287]

5 / THE BATH OF THE HIGH PRIEST

To the Jews of Jerusalem the Fountain of Gihon is known as the Bath of Ishmael the High Priest. They relate that on the Day of Atonement, before entering the holy of holies, the high priest used to dip his body and purify himself in its waters.*

It is said of the Fountain of Gihon: "It was the ritual bath of Rabbi Ishmael the high priest, who was among the 'ten martyrs of Israel.' And a big fountain fills it with water every day before the break of dawn; and the waters were sweet and pure from the moment they gushed forth from the spring till sunrise. But after the sun shined and flashed its rays over the surface, they became so salty that no man could drink from them."[288]

6 / THE POOL OF SILOAM

The waters of Gihon flow through a tunnel hewn in the mountain beneath the biblical Jerusalem, the city of David, to the Pool of Siloam, which in the olden days was enclosed in the wall. The Jews call this pool *Breichat ha-Shiloah* (or *Shelah*), which probably means "the Pool of the conducted" (Water). The name Shiloah was corrupted into Siloam (fig. 87).

The waters of Siloam were renowned for their sweetness, and they were credited with strong powers of purification.

---

* Actually the ritual bath of the high priest was in the Temple courtyard; see legend VIII:2.

FIG. 87. BIBLICAL TUNNEL TO POOL OF SILOAM

After the destruction of Jerusalem, when its Jewish inhabitants were exiled to Babylon, the prophet Jeremiah appeared before them and said: "Had you been worthy, you would yet be dwelling in Jerusalem and drinking from the Siloam, whose waters are pure and sweet. But since you were unworthy, you are in exile in Babylon, and drink from the Euphrates, whose waters are impure and evil-smelling.

"Had you been worthy, you would yet be dwelling in Jerusalem, uttering songs and praise to the Holy One, blessed be He. But since you were unworthy, you are in exile in Babylon and utter lamentations. . . . Alas!"[289]

7 / SILOAM IN THE END OF DAYS

The vessels of the Temple, hidden away in many different places in neighboring lands, shall be revealed in the end of days, at the time of the eternal resurrection.

"At that time a great stream shall flow forth from the Holy Temple, and its name is Gihon. It shall run through the great and awful desert and unite there with the Euphrates. And immediately, all the vessels shall rise and be revealed—may it be speedily in our day, Amen."[290]

8 / SILOAM ON THE SABBATH

A Christian traveler who went to Jerusalem from Bordeaux, France, in 333 describes the Pool of Siloam and says: "This spring runs for six days and nights, but on the seventh day, which is the Sabbath, it does not run at all, either by day or night."[*][291]

9 / WHENCE THE WATERS OF SILOAM?

"He who comes to visit Jerusalem,
shall bathe in the fount of Siloam,
which springs from the Garden of Eden."

The Arabs call the Pool of Siloam by the name *Ain Silwan*—the Spring of Consolation. It is said that if anyone who is sad and oppressed drinks its waters, he is relieved and consoled, because this spring derives its water from the Garden of Eden.

The Arab poet of the desert, Ruba son of Ajaj, who lived in the eighth century, says in his despair: "Were I made

---

[*] Similar to the well-known legend of the Sabbation or Sambbation, the river of the Sabbath, which flows with a strong current on weekdays, carrying along stones and rubble with tremendous force, and rests on the Sabbath.

to drink the water of Silwan, even then I should not be comforted!"

The Moslem geographer Makadissi, a Jerusalemite, writes in 985: "It is said that on the night of Arafat [when Moslem pilgrims gather on the Mount of Arafat near Mecca], the water of the holy Well of Zamzam [which was shown to Hagar and her son Ishmael, and is near the mosque of Mecca] flows underground to the water of the spring of Siloam. And the people hold a festival here on that evening."

It is said that anyone who washes from head to foot in the water of Siloam obtains relief from his pains, and will even recover from chronic maladies.[292]

10 / EIN ROGEL—FULLER'S SPRING

South of ancient Jerusalem, in the Brook of Kidron, is Ein Rogel, one of the sources of water for Jerusalem in the biblical period. Ein Rogel was called in Aramaic *Ein Katzra—Fuller's Spring*—because women came here to do their laundry (a fuller is a launderer), as is the custom of Arab women today.

The Bible commentators explain the name Rogel as deriving from the Hebrew word *regel*—foot—because the women used to wash the clothes with their feet at this spring (fig. 88).

Adonijah son of Haggith, who planned to usurp the throne of Israel after the death of his father, King David, went to Ein Rogel, as it is told in the Book of Kings: "And Adonijah slew sheep and oxen . . . beside En-rogel; and he called all his brethren the king's sons."

The commentarian Isaac Abarbanel relates: "And at this spring the women wash their clothes. Therefore it is called the Fuller's Spring. They rub their garments by foot, and because the youths desire to go to that place to see the feet of the maidens who come to the spring, Adoniyah went there, to delight in love."[293]

FIG. 88. EIN ROGEL IN BROOK OF KIDRON, JERUSALEM (1839)

11 / THE WELL OF JOB

Job was a perfect and upright man. To him seven sons and three daughters were born, and he had sheep and cattle and camels in great abundance. God wanted to try Job and to see if he was faithful to Him. His sons and daughters died, and all his possessions were lost within a short time. In spite of this Job did not sin, nor did he murmur against the Lord. God added to his troubles, and covered his body with boils; the people deserted him, even his best friends. Only his wife remained with him.

And Job left his country and wandered with his wife; they were sustained with what was offered by the way. During his wanderings he went to Jerusalem, whose inhabitants were pious and generous. They took pity on poor, afflicted Job, and they fed him and tried to comfort him. Only at nightfall did Job and his wife leave the city, for it was the law of Jerusalem that no one who was afflicted in body should sleep within the walls. So Job slept each night near the Brook of Kidron.

God then decided to put Job to a final trial to test his faith in Him. So the Lord caused his wife to turn against Job, and this woman who had been his comforter and faithful friend wearied of her bitter fortunes, and said to Job: "Dost thou still retain thine integrity, curse God and die!" Job did not murmur against this new ordeal, although his heart was torn with grief. But he said to her: "Thou speakest as one of the foolish women. What! Shall we receive good at the hand of God and shall we not receive evil?"

God was greatly pleased now that He had proved Job and He said: "It is time to heal him from his sickness and to reward him for his faith and trust." On the spot where Job was wont to sleep, God caused a spring of fresh water to flow and commanded Job to wash in the water. Job did as the Lord commanded him, and his flesh became healthy and firm.

The waters from this spring continued to flow and were given as a reward to the generous inhabitants of Jerusalem. They called it the Well of Job, and thus it is known to this day.[294]

12 / WELL OF JOB—WELL OF JOAB

Jewish pilgrims of the Middle Ages describe the Well of Job, which they call after Joab son of Zeruiah, one of King David's most famous warriors. A Karaite pilgrim who went to Jerusalem in 1641 relates: "And we saw a fine well . . . called in the Ishmaelite language "The Well of Job," after Job the righteous. And I heard from the mouth of a gentile youth that this is the well of Joab . . . and I, too, am inclined to think so. . . . If there falls a rain, the waters fill up the well, which is very deep, and they also fill up the pool. Then people come out to the well to eat and drink and make merry, because this is a sign of a season of abundance and plenty."

Another Karaite, who was in the Holy City in 1654, also tells of this well: "And the Ishmaelites say that this is the well of Job. . . . They do not know and will not understand that it is the well of Joab, as Israel's tradition has handed down from generation to generation; but the gentiles have interchanged the letters: Job—Joab."

In very rainy years the waters of the Well of Job overflow and stream into the ravine of the Brook of Kidron. This is a sign of a blessed year, of plentiful crops and of an abundance of bread and vegetables. On such occasions, therefore, from the most ancient times, crowds of Jerusalemites were wont to repair to the Well of Job and sit on the banks of the streaming waters, reveling in its refreshing coolness, enjoying a festive meal, and making merry all day long. The Turkish government used to send a military band, which entertained the people with gay tunes.[295]

13 / THE WELL OF NEHEMIAH

When the men of Judah were exiled from Jerusalem, Jeremiah the prophet commanded the exiled priests to take the everlasting fire of the altar in the Temple and hide it, until the days of the return to Israel. They did so, and no man knew where it was hidden, save the priests.

When Nehemiah went to Jerusalem, he brought with him some of the young priests descended from those who had served in the sanctuary. And they sought the fire.

Descending the Well of Job, which is in the Brook of Kidron, they found water half frozen in a little hollow in the wall.

They took this water into the Temple and sprinkled it upon the altar. The everlasting fire suddenly kindled itself anew, to the great joy of all Israel.

Ever since then, the Well of Job has also been known as the Well of Nehemiah.[296]

XXVIII

THE MOUNT OF OLIVES AND SCOPUS

Jerusalem is entirely surrounded by mountains, as described by the ancient psalmist: "As the mountains are round about Jerusalem,/So the Lord is round about His people,/From this time forth and for ever."

The mountain rising to the east of the city is the Mount of Olives, or Olivet. Its northern extension is Mount Scopus, the Greek translation of the Hebrew name *Ha-Zofim*—the Overlooker. The mountain was thus named because of its prominent position overlooking Jerusalem and all its surroundings.

1 / THE PLACE OF RESURRECTION

"When shall we be glad and joyful?—When the feet of the divine Presence shall stand upon the Mount of Olives."

The Mount of Olives shall be the place of the resurrection of the dead at the end of time. Therefore it has been a chosen burial place for many generations, and its slopes are covered by the largest and most ancient cemetery of the Jewish world.

Zechariah the prophet foresees Jerusalem and the Mount of Olives in the end of days: "Behold, a day of the Lord cometh. . . ./And His feet shall stand in that day upon the mount of Olives,/Which is before Jerusalem on the east,/And the mount of Olives shall be cleft in the midst thereof/Toward the east and toward the west,/So that there shall be a very great valley; . . ./And half of the mountain shall remove toward the north,/And half of it toward the south. And ye shall flee to the valley of the mountains; . . ./And it shall come to pass in that day,/

FIG. 89. MOUNT OF OLIVES (C. 1900)

At bottom, words of the prophet Zechariah: "And his feet shall stand in that day upon the mount of Olives" (Zechariah 14:4). At foot of mountain stands wall of Jerusalem with Gate of Mercy (Golden Gate) in center. Beyond wall, Hand of Absalom; on right, Beth ha-Hofshit and tomb of Zechariah.

That living waters shall go out from Jerusalem. . . ./And the Lord shall be King over all the earth. . . ./But Jerusalem shall dwell safely."

"Valley of the mountains" is apparently the Brook of Kidron, which flows between the Mount of Olives and

Mount Moriah. Azel is the name of a place which was on Olivet, or near it. One belief holds that it was named after Azel, a descendant of King Saul, as is told in the Book of Chronicles: "And Azel had six sons."

A Christian historian of the fifth century tells of a village called Azel which lay on the slope of Olivet. A valley which descends toward the southern part of Olivet to the Brook of Kidron is called in Arabic *Wadi Yazul*. This name may be an echo of the ancient name Azel.[297]

2 / THE WANDERING OF THE DIVINE PRESENCE

After the destruction of the Temple, the divine Presence departed from it, weeping and lamenting its fate. Before it ascended to the firmament, the divine Presence wandered over several places in the Temple courtyard and in Jerusalem.

The ancients tell us: "Ten journeys were made by the divine Presence: from cherub to cherub; from the cherub to the threshold of the house; from the threshold of the house to the cherubim; from the cherubim to the East Gate; from the East Gate to the court; from the court to the roof; from the roof to the altar; from the altar to the wall; from the wall to the city [of Jerusalem] and from the city to the Mount of Olives,—as it is written in the prophecy of Ezekiel: 'And the glory of the Lord went up from the midst of the city, and stood upon the mountain which is on the east side of the city.'

"Three and a half years did the divine Presence dwell on the Mount of Olives, expecting Israel to repent . . . but they did not confess their sins; and an echo from heaven was heard declaring [the words of Jeremiah]: 'Return, O backsliding children!' [and the words of Malachi]: 'Return unto Me, and I will return unto you!' And as they did not make repentance, the echo said [the words of Hosea]: 'I will go and return to My place!'

"Three and a half years, while the enemy surrounded Jerusalem did the divine Presence rest on the Mount of Olives, and every day it called out [the words of Isaiah]: 'Seek ye the Lord while He may be found,/Call ye upon Him while He is near!' But they [Israel] did not make repentance. And when the divine Presence saw that Israel remained obdurate, it ascended to the firmament alone."[298]

3 / THE CONSOLER ON THE MOUNT OF OLIVES

Consoler (in Hebrew, *Menahem*) is the nickname of the Messiah of Israel. And his father is called *Amiel*—"My nation to God." Menahem the son of Amiel will appear in the end of time on the Mount of Olives, before the gates of Jerusalem. And the exiles shall return and ascend to the mountain, and see the redemption of Zion and Jerusalem.

A poet describes the appearance of Messiah—the Consoler: "In those days, at that time,/In the fifth month, the month of Ab,/The Pure, dressed in his robes of vengeance,/By his wrath the Mount of Olives will be cleft./Messiah comes forth in his majesty,/As the sun shines in its strength."[*][299]

4 / PRIVILEGES ON THE MOUNT OF OLIVES

A famous cabalist, Rabbi Abraham Azulai, who lived in the Holy Land in the seventeenth century, relates: "There is a tradition which says that when the Messiah returns to the land of Israel with the army of Jewish exiles, he will find here seven thousand sons of Israel.

"On that day, the dead of the land of Israel will come to life; the walls of Jerusalem will disappear, and the Messiah will rebuild them with precious stones and pearls. The resurrected dead will return to a new spiritual creation . . . like Adam, the first man, before he sinned . . . and they will all float in the air, and fly like angels . . . to

* See legends XXV:1–4.

go and live in the Garden of Eden, to learn Torah from the Holy One, blessed be He.

"Then the Jews of the Diaspora will gather together, troubled and disturbed . . . and they will murmur against the king, the Messiah, saying: 'Are we not sons of Israel as well as they? Why are they privileged with the spirituality of body and soul? . . .'

"And the Messiah will answer: 'They . . . after much wearying effort tried to come to the land of Israel, that they might be privileged with a pure soul, and they did not fear for their bodies or for their worldly goods, and you feared lest harm come to your bodies . . . therefore have you remained corporeal.' "[300]

5 / NO WORMS IN THE MOUNT OF OLIVES

It is commonly believed that worms do not disturb the sleep of the dead buried on the Mount of Olives and do not decay their bodies.

The sages of Israel tell: "Seven were free from rot and decay, their bodies were not touched by worms, and these are Abraham, Isaac, Jacob, Moses, Aaron, Miriam, and Benjamin son of Jacob." Some add to them King Saul and Jonathan his son.

Rabbi Farhi the Jerusalemite, around 1838, describes the virtues of the Holy Land in his book *Excellence of Jerusalem*: "After the death of man, worms do not disturb his body. And there is no better gift, for the sages, blessed be their memory, have already said: 'Worms are painful to the body of the dead as needles to the flesh of the living, and happy is the man who merited burial in the land of Israel, and is thus saved from such punishment.' "[301]

6 / JUDGMENT ON THE MOUNT OF OLIVES

After the body of the dead is laid in the grave, angels seize it and beat and smite it, causing it very severe pains.

FIG. 90. JEWISH CEMETERY ON MOUNT OF OLIVES (1942)
Opposite wall of Jerusalem. Between Mount of Olives and Jerusalem
lies Valley of Jehoshaphat. In distance, left of wall, is Mount Zion.

"The smiting in the grave is worse than the agony of
Gehenna." However, those who die and are buried in the
land of Israel are free from the castigation of the grave
(*hibutt ha-kever*).

The elders said: "Whoever lives in the land of Israel
and dies on the eve of Sabbath before the sun sets when
the shofar is blown does not suffer the judgment of the
grave. And in what way is that judgment conducted?
When a man dies, three ministering angels come to him.
One says: 'A righteous man has passed away!' And one
says: 'Peace shall come!' And one says: 'Go forward!'

"And if the man during his life has been completely wicked, five angels of destruction come to him. One sits on his grave and says: 'The wicked shall return to the grave!' and he beats him with his hand and asks for his name. . . . Forthwith, he quickens the body back to life, breathes in its soul and puts it to trial, and with a chain, partly iron and partly fire, he flagellates him three times. First his bones fall apart; then they are dispersed. Then the ministering angels reassemble his body again, and they bring his soul and throw it back into the body and beat him for the third time. Then they put him to trial and pass judgment on his every deed."[302]

7 /EARTH FROM THE MOUNT OF OLIVES

Jews of the Holy Land used to send abroad small bags of earth taken from the Mount of Olives. The Jews in the Diaspora would place some of this earth in their graves, in the belief that it would prevent worms and was graced with merits which would be propitious for the resurrection of the dead at the end of days.

When departing from Jerusalem, Jews used to take with them soil from the Mount of Olives, as a talisman of special merit for their journey. The author of a booklet, *Seeker of the Peace of Jerusalem*, about 1710, praises the Mount of Olives and says: "And whoever traveled from the land of Israel to foreign countries would take with him white earth from this mountain—I too took some with me—to fulfill the words of Psalms: 'And favor the dust thereof.' "

A messenger on behalf of the Jewish communities from Jerusalem, who wandered through many countries around 1700, used to distribute soil from the Mount of Olives to the people in the lands of the dispersion. It is told that one messenger from Jerusalem, who visited Russia at the beginning of the nineteenth century, used to take in payment for the earth from the Mount of Olives the same amount in gold.

A Hungarian Jew wrote in his will: "Place the holy earth from the Mount of Olives which is in the paper in my shroud, and write upon it; 'Earth from our rabbi and teacher Obadiah.' He promised me it was taken from the Mount of Olives in Jerusalem. And this earth shall spread over me, over my head and all my body and my limbs, completely, that the words of the Torah may be fulfilled: 'And doth make expiation for the land of his people.' "[303]

8 / THE LAND OF THE LIVING

The psalmist sang: "I have cried unto Thee, O Lord./ I have said 'Thou art my refuge,/My portion in the land of the living.' "

From here we learn that the land of Israel is also known as "the land of the living." And why is it thus called? Because those who die in the land of Israel shall be the first to rise again in the days of the great resurrection when the Messiah comes.

"To be buried in Jerusalem is like being buried beneath the throne of the Lord."

"He who is buried in the soil of the Holy Land is assured of his portion in the eternal life."

"Whoever is buried in the land of Israel is deemed to be buried under the altar [of the Temple]."

In the end of time, the righteous will sprout and rise from the soil of Jerusalem. And they will be like unto the wheat: as the seeds of wheat which are sown naked grow wrapped and clad in husks, so the righteous, who are buried in their garments, shall come forth fully dressed.

For the psalmist says: "And may they blossom out of the city like grass of the earth"—and by "the city" only Jerusalem can be meant.[304]

9 / THE ROLLING IN TUNNELS

The sages of Israel explain the words of Isaiah: " 'Thy dead shall live.'—This refers to the dead of the Land of Israel. 'My dead bodies shall arise.'—These are the dead outside of the Land."

What will the Almighty do with the righteous who die in the lands of exile, far away from the Holy Land? They will roll through tunnels to the Holy Land. This is called in Hebrew *gilgul mehilot*—rolling in tunnels.

"Would not the righteous outside the land [of Israel] be revived?—[They will be revived] by rolling [to the land of Israel] . . . tunnels will be made for them underground."

At the end of time the Almighty will create underground tunnels from one end of the earth to the other, leading to Zion. He will then command His ministering angels to bear the righteous through these tunnels into the land of Israel, where they will rise and atonement will be granted to them.[305]

10 / RESURRECTION ON THE MOUNT

"At the time of the resurrection, the Almighty, blessed be He, shall descend from the upper heavens and shall sit upon his throne in Jerusalem and the Holy One shall call to his ministering angels and say: 'My children! I created you purposely for this hour.'

"The angels shall answer: 'Lord of the universe, we stand here before Thee, to do Thy will!'

"And the Holy One shall command: 'Go ye, and journey to the ends of the world, and raise up the corners of the earth; give pardon to the righteous in lands of the exile, and bring before me in the land of Israel each just man, who devoted every day of his life to the sanctification of My Name. . . .'

"How shall the dead be resurrected in the world to come?—The Holy One shall take in His hand a great trumpet [shofar], 1,000 cubits in its measurements, and He shall blow it:

"At the first blast—the whole world will quake.

"At the second blast—the soil crumble.

"At the third blast—their bones will join together.

"At the fourth blast—their limbs will become warm.

"At the fifth blast—their skin will cover them.

"At the sixth blast—spirit and soul will enter their bodies.

"At the seventh blast—they will stand on their feet, clothed in their garments."[306]

11 / THE PROCESSION ON THE MOUNT

In the Middle Ages there was a custom among the Jews to climb the Mount of Olives in a great procession during the Feast of Tabernacles, on the day of Hoshana Rabba. The procession was accompanied with song, and circled seven times the summit of the mount, which commands a beautiful view of Mount Moriah and the Temple site.

Men of priestly families (Cohanim), descendants of Aaron, the high priest, dressed in silks, led the throng, fulfilling their honorable service in the ceremony. Apparently there were many who pretended to be Cohanim in order to enjoy this great honor. Rabbi Hai Gaon, in the tenth century, tells derisively of those self-styled sons of priestly families.

Once he himself went along in the procession and at one point burst into laughter. When asked the reason for his behavior, he related: "Elijah the prophet walked with me and talked to me. And I asked him, 'When will the Messiah of Israel come?' 'When the Mount of Olives is circled by real priests of Israel. Look at those priests whom you see richly garbed and marching haughtily. Not one is of the seed of Aaron the high priest. Only one, who marches behind them all . . . in poor clothes, not seeking after honor . . . limping, and with one eye missing—he is truly a Cohen, a descendant of Aaron.'

"Then I laughed," concluded Rabbi Hai, "because among them all, the only real priest was that cripple."[307]

12 / MOUNT OF ANOINTMENT—MOUNT OF CORRUPTION

The Mount of Olives is named for the groves of olive trees which grew on its slope. The groves have been destroyed, and only a few ancient trees have remained in the garden of Gethsemane. The name Gethsemane is a corruption of the Hebrew *gath-shanna*, oil press.

The southern part of the Mount of Olives was named the Mount of Anointment, in Hebrew *Har ha-Mish-ha*, for here was prepared the finest olive oil which was used to anoint kings and high priests of Israel. The Mount of Anointment commands a beautiful view of Jerusalem of the biblical period: the city of David and the Ophel.

The Mount of Anointment was at a certain period the center of the cult of idol worship; idolators gathered there to perform their abominable practices. Therefore the beautiful name *Mish-ha*—Anointment—was changed into *Mash-hit*—Corruption.

The prophet Jeremiah calls to the enemy of Israel: "Behold, I am against thee,/O destroying mountain [*Har ha-Mashhit*], saith the Lord,/Which destroyest all the earth,/And I will stretch out My hand upon thee,/And roll thee down from the rocks,/And will make thee a burnt mountain./And they shall not take of thee a stone for a corner,/Nor a stone for foundations,/But thou shalt be desolate forever."

Josiah, king of Judah, brought an end to the cult of the heathen gods in this place, as it is told in the Book of

Kings: "And the high places that were before Jerusalem, which were on the right hand of the mount of corruption, which Solomon the king of Israel had builded for Ashtoreth the detestation of the Zidonians, and for Chemosh the detestation of Moab, and for Milcom the abomination of the children of Ammon, did the king defile. And he broke in pieces the pillars, and cut down the Asherim [sacred trees]."[308]

13 / THE DOVE AND THE OLIVE

During the time of the flood in the days of Noah the righteous, the Mount of Anointment remained uncovered by the waters. From this mountain the dove brought the olive leaf to the ark (fig. 91).

It is told in the Book of Genesis: "And the dove came in to him at eventide; and lo in her mouth [was] an olive-leaf freshly plucked off."

FIG. 91. DOVE AND OLIVE LEAF (2D CENTURY)
Picture in mosaic floor of synagogue of Gerassa, Jordan. Below dove are written (in Greek) the names Japhet and Shem, sons of Noah the righteous.

Where did she get it? From the Mount of Anointment, for the land of Israel was not flooded.

Why did the dove particularly choose an olive leaf, whose taste is very bitter? The dove said to the holy One, blessed be He: "Lord of the universe, may my food be bitter as the olive, but given by your hands, rather than sweet as honey, and given by human beings."[309]

14 / FLARES ON THE MOUNT

After the sages in Jerusalem determined the first day of the new month, their messengers ascended the Mount of Olives. There, on the lofty peak of the Mount of Anointment, they kindled the first flare, after which the flares on other mountains in the land were lit.

"After what fashion did they kindle the flares?—They used to take long cedar-wood sticks and rushes and oleaster-wood and flax-tow; and a man bound these up with a rope and went up to the top of the mount and set light to them. And he waved them to and fro and up and down, until he could see his fellow doing the like on the top of the next mount. And so, too, on the top of the third mount.

"And from what place did they kindle the flares?—From the Mount of Olives."[310]

15 / CEDARS AND CINNAMON TREES

There were two cedars on the Mount of Olives; beneath one of them were four stalls for a seller of birds for ritual offerings.

The leper had to offer, as told in the Torah, "two living clean birds and cedar-wood . . . and the poor if his means suffice not for a lamb, then he shall bring . . . two turtledoves, or two young pigeons."

When Nebuchadnezzar, king of Babylon, destroyed the

Temple, he uprooted the cedars and replanted them in his land. When he died, the trees rejoiced, as the prophet Isaiah says: "The cypresses rejoice at thee,/And the cedars of Lebanon:/'Since thou art laid down,/No feller is come up against us.'"

It is told that cinnamon trees also grew in Jerusalem in days of old. "Cinnamon used to grow in the land of Israel, and the goats and hinds ate it."

The fuel logs of Jerusalem were of the cinnamon tree, and when they were burnt, their fragrance pervaded the whole of the land of Israel. But when Jerusalem was destroyed, they were hidden, only as much as a barley grain being left. It is to be found in the Queen of Zimzemai's treasury.[311]

16 / JEREMIAH ON MOUNT SCOPUS

The birthplace of Jeremiah the prophet, Anathoth, was east of Scopus and Jerusalem. A road from Anathoth runs upon the heights of Scopus and then leads down to Jerusalem.

Along this road Jeremiah used to pass on the way from his home in Anathoth to Jerusalem, the capital. He also traversed it during the critical days when the Babylonian forces were besieging the city.

"At that time the Lord said to Jeremiah: 'Arise and go to Anathoth!' . . . After Jeremiah had departed from Jerusalem, an angel descended from heaven, placed his feet on the wall of the city, and wrecked them. Then he cried: 'Let the enemies come and enter the Temple which the Lord no longer inhabits. . . . Let them pillage and destroy it. . . . Let them enter the vineyard and trample the grapes that the watchman has deserted. . . . So that you shall not praise yourselves and boast: 'We have conquered it!' For a conquered city have you conquered; and a dead people have you killed!

"When Jeremiah the prophet went out of Anathoth to come to Jerusalem, he lifted his eyes and beheld smoke rising from the Temple. He thought: 'It must be that Israel has repented, and is offering sacrifices, for lo, the smoke of the incense ascends!'

"He continued till he reached Mount Scopus; there he saw that the Temple had been reduced to piles of stones, and the wall of Jerusalem destroyed. He began to wail, crying: 'O Lord, thou hast enticed me, and I was enticed,/ Thou hast overcome me, and hast prevailed;/I am become a laughing-stock all the day.'

"After the destruction of Jerusalem, Jeremiah relates: 'When I came to Jerusalem, I saw a woman sitting solitary on the mountain top, clothed in black, her hair dishevelled. She wept and beseeched: "Who shall comfort me?"— And she told me: "I am the mother of Zion!"'

"Why was the prophet named Jeremiah?—Because in his day Jerusalem became eremia [a Greek word which means]—desolation."[312]

17 / WHOEVER SEES JERUSALEM

From the height of Mount Scopus there unfolds a splendid view of Jerusalem and of Mount Moriah, upon which once rose in glory the first and the second Temples of Israel.

Pilgrims going to Jerusalem from the northeast, when gazing from Mount Scopus on Jerusalem in her destruction, used to rend their garments as a sign of mourning, and read the words of Isaiah the prophet: "The holy cities are become a wilderness,/Zion is become a wilderness,/ Jerusalem a desolation./Our holy and our beautiful house,/ Where our fathers praised Thee,/Is burned with fire;/ And all our pleasant things are laid waste."

The sages commanded: "He who views Jerusalem from Mount Scopus—must rend [his garment]."

OR
F. de Iordan
M. Morte
Cite de Tyberiade
Hyerico
Bethanie
Samarie
Iosaphat
M. Sion
Bethleem
Hebron
Cite de David
Rama
Lida
Iaffa
Champ
Mer Mediterranee
S
M
OC

Whoever rends his garment must let the tear remain as a memorial; he is forbidden to join the edges together and mend it. The ancients said: "Ten rends are forbidden to be joined . . . and for Jerusalem and for the Holy Temple" (fig. 92).³¹³

FIG. 92. WAYS TO JERUSALEM (1615)

In center, Jerusalem, *Hierusalem,* a walled city; also indicated by its biblical name, city of David, *cité de David.*

At bottom, on coast of Mediterranean, *Mer Méditerranée,* pilgrims land at Jaffa. One kneels to kiss holy soil. Above Jaffa is Ramla, marked *Rama,* the name known to medieval pilgrims. Lydda, *Lida,* is farther up coast and above it, Castle of Maccabees.

Jerusalem is bounded on east by Valley of Jehoshaphat and on south by Mount Zion, rising above Pool of Siloam. Farther on right is Bethlehem, with Hebron depicted immediately below it and Field of Damascus, *Champ Damascene,* from whose soil God created the first man, strangely pictured almost on shore of Mediterranean Sea.

East of Jerusalem rises the Mount of Offense (Mount of Olives) and beyond it, village of Bethany, on the way to Jerisho, *Hyerica.* Famed monastery of Saint Saba is drawn near shore of Dead Sea, *Mer Morte,* which receives sweet waters of Jordan River, flowing out of Sea of Galilee, next to town of Tiberias, *cité de Tyberiade.*

XXIX
ROADS
TO JERUSALEM

"The midst thereof being paved with love,
for the daughters of Jerusalem."

1 / DAUGHTERS IN THE VINEYARDS

Roads from Jerusalem lead into the surrounding regions, which are covered with vineyards and olive groves.

In days of old there was a custom widespread in Israel: twice a year the daughters of Jerusalem would dress in white and go out to dance in the vineyards.

"There were no happier days for Israel than the fifteenth of the month Ab and the Day of Atonement, for on them the daughters of Jerusalem used to go forth in white garments, and these were borrowed, that none should be abashed which had them not. . . .

"And the daughters of Jerusalem went forth to dance in the vineyards. And what did they say?—Young man, do not lift up thine eyes on beauty, but set thine eyes on family, for [it is said in the Book of Proverbs] 'Grace is deceitful and beauty is vain;/But a woman that feareth the Lord, she shall be praised!'

"Our Rabbis have taught: "The daughter of the king borrows [the garments] from the daughter of the high priest.

"The daughter of the high priest from the daughter of the deputy high priest.

"And the daughter of the deputy high priest from the daughter of the anointed for battle [chaplain of the army in time of war].

"And the daughter of the anointed for battle from the daughter of an ordinary priest.

"And all Israel borrow from one another, so as not to put to shame anyone who may not possess [white garments].

"The beautiful amongst them called out: 'Set thine eyes on beauty, for the quality most to be prized in woman is beauty.'

"Those of them who came of noble families called out: 'Look for [a good] family, for woman has been created to bring up a family.'

"The ugly ones amongst them called out: 'Carry off your purchase in the name of heaven, only on one condition that you adorn us with jewels of gold.'"

Why was the fifteenth of the month of Ab chosen for this celebration? Tradition tells that on this day, the children of Israel completed their forty-year journey in the Sinai Desert.

Others say that on this day the guards on the roads, who prevented the people of Israel from going up to Jerusalem, were abolished.[314]

2 / THE ROADS OF ZION MOURN

In ancient days many roads led to Jerusalem from all parts of Israel. At festival time thousands of pilgrims thronged these roads, streaming into the capital city and the Temple and visiting the holy shrines, to fulfill the commandment of appearance before the Lord in His exalted habitation. The pilgrims brought with them the produce of their labor, the firstfruits of their fields and groves and vineyards, as a donation to the priests and Levites who served the Lord of hosts in the city of God.

The pilgrimage was magnificent and brought great joy to the hearts of the participants. The psalmist expresses the emotion it evoked: "These things I remember, and pour out my soul within me,/How I passed on with the throng, and led them to the house of God,/With the voice of joy and praise, a multitude keeping holyday./ . . . O my God, my soul is cast down within me;/therefore do I remember Thee from the land of Jordan,/And the Hermons."

The rabbis asked: "What is the meaning of the verse [in the Song of Songs]?—'How beautiful are thy feet!'— It means: How comely are the feet of Israel when they go up on the festival pilgrimage."

With the destruction of the nation, the roads to Jerusalem, winding above mountain slopes in regions covered with forests and fragrant vegetation, became ruined. Rains washed away the soil, and bare rocks and stones projected. The fresh verdure disappeared, and the countryside turned gray and pale. The roads of Zion, once bustling with wayfarers were desolate, as told in Lamentations: "The ways of Zion do mourn,/Because none come to the solemn assembly."

"The community of Israel spoke before the holy One, blessed be He: In the past I used to go up to Jerusalem along well-kept roads—but now through thorny hedges. . . .

"In the past, I used to go up, and the trees formed a covering above my head—but now I am exposed to the sun. . . .

"In the past I used to go up in the shade of the Holy One, blessed be He—but now in the shadow of the [oppressive] governments."[315]

3 / THE HIGHWAYS LIE WASTE

The people of Israel expressed their sorrow for the destruction of the land, and remembered the days of their glorious past: "In days gone by, I used to go with my basket of firstfruits, and in the early morning, the people rose and called to one another: 'Come, let us go up to Zion!'—and now I come and depart amid silence.

"In days gone by, I used to go up before the Lord with music and song—and now I come and depart in tears.

"When the Temple existed, we would ascend unto the Lord during the festivals—we and our children would come in great multitudes, and the nations were inarticulate before us—and now we are so before them.

"Isaiah the prophet laments: 'The highways lie waste,/ The wayfaring man ceaseth.'

"The ministering angels said to the Holy One, blessed be He: 'Roads to Jerusalem which I repaired, always teeming with travelers—how are they now desolate!'

" 'Roads which Israel used to traverse on the holy days —how are they now deserted!

" 'For Thou hast rejected Jerusalem and Zion, after Thou hadst chosen them.' "[316]

4 / THORNS ON THE ROADS

In the land of Israel grows a thorny shrub called in Hebrew *heiga* (plural *heigim*). In olden days hedges of it were grown as fences to protect groves and gardens. However, *heigim* which spread in fields were uprooted because they damaged the plantations. The sages of Israel speak about "those who trim *heigim*."

With the destruction of the Temple the pilgrimages ceased, and the forsaken roads leading to Jerusalem became covered with *heigim*, this thorny shrub.

Legend finds a hint about the *heigim* on the roads in

the words of Isaiah the prophet to Jerusalem: "Ah, Ariel, Ariel, the city where David encamped!/Add ye year to year,/Let the feasts come round."

The Hebrew word for feast is *hagim*; the legend says: "Do not read *hagim*—feasts—but *heigim*—thorny shrubs."

"Years came and years passed. The children of Israel do not go up to Jerusalem for their pilgrimage in the feasts, and the roads grew thorny shrubs."[317]

5 / WHERE ARE THE STONES FROM?

On the outskirts of Jerusalem and on the sides of the roads leading to her, many stones are scattered and strewn. Where did all these stones come from? Who put them along the roadsides?

It is told that when any Jew in exile remembers Jerusalem in her destruction, he feels as if a heavy stone presses his saddened heart. If the blessed day should come when he is granted the privilege of ascending to Jerusalem, the first glance at his desired site relieves him of his burden. It is as if the very stone that pressed him is lifted. He takes the stone and places it on the roadside as a faithful testimony that here he was comforted by the sight of the Holy City.

One wish is in his heart, and one prayer on his lips: to see his city, Jerusalem, rebuilt and flourishing. And he recites the words of the psalmist: "Thou wilt arise, and have compassion upon Zion;/ For it is time to be gracious unto her, for the appointed time is come./For Thy servants take pleasure in her stones,/And love her dust./ . . . When the Lord hath built up Zion,/When He shall hath appeared in His glory . . ./That men may tell of the name of the Lord in Zion,/And His praise in Jerusalem . . ./The children of Thy servants shall dwell securely,/And their seed shall be established before Thee."[318]

6 / YE MOUNTAINS OF ISRAEL

Joel prophesies: "And it shall come to pass in that day,/ That the mountains shall drop down sweet wine,/And the hills shall flow with milk,/And all the brooks of Judah shall flow with waters."

The prophet Ezekiel calls: "Ye mountains of Israel, hear the word of the Lord God: Thus saith the Lord God to the mountains and to the hills, to the streams and to the valleys, to the desolate wastes, and to the cities that are forsaken, which are become a prey and derision to the residue of the nations that are round about. . . .

"But ye, O mountains of Israel, ye shall shoot forth your branches, and yield your fruit to My people Israel; for they are at hand to come. For behold, I am for you, and I will turn unto you, and ye shall be tilled and sown; and I will multiply men upon you, all the house of Israel, even all of it; and the cities shall be inhabited, and the waste places shall be builded; and I will multiply upon you man and beast, and they shall increase and be fruitful; and I will cause you to be inhabited after your former estate, and will do better unto you than at your beginnings."

"When the Holy One, blessed be He, shall redeem Israel, three days before the coming of the Messiah, Elijah the prophet shall appear on the mountains of Israel, weeping and mourning for them, saying: 'O mountains of the Holy Land! How long shall ye remain barren and desolate?'

"And his voice is heard till the ends of the earth—

"And then he proclaims: Peace has come to the world!"[319]

THE ANCIENT SOURCES

THE BIBLE. It is divided into three parts: *Torah* or Pentateuch, *Nebiim* (Neviim) or Prophets, and *Ketubim* (Ketuvim) or Writings (Hagiographia); hence the Hebrew name of the Bible: *Tanakh*. The English translation used in *The Legends of Jerusalem* is by The Jewish Publication Society of America, Philadelphia.

RASHI. The most popular commentator on the Bible. Rashi is the acronym taken from his full name: *Rabbi Shelomo Izhaki*. He lived at the end of the eleventh century in France.

RADAK. Another commentator on the Bible. Radak is contracted from *Rabbi David Kimchi*. He lived in the thirteenth century in Narbonne, France.

JOSEPHUS. The Jewish historian Joseph ben Mattitiahu Hacohen. He was born in Jerusalem about 38 c. e. and took part in the revolt against Rome. His various treatises on the history of the Jews have survived in Greek and have been widely translated. His main works are *Antiquities of the Jews* and *Wars of the Jews against the Romans*.

MISHNAH. From the Hebrew *shano*, to study. This is a literary creation written in Hebrew, mainly in the second century, and compiled in the Galilee in 200 c. e. The Mishnah, sometimes called in the plural Mishnayot, is divided into six orders (Hebrew S*hisha* S*edarim,* which gave rise to the contracted name: *Shas*). Each order (*seder*) contains various tractates (*masekhot*), sixty-three tractates in all. The English translations used here are by H. Danby (Oxford, 1933) and P. Blackman, (New York, 1965).

TOSEFTA. The Aramaic form of the Hebrew *tosefet*, which means supplement. It is an addition to the Mishnah, which was compiled and edited in Eretz Israel at the end of the fourth century.

TALMUD. From the Hebrew *lamod*, to learn; Talmud-learning. A vast collective literary creation to which hundreds of sages contributed during the course of several generations. There are two Talmuds, each produced by a different school of study, one in Eretz Israel and the other abroad:

Talmud Yerushalmi was compiled in Eretz Israel, mainly in the Galilee; it is named Yerushalmi Jerusalemite, as an expression of longing for the capital then held by foes. It is sometimes called the Palestinian Talmud. It was completed at the end of the fourth century, under Byzantine rule. Mainly written in Aramaic, it is about one-third the size of the Talmud Babli. The only existing translation was by M. Schwab into French, eleven volumes, published in 1871–89, Paris.

Talmud Babli (or *Bavli*), the Babylonian Talmud, was compiled in Babylon (Hebrew *Babel* or *Bavel*) at the end of the fifth century. Written in Aramaic and Hebrew, it is a comprehensive treatise of Judaic laws and a treasury of Jewish folklore. The English translation of the whole Babylonian Talmud was done by a number of scholars under the editorship of I. Epstein and published in 1935–52 by Soncino Press, London.

ABBOTH DE-RABBI NATHAN. A collection of folk tales concerning the forefathers, *abboth* or *avot* in Hebrew, and named after its compiler, Rabbi Nathan, who lived in the third century. There are two versions of the work, A and B. They were published by S. Schechter in 1887. The English translation of version A was published by A. Goldin in 1955, New Haven.

MECHILTA DE-RABBI ISHMAEL. *Mechilta* is Hebrew-Aramaic for collection. This *mechilta* is named for the sage mentioned in its opening sentence: "Rabbi Ishmael says. . . .' It is a collection of interpretations of the Book of Exodus, written in approximately the eighth century. An English translation by J. Z. Lauterbach was published by the Jewish Publication Society in 1933–35, Philadelphia.

MECHILTA DE-RABBI SHIMON BAR-YOHAI. A collection of commentaries on Exodus compiled about the fifth century and attributed to the famous rabbi of the second century who lived in Eretz Israel. His tomb, in the Galilee, is venerated to this day.

MIDRASH TANAIM. The Hebrew word *midrash* is derived from *darosh*, to inquire, to investigate. *Tanaim* (singular *tana*) is the title accorded to the sages of the Mishnah period. *Midrash Tanaim* is a collection of exegeses to Deuteronomy.

TANHUMA. A collection of legendary explanations to the Torah (Pentateuch) written by Tanhuma son of Abba, in the fourth and fifth centuries.

PESIKTA DE-RAB KAHANA. *Pesikta* is Hebrew-Aramaic for "portion." This was written in the sixth and seventh centuries and attributed to Rabbi Kahana. The English translation by W. G. Braude was published in New Haven.

MIDRASH RABBA. *Rabba* is similar to *Rabbati*. This is a large collection of various homiletics on Torah quotations (Five Books of Moses) and the Five Scrolls. It was composed by various rabbis who lived from the fourth to the twelfth centuries.

Its first five volumes deal with the Five Books of Moses: *Bereshith Rabba* is about Genesis, approximately fifth century; *Sheimoth Rabba* is about Exodus, approximately tenth century; *Va-Yikra Rabba* is about Leviticus, approximately seventh–ninth centuries; *Ba-Midbar Rabba* is about Numbers, approximately eighth–ninth centuries; *Debarim Rabba* is about Deuteronomy, approximately eighth–ninth centuries.

The next five volumes deal with the Scrolls: *Shir ha-Shirim Rabba* is about the Song of Songs, approximately seventh–eighth centuries; *Ruth Rabba* is about the Book of Ruth, approximately seventh–tenth centuries; *Eicha Rabba* is about the Book of Lamentations, approximately fifth century; *Koheleth Rabba* is about the Book of Ecclesiastes, approximately seventh century; *Esther Rabba* is about the Book of Esther, approximately fifth century.

An English translation was prepared under the editorship of H. Freedman and M. Simon and published in ten volumes, in 1939, by Soncino Press, London.

MIDRASH TEHILLIM. Relates to the Book of Psalms (Hebrew, *Tehillim*). *Shoher Tov* (Hebrew for "seeketh good") is another name of *Midrash Tehillim* because it opens with the following verse: "He that diligently seeketh good seeketh favor" (Proverbs 11:27). *Midrash Tehillim* was composed in the ninth–tenth centuries approximately, probably in Eretz Israel. The English translation was prepared by W. G. Braude and published in two volumes in 1957, New Haven.

PIRKE RABBI ELIEZER. *Pirke* is Hebrew for "chapters."

This is attributed to Eliezer son of Hyrcanos, a prominent sage. It is a collection of homiletics and tales and was written about the ninth century in Eretz Israel. The English translation done by G. Friedlander appeared in 1916, London.

ZOHAR. Hebrew for splendor. This is a collection, written partly in Aramaic and partly in Hebrew, of mystical commentaries on the five books of the Torah, the Pentateuch. It is attributed to the above-mentioned Rabbi Shimon bar-Yohai, although in fact it was composed in Spain, in the thirteenth century by Rabbi Moses de Leon, probably from earlier sources.

The *Zohar* is the fundamental book of the cabala—Jewish mysticism. Its adepts are called cabalists. *Kabbala* is Hebrew for reception. Every generation was supposed to receive the secrets of mysticism from the generation preceding it. The English translation of the *Zohar* was done by H. Sperling and M. Simon and published in five volumes by Soncino Press in 1931–34, London.

YALKUT SHIMONI is a comprehensive collection (in Hebrew, *yalkut*) of legendary commentaries and rabbinical sayings covering all the books of the Bible. It was edited by Rabbi Shimoni, "chief of the preachers" of Frankfurt, Germany, in the thirteenth century.

BEIT HA-MIDRASH. Hebrew for the house of study; the name of a modern publication of various small Hebrew tractates of later periods, edited by A. Yellinek. The six volumes of *Beit ha-Midrash* were originally published in 1853–77, Germany.

ABBREVIATIONS

JJS—*Journal of Jewish Studies*

JQR—*Jewish Quarterly Review*

MGWJ—*Monatsschrift für Geschichte und Wissenschaft des Judentums*

MPCC—*Migne, Patrologiae Cursus Completus*

PEQS—*Palestine Exploration Fund, Quarterly Statement*

PPTS—*Palestine Pilgrims Text Society*

QDAP—*Quarterly of the Department of Antiquities in Palestine*

REJ—*Revue des Études Juives*

ZDPV—*Zeitschrift des Deutschen Vereins Palästina*

SOURCES OF THE LEGENDS

The sages of Israel said:
"He who acknowledges his authorities brings
redemption to the world."
"Trace your source even as far as to Moses—
if you can!"
"If a man devotes himself with his whole soul to
anything—it is named after him."

1. *JERUSALEM WAS THE BEGINNING:* Ezekiel 5:5.
   Proverbs 3:19. Tosefta, Yom ha-Kippurim 3:6. Yerushalmi,
   Yoma 8:4. Babli, Yoma 54b. *Midrash Tehillim,* ed. Buber,
   p. 140. Psalms 50:2. Jeremiah 9:10. Isaiah 2:2; 28:16.
2. *MIDDLE OF THE EARTH:* Ezekiel 38:12. *Midrash Tan-*
   huma, Kedoshim 10. A. J. Wensinck, *The Ideas of the*
   Western Semites concerning the Navel of the Earth, 1917.
   W. H. Roscher, *Der Omphalosgedanke bei verschiedenen*
   Voelkern, 1918.
3. *THE NAVEL OF THE WORLD: Koheleth Rabba* 1:1.
   "Midrash Be-Hochma Yasad Eretz," *Beit ha-Midrash* (ed.
   Yellinek), V, p. 63.

4. *THE EYE OF THE WORLD: Bereishith Rabba* 63:14. *Masecheth Eretz Zutta* 9. *Mahzor Vitri*, 1893, p. 723. Il Heilperin, *Arachei ha-Kinuim*, 1806, p. 53.

5. *WHO SET UP THE STONE?:* Psalms 48:3. *Zohar*, II, 1867, p. 222; III, p. 131.

6. *WHERE IS THE SOURCE OF SPRINGS?:* Babli, Taanith 10a. Yerushalmi, Yoma 8:5. Psalms 87:1–7.

7. *THE "NAME" ON THE STONE: Abboth de-Rabbi Nathan* (1) 36. *Pesikta de-Rab Kahana* 148a. Ecclesiastes 3:11. The Aramaic translation (*Targum Yerushalmi*) to Exodus 28:30. S. Krauss, *Das Leben Jesu*, 1902, pp. 40, 116, 279.

8. *THE STONE—JACOB'S PILLAR:* Genesis 28:11. Translation of Yonathan ben Uziel, and Rashi commentary. *Bereishith Rabba* 69:6. *Midrash Tehillim* 91:7. Genesis 28:22. *Sifri, Debarim* 354.

9. *WHERE WERE THE TABLETS HEWN?: Zohar*, I, 1895, p. 231b. Exodus 31:18.

10. *THE HOLY ARK ON THE STONE: Tosefta, Yom ha-Kippurim* 3:6. Yerushalmi, Yoma 8:4. Babli, Yoma, 54b. *Va-Yikra Rabba* 20:4. *Shir ha-Shirim Rabba* 3:18.

11. *THE ANGEL ABOVE THE STONE:* 1 Chronicles 21: 15–28. 2 Samuel 24:20–24. 2 Chronicles 3:1. William of Tyre.

12. *JONAH SAW THE STONE:* Jonah 2:5–8. *Pirke Rabbi Eliezer* 10. *Yalkut Shimoni, Jonah* 1.

13. *THE STONE AND WEAVING:* Yerushalmi, Pesahim 4:1; Taanith 1:6. Babli, Sanhedrin 26b. Psalms 11:3. J. Caro, *Shulhan Aruch: Orah Haim*, 551:8.

14. *CHERUBIM ABOVE THE STONE: Zohar*, I, 1895, p. 231b. Psalms 125:1–2.

15. *THE CROWN ON THE STONE:* Ezekiel 25:14. Y. Eben Shemuel, *Midrashei Geulah*, 1943, p. 312.

16. *THE FOUNDATION STONE AND PARADISE:* Mujir ed-Din, *Kitab a-Uns ej-Jalil be-Taarikh a-Kuds wal-Khalil*, 1866.

17. *THE STONE RESTS ON A WHALE:* Ibid.

18. *THE STONE—SOURCE OF WATERS:* Ibid.

19. *THE TONGUE OF THE ROCK:* Koran 17:1. C. Schick, *Beit el-Makdas*, 1887, p. 9. T. W. Arnold, *Painting in Islam*, 1928, p. 117–22.

20. *MUHAMMAD'S FOOTPRINT:* PPTS, V, p. 23.

21. *ENOCH'S FOOTPRINT:* Koran 19:58. Genesis 5:23–24. C. Wilson, *Ordnance Survey of Jerusalem, Notes*, 1865, p. 35.

22. *THE FOUNDATION STONE HOVERS:* Mujir ed-Din, *Kitab a-Uns. Otzar Massaoth*, ed. Eisenstein, 1926, p. 195. M. Hagiz, *Parashath Eleh Massai*, 1733. T. Tobler, *Topographie von Jerusalem*, I, 1853, p. 531. *MGWJ*, 1925, p. 51.

23. *THE STONE AND MESSIAH: Das treue Zions-Waechter*, III, 1847, Nos. 40–44.

24. *THE HOLY CAVERN: David ha-Reubeni*, ed. Eshcoli, 1940, p. 25.

25. *WELL OF THE SOULS:* Radbaz, *Sheeloth Ve-Teshuboth*.

26. *THE STONE OF EDEN: Voyages d'Ali Bey el-Abassi*, III, 1814, p. 143. Abd al-Rabbih, *Al-Ikd al-Farid*, 1876, p. 164. Mujir ed-Din, *Kitab a-Uns*, p. 200. *Al-Hadra al-Unsia fi Rihlah al-Kudsiya*, ed. Cairo, p. 28. Schick, *Beit el Makdas*, p. 15. T. Canaan, *Mohammedan Saints and Sanctuaries in Palestine*, 1927, p. 28.

27. *WHEN THE CANDLABRUM FELL: Journal of the Royal Asiatic Society*, XIX, 1887, p. 287.

28. *WHY DOES THE DOME TARNISH?:* I heard this legend in Jerusalem in 1940.

29. *THE CRESCENT ON THE DOME: David ha-Reubeni*, ed. Eshcoli, p. 26. Moses Bassola, *Massaoth Eretz Israel*, ed. Ben-Zvi, p. 91. *Kobetz al-Yad*, IV, 1888, pp. 27, 31. J. Doubdan, *Le Voyage de la Terre-Sainte*, 1666. *PEQS*, 1923, p. 188.

30. *THE BIRDS WHICH TURNED INTO STONE:* 1 Kings 5:13. Rashi's commentary to Kings 3:15. *QDAP*, 1939, p. 88. J. Burton, *Inner Life of Syria*, II, 1875, p. 89. G. H. Hanauer, *Folklore of the Holy Land*, 1907, p. 47.

31. *THE CANDLES AT THE TEMPLE SITE: Otzar Mas-saoth*, pp. 100, 121.

32. *SIGHS FROM THE TEMPLE SITE:* Josef ben Josef, *Kessef Razuf*, 1926, p. 169b. *Ha-Maamer* (ed. Lunz), III, 1920, p. 107. Isaiah 51:9; 52:1.

33. *VOICES FROM THE TEMPLE SITE: Beit ha-Midrash* (ed. Yellinek), VI, p. 149. *Kobetz al-Yad*, IV, p. 47.

34. *SOLOMON'S STUDY HOUSE:* Koran, Al-Isra (Benei Israil) 17:1. B. Schrike, *Die Himmelsreise Muhammed's: Der Islam*, VI.

35. *BETWEEN THE PILLARS:* J. Goldziher, *Muhammed-anische Studien*, II, 1896, p. 408.

36. *PRAYER PLACE OF ZECHARIAH:* 2 Chronicles 24: 20–21. *Itinerarium Burdigalense*, ed. Geyer, 1898. Jerome's commentary to Matthew 23:35. Luke 11:51.

37. *KING DAVID'S TRIBUNAL:* Al-Rabbih, *Al-Ikd*, p. 338. Yakut, *Mujam al-Buldan*, IV, p. 598. Al-Mukaddasi, *Ahsan al-Takassim fi Muarif al-Akalim*, pp. 46, 163.

38. *THE SCALES OF JUDGMENT:* I heard this legend from one of the attendants in the Mosque of Omar (Dome of the Rock) in 1927.

39. *THE THRONE OF SOLOMON:* Al-Rabbih, *Al-Ikd*, p. 338. Yakut, *Mujam al-Buldan*, IV, p. 598. Al-Mukaddasi, *Ahsan al-Takassim*. Nasir Khosrau, *Sefer Nameh*, 1881. Babli, Nedarim 25a. G. Weil, *Biblische Legenden der Muselmänner*, 1845, p. 215.

40. *KING SOLOMON'S STABLES:* F. Fabri, *Evagatorium in Terrae Sanctae.* Guy le Strange, *Palestine under the Moslems*, 1890, p. 167.

41. *THE CRYPT OF THE DEVILS: Itinerarium Burdiga-lense*, p. 21.

42. *THE FRAGMENT OF THE ROCK:* Mujir ed-Din, *Kitab a-Uns.*

43. *THE WELL OF THE LEAF:* Le Strange, *Palestine under the Moslems*, p. 198.

44. *WEEPING FROM THE WELL: Ha-Maamer* (ed. Lunz), III, p. 91.

45. *THE POOL OF ISRAEL:* M. Reisher, *Shaarei Yerusha-laim*, 1879.

46. *THE HOLY NETTLE TREE:* This legend was told to me by an Arab in the vicinity of Bethlehem, in 1928.
47. *PRAYER IN THE GATES:* Ms. in the Bodley Library, Oxford (Ms. Heb. e. 25. fol. 77). *Sefer ha Yeshub*, 1944, p. 128. Psalms 99:5.
48. *THE GATE OF MERCY:* "Travels of Rabbi Petahyia." *Otzar Massaoth.*
49. *THE GRAVEYARD AROUND THE GATE:* Zechariah 9:9. Babli, Baba Mezia 114b. *Midrash Mishlei* 4:9.
50. *THROUGH THE GATE OF MERCY: Kobetz al-Yad*, IV, p. 27.
51. *SUPPLICATION AT THE GATE:* Ashtori ha-Parhi, *Kaftor Va-Perah*, ed. Lunz, p. 114.
52. *WHO BUILT THE GATE OF MERCY?:* Prudentius, "Dittocheum," *MPCC*, Series Latina 60, 110. Baldi, *Enchiridion Locorum Sanctorum*, 1935.
53. *GATE OF ETERNAL LIFE:* Niebuhr, *Reisebeschreibung nach Arabien*, III, 1837, p. 52.
54. *THE GOLDEN GATE:* Matthew 21:9. Acts 3:2; 10. Psalms 118:25–26. *MPCC*, Series Latina 110, 133.
55. *THE GOLDEN GATE IN THE END OF DAYS:* "Ma'ase Daniel," *Beit ha-Midrash* (ed. Yellinek), V, p. 128.
56. *THE GATE OF THE TRIBES:* Psalms 122:2–4. *Midrash Tehillim* 123:3.
57. *THE GATE OF SIN:* Koran, The Cow 2:55.
58. *HEIGHT OF ISRAEL:* Micah 4:1–2. Isaiah 2:3; 66:20. Daniel 11:45. Ezekiel 20:40.
59. *MOUNT OF MYRRH:* Genesis 22:2. Song of Songs 4:6.
60. *MOUNT OF LIGHT:* Ezekiel 43:2. Psalms 50:2. Bereishith Rabba 3:4. "Midrash Konen," *Beit ha-Midrash* (ed. Yellinek), II, p. 27.
61. *MOUNT OF AWE:* Babli, Taanith 16a. *Bereishith Rabba* 55. Psalms 68:36.
62. *MOUNT OF INSTRUCTION:* Psalms 84:7. Isaiah 2:3.
63. *MOUNT OF APPEARANCE:* Genesis 22:14.
64. *MOUNT OF EXCHANGE: Yalkut Shimoni, Shir ha-Shirim*, 988. Leviticus 27:10.
65. *MOUNT OF SPICES:* Song of Songs 8:14. The Aramaic translation and Rashi's commentary.

66. *WHERE WAS ADAM CREATED?:* Genesis 2:7. *Targum Yerushalmi*, I. *Midrash Tehillim* 92:6. *Pirke Rabbi Eliezer* 20.

67. *THE ABODE OF ADAM:* Genesis 3:24. *Midrash Tehillim* 92:6.

68. *NOAH ON MOUNT MORIAH:* *Midrash Tehillim* 92:6.

69. *ABRAHAM ON MOUNT MORIAH:* Genesis 22:1–4. *Sheimoth Rabba* 80:15.

70. *ISAAC'S SACRIFICE:* Genesis 22:3; 11–13. *Bereishith Rabba* 55:8. Exodus 14:21. *Koheleth Rabba* 10:8.

71. *MORIAH IN THE EXODUS:* *Mechilta*, ed. Lauterbach, I, pp. 216, 223, 233.

72. *BENJAMIN AND MOUNT MORIAH:* Psalms 68:16–17. Genesis 49:27. *Bereishith Rabba* 97:99.

73. *TEMPLES IN BENJAMIN'S PORTION:* Deuteronomy 12:5; 33:12. *Mechilta de-Rabbi Ishmael*, IV, 1931, p. 216. *Bereishith Rabba* 99:1. *Abboth de-Rabbi Nathan* (A) 38; (B) 43. Babli, Zebahim 54b; 118b. 2 Samuel 12:28. Psalms 84:2.

74. *THE PURCHASE OF MOUNT MORIAH:* Deuteronomy 12:8. 2 Samuel 24:24. 1 Chronicles 21:25. *Sifri* 81. Babli, Zebahim 116b. *Agadath Shir ha-Shirim*, ed. Schechter, p. 33.

75. *WHY WAS THE TEMPLE ON MOUNT MORIAH?:* *Va-Yikra Rabba* 13. 2 Chronicles 3:1. The legend appears first in the description of travels by A. de Lamertine, *Voyage en Orient*, I, 1875, p. 329. See also A. Kopish, *Gesammelte Werke*, I, 1856, p. 23. *Gedichte von Aug. Kopish*, p. 149. Israel Kosta, *Mikveh Israel*, 1851, p. 30. S. B. Hutzin, *Maaseh Nissim*, 1890, p. 53. A. Schreiber, "La legende de l'emplacement du Temple de Jerusalem," *REJ*, IX, 1948–49, pp. 108–9.

76. *THE FOUNDATION ON THE ABYSS:* Babli, Makkoth 49a; Sukkah 49a; 53a.

77. *KING DAVID AND THE ABYSS:* Yerushalmi, Sanhedrin 3:10.

78. *BUILDING THE TEMPLE:* *Sifra* 1. Babli, Taanith 23a.

79. *STONES BUILT THE TEMPLE:* 1 Kings 6:7; 8:13. *Pesikta Rabbati* 6, p. 28a.
80. *HOW DID THE TEMPLE APPEAR?:* Babli, Sukkah 51b; Baba Bathra 4a. *Sheimoth Rabba* 36:1.
81. *CEDARS IN THE TEMPLE:* 1 Kings 6:15. Psalms 92:14. Zechariah 11:2.
82. *LIGHT FROM THE TEMPLE: Tanhuma* 7. 1 Kings 6:4. Jeremiah 11:16. *Yalkut Shimoni, Isaiah* 501.
83. *THE CURTAIN TO THE ENTRANCE:* Mishnah, Shekalim 8:5. Tosefta, Shekalim 3:13. Exodus 26:1, 36. Yerushalmi, Shekalim 8:4. Josephus Flavius, *Wars*, V, 8, 4. *Pesikta Rabbati*, p. 131a.
84. *THE GOLDEN CANDLESTICK:* Mishnah, Yoma 3:10. Tosefta, Yom ha-Kippurim 2:3. Babli, Yoma 37b.
85. *THE VINE ON THE ENTRANCE:* Babli, Holin 92a. Mishnah, Middoth 3:8 and Tifereth Israel commentary.
86. *THE SAPPHIRE ON THE ROOF:* Mujir ed-Din, *Kitab a-Uns.*
87. *THE RAVEN DESTROYERS:* Leviticus 11:13–15. Mishnah, Middoth 4:6. Babli, Shabbath 90a; Minahoth 107a. *Abboth de-Rabbi Nathan* (B), 39. Josephus, *Wars*, V, 5, 6. 2 Chronicles 4:13. S. Liberman, *Hellenism in Jewish Palestine*, 1950, p. 164.
88. *THE SANHEDRIN IN THE CENTER:* Lamentations 1:6. *Eicha Rabba* 1. Song of Songs 7:2–3. *Shir ha-Shirim Rabba* 3:4. Babli, Sanhedrin 36a. *Ba-Midbar Rabba* 1:4.
89. *THE BATH OF THE HIGH PRIEST:* Leviticus 16:4. Mishnah, Middoth 4:3; Parah 3:8. Babli, Yoma 31a–b; 34b.
90. *THE CHAMBER OF PARVAH:* Mishnah, Middoth 5:3. Babli, Yoma 38a; Holin 62b.
91. *THE CHAMBER OF SECRETS:* Mishnah, Shekalim 5:6.
92. *CHAMBER OF THE HEARTH:* Mishnah, Tamid 1:1; Shabbath 1:11.
93. *CHAMBER OF THE INCENSE-MAKER:* Babli.
94. *THE FIRE ON THE ALTAR:* Babli, Yoma 21a–b.
95. *WHO KINDLED THE FIRE?:* Babli, Yoma 21b.

96. *WOOD FOR THE TEMPLE:* 1 Chronicles 2:54. Babli,
    Taanith 28a.
97. *THE OFFERING OF FIRSTFRUITS:* Babli, Taanith 28a.
98. *CENSUS IN ISRAEL:* Tosefta, Pesahim 4:3. Babli, Pesa-
    him 64b. *Eicha Rabba* 1:2.
99. *PASSOVER OF THE CRUSHED:* Mishnah, Abboth 5:8.
    Babli, Pesahim 64b.
100. *CRIES FROM THE TEMPLE:* Babli, Pesahim 57a; Keri-
    toth 28a–b.
101. *WHEN DID THE GATES OPEN?:* Psalms 24:7–8; 87:2.
    Babli, Sanhedrin 107b. 2 Chronicles 6:41.
102. *THE EASTERN GATE:* Ezekiel 43:1–4; 44:1–2. Mish-
    nah, Berachoth 9:8. *Pesikta de-Rab Kahana*, ed. Buber,
    p. 137a. *Eicha Rabba, Petihta* 28.
103. *SHECHINA AT THE EASTERN GATE:* Ezekiel 11:1,
    10:18–19. *Eicha Rabba, Petihta* 25.
104. *THE EASTERN GATE ON SABBATH:* Ezekiel 46:1.
    Pirkei Rabbi Eliezer 51.
105. *GATE OF NICANOR:* Mishnah, Middoth 2:3; 3:10;
    Yoma 3:7. Josephus, *Wars*, V, 5, 3. Tosefta, Yom ha-
    Kippurim 2:4. Yerushalmi, Yoma 3:4. Babli, Yoma 38a.
    E. Wiesenberg, "The Nicanor Gate," *JJS*, III, 1952, pp.
    14–29.
106. *GATES OF BRIDEGROOMS AND MOURNERS:* Psalms
    24:9. *Abboth de-Rabbi Nathan* (B) 43. *Pirke Rabbi
    Eliezer* 17. *Masecheth Sofrim* 18:9. Bassola, *Massaoth
    Eretz Israel*, ed. Ben-Zvi, p. 56.
107. *THE SHUSHAN GATE:* Mishnah, Middoth 1:3. Babli,
    Minahoth 98a.
108. *THE WATER GATE:* Mishnah, Middoth 2:6. Tosefta,
    Sukkah 3:3; 4:9. Ezekiel 47:1. Zechariah 14:8.
109. *GATE OF THE SUN:* Jeremiah 19:2. Yerushalmi, Eiru-
    bin 5:1.
110. *THE GATE WITH SEVEN NAMES:* 2 Kings 11:6.
    Lamentations 4:15. 2 Chronicles 23:8. Jeremiah 19:2.
    Ezekiel 40:15. Jeremiah 39:3; 26:36. Ezekiel 9:2.
111. *THE GATES SUNK:* Lamentations 2:9. *Eicha Rabba*
    2:13.

112. *ARIEL:* 1 Kings 14:21. Psalms 132:13. Isaiah 29:1. Mishnah, Middoth 4:3.
113. *DEVIR:* 1 Kings 8:6. Yerushalmi, Berachoth 4:5. *Bereishith* Rabba 55:9.
114. *HADOM HADONAI:* Isaiah 66:1. 1 Chronicles 28:2. Psalms 132.7. Lamentations 2:1.
115. *LEVANON:* 2 Chronicles 9:15–16. Deuteronomy 3:25. Zechariah 11:1. Isaiah 10:34. *Sifri, Debarim* 28. Isaiah 1:18.
116. *YEDIDUT:* Isaiah 5:1; 8:1. Isaiah 41:8. Jeremiah 12:7. Deuteronomy 33:12. 2 Samuel 12:24–25. Psalms 84:2–3. *Abboth de-Rabbi Nathan* (II) 63. *Midrash Tanaim,* p. 215.
117. *LEV HAOLAM:* Jeremiah 4:18. 1 Kings 9:3. *Zohar,* I, Lech-Lecha 84b.
118. *AF HAOLAM:* Song of Songs 7:5.
119. *ZAVAR HAOLAM:* Songs of Songs 7:5. Lamentations 5:5. Isaiah 8:8. *Zohar,* I, Vaigash 209b.
120. *TALPIOT:* Songs of Songs 4:4. *Shir-ha-Shirim Rabba,* 4:6. Babli, Berachoth 30a.
121. *APIRION:* Song of Songs 3:9–10.
122. *SIGNS OF DESTRUCTION:* Josephus, *Wars,* VII, 8, 3.
123. *PORTALS OPENED BY THEMSELVES:* Babli, Yoma 39b. Yerushalmi, Yoma 6:3. Josephus, *Wars,* VI, 6, 3.
124. *SQUARE—AN OMEN OF DESTRUCTION:* Josephus, *Wars,* VI, 5, 4.
125. *A THREAD OF CRIMSON:* Mishnah, Yoma 6:8; Shabbath 9:3. Isaiah 1:18. Babli, Rosh ha-Shanah 31b.
126. *ANGELS LIT THE FIRE:* Mishnah, Taanith 8:9. *Pesikta Rabbati* 15, p. 131a. Babli, Taanith 29a. Isaiah 22:1.
127. *WHERE ARE THE KEYS?:* Babli, Taanith 29a. Isaiah 22:1. *Beit Eked ha-Agadoth* (Horowitz-ha-Levi), I, 1881, p. 36.
128. *THE DIVINE PRESENCE LEAVES: Pesikta de-Rab Kahana,* 1868, p. 115. *Yalkut Shimomi, Ezekiel* 350.
129. *THE DIVINE PRESENCE IS AS A BIRD:* Ecclesiastes 12:4. *Eicha Rabba, Petihta* 23. *Yalkut Shimoni, Psalms.*
130. *THE DIVINE PRESENCE REBUKES: Shir-ha-Shirim Rabba* 4:2. *Seder Eliyahu Zuta,* 1904, supplements, p. 31.

131. *ARIEL DESTROYED AND REBUILT: Pesikta de-Rab
~~Kahana,~~ ed. Buber, p. 116. Jeremiah 4:7; 1:3; 31:13.
Isaiah 29:1. Amos 3:8. Psalms 147:2.

132. *WHEN WAS THE TEMPLE DESTROYED?:* Mishnah,
Taanith 4:6. Babli, Taanith 30b; Megillah 8a. *Pesikta
Rabbati* 38. Jeremiah 31:12. Yerushalmi, Taanith 4:9;
Megillah 1:6.

133. *FROM THE DAY OF DESTRUCTION:* Babli, Yoma 9b;
Baba Bathra 12b; 25b; Taanith 19b; Berachoth 32b; 58b;
59a; Abodah Zarah 3b. Mishnah, Zuta 9:12; 15. *Abboth
de-Rabbi Nathan* (A) 4; (B) 5. *Pirke Rabbi Eliezer* 34.
Derech Eretz (Eliyahu Zuta), I, p. 9. Psalms 122:6. *Midrash Zuta*, p. 63.

134. *MOURNERS FOR THE TEMPLE:* Babli, Taanith 30b.
Tosefta Zuta 15:11. Psalms 121:6–9.

135. *WOE TO US THAT IT IS DESTROYED:* Hosea 6:6.

136. *THE HOLY ARK: Abboth De-Rabbi Nathan* (A) 41.
Selihoth Le-Erev Rosh ha-Shanah, attributed to Rabbi
Gershom Meor ha-Golah. Tosefta, Yom ha-Kippurim 3:7.
Babli, Zuta 13a; Yoma 54a. Yerushalmi, Shekalim 6:1.
Rambam, *Mishneh Torah, Hilchoth Beth ha-Behira* 4:1.
Relandus, *De spoliis templi Hierosolymitani*, 1716. J.
Levi, "The Fate of the Temple Vessels after the Destruction of the Second Temple," *Kedem*, II, 1945, pp. 123–25.

137. *THE HOLY CURTAIN:* Josephus, *Wars*, VII, 8, 7.
Tosefta, Yom ha-Kippurim 3:8. Babli, Gittin 56b; Sukkah 5a.

138. *THE GOLDEN MENORAH:* Yerushalmi, Shekalim 6:1.
REJ, XIII, 1886, p. 55.

139. *PILLARS FROM THE TEMPLE: Bereishith Rabba* 33:1.
Travels of Rabbi Benjamin of Tudela.

140. *THE GOLDEN PLATE:* Exodus 28:36; 39:30. Babli,
Sukkah 8a.

141. *KING SOLOMON'S THRONE:* Esther Rabba 1:10.

142. *VESSELS IN BABYLON:* Naftali ben Yitzchak Elhanan,
Emek ha-Melech, 1644, p. 14.

143. *THE TEMPLE OF HEAVEN AND OF EARTH:* Exodus

15:17. *Midrash Tehillim* 30, ed. Buber, p. 117. *Tanhuma,* *Va-Yakhel* 7. Yerushalmi, Berachoth A. Aptowitzer, "The Upper Temple in Legend," *Tarbitz*, II, 1931, pp. 137–53; 257–87.

144. *THE HEAVENLY TEMPLE:* Psalms 96:6. "Perek Masiah," *Beit ha-Midrash* (ed. Yellinek), III, p. 68.

145. *SERVICE IN THE CELESTIAL TEMPLE:* Babli, Hagigah 12a. Ein Yaacob.

146. *MOSES IN THE TEMPLE OF HEAVEN: Pesikta Rabbati* 20, ed. Ish-Shalom, p. 98a. *Beit ha-Midrash,* VII, p. xxii.

147. *DAVID IN THE TEMPLE OF HEAVEN:* "Pirkei Halachoth Rabati," *Batei Midrashoth*, ed. Wertheimer, 1946, pp. 78, 93.

148. *POSSESSION OF THE TRIBES:* 1 Kings 11:32. Deuteronomy 18:5. Babli, Megillah 26a; Baba Kama 82a. *Midrash Tanaim*, p. 48. *Koheleth Rabba* 12:7. *Eicha Rabba, Petihta* 23. *Abboth de-Rabbi Nathan,* 1st ed. Tosefta, Maaser Sheni 1:12.

149. *HOW DID DAVID CONQUER?:* Midrash Tehillim 18:24, ed. Buber, p. 152. 2 Samuel 5:5. 1 Chronicles 11:6. 2 Samuel 22:30. Psalms 18:1; 30. Rashi brings this legend in the name of *Midrash Tehillim* in his commentary on Psalms 18:30. In *Yalkut Shimoni, Samuel* 161, this legend is mentioned, and instead of Jebus, the name Gimzo is given. Gimso was at the site of the Arab village Jimzu, near Lod and Ben-Shemen. There is no information that David fought there. Ahaz, king of Judah, fought at Gimzo and conquered it. See 2 Chronicles 28:18.

150. *CUSTOMS AND MANNERS:* Tosefta, Berachoth 4:8. Babli, Sukkah 41a–b.

151. *MARKETS IN JERUSALEM:* Babli, Pesahim 7a. *Eicha Rabba* 1:29.

152. *THE SPICE MARKET:* Babli, Ketuboth 66b; Shabbath 42b; Yoma 38a. Isaiah 3:16.

153. *REGULATIONS IN ANCIENT JERUSALEM:* Babli, Baba Kama 82b. Mishnam Abboth 5:5. *Abboth de-Rabbi Nathan* (A) 35.

154. *THE COIN OF JERUSALEM:* Babli, Baba Kama 97b.

155. *THE GOLDEN CITY:* Mishnah, Shabbath 6:1; Eduyoth 2:7; Kelim 11:8. Babli, Nedarim 50a; Shabbath 59a. Yerushalmi, Shabbath 6:1.

156. *WHAT SHALL BE SOLD?:* Babli, Baba Bathra 75a.

157. *STONE OF INQUIRY:* Mishnah, Taanith 3:8. Babli, Baba Mezia 28b. Yerushalmi, Taanith 3:9. Rambam, *Mishneh Torah (ha-Yad ha-Hazaka), Gezeila Ve-Abeidah* 3:1.

158. *LODGE OF ACCOUNTANTS:* Sheimoth Rabba 52:8. Psalms 48:2–3. Isaiah 51:3. S. Gandz, "The Hall of Reckonings in Jerusalem," *JQR*, XXXI, 1941, pp. 385–407.

159. *COURT AT BETH YAAZEK:* Numbers 10:10. Isaiah 5:1–2. Mishnah, Rosh ha-Shanah 2:5–8. Babli, Rosh ha-Shanah 23b; Sanhedrin 42a. Yerushalmi, Sanhedrin 1, 2.

160. *THE ARMORY OF JERUSALEM:* Nehemiah 3:19. Commentary of Benyamin ben Yehudah ha-Romi, *Kobetz al-Yad,* VII, 1896–7, p. 28. Leviticus 26:6.

161. *TOWER OF THE HUNDRED:* Nehemiah 3:1; 12:29. Commentary of Benyamin ben Yehudah.

162. *TOWER OF THE OVENS:* Nehemiah 3:11; 12:38. Commentary of Benyamin ben Yehudah.

163. *PILGRIMS IN JERUSALEM:* Mishnah, Abboth 5:8; Ohaloth 14:1. Babli, Baba Kama 82b; Megillah 26a. *Abboth de-Rabbi Nathan* (A) 35.

164. *OATH IN HOLY JERUSALEM:* Mishnah, Ketuboth 2:9. Tosefta, Nedarim 1:2–3. Babli, Ketuboth 3b; Baba Batra 166a; Kidushin 71a. Strack-Bilerback, *Kommentar zum Neuen Testament,* I, 1922, p. 333. Matthew 5:35.

165. *WONDERS OF THE WALLS:* Isaiah 62:6. *Abboth de-Rabbi Nathan* (B) 39. Mujir ed-Din, *Kitab a-Uns,* pp. 393, 113.

166. *WATCHMEN ON THE WALLS:* Isaiah 60:18; 62:6. *Sheimoth Rabba* 18:5.

167. *KING OF BABYLON TO JERUSALEM:* Ezekiel 21:26. *Koheleth Rabba* 12:7. *Eicha Rabba, Petihta,* 23. *Yalkut Shimoni, Ezekiel* 361. *Midrash Tehillim* 79:2. ed. Buber, p. 180.

168. *THE FATE OF THE DESTROYER OF JERUSALEM:*
Babli, Gittin 56b. *Abboth de-Rabbi Nathan* (B) 7.
169. *AN ANGEL BROKE THROUGH: Pesikta Rabbati* 26,
1880, pp. 131, 1.
170. *FROM THE WALL TO THE TEMPLE:* Leviticus 26:19.
Shir ha-Shirim Rabba 4:6. Yerushalmi, Taanith 4. Jeremiah 1:11; 51:51.
171. *WITHIN THE STRAITS:* Lamentations 1:3. *Eicha
Rabba* 1:29. Deuteronomy 32:24. Psalms 91:56.
172. *WHY WAS JERUSALEM DESTROYED?:* Babli, Shabbath 119b; Yoma 9b. Tosefta, Minahoth 13:22; Zuta 15:11.
Yalkut Shimoni, Isaiah 394. *Sefer Eliyahu Zuta*, ed. Ish-
Shalom, p. 168.
173. *RENDING THE GARMENTS:* Tosefta, Baba Bathra
2:17. Isaiah 9:9. Caro, *Shulhan Aruch, Orah Haim* 561.
174. *THE MOURNERS FOR JERUSALEM:* Psalms 137:5.
Isaiah 61:3. Tosefta, Zuta, 15:11.
175. *THE COMFORTING OF JERUSALEM:* Isaiah 52:1.
Rashi commentary. *Pesikta de-Rab Kahana,* 1868, p. 127b.
Pesikta Rabbati, 1880, p. 138b. *Yalkut Shimoni, Isaiah*
443. Hosea 14:6; 9:16; 13:7. Joel 4:17–18. Amos 9:11; 5:2.
Micah 7:18; 1:5. Nahum 2:1; 1:11. Habbakuk 3:13; 1:2.
Zephaniah 1:12, 15; 3:14; 1:2. Haggai 2:19; 1:6, 11.
Zechariah 1:15, 2. Malachi 3:12; 1:10. Isaiah 40:1, 9.
176. *WHEN WILL JERUSALEM BE RESTORED?:* Babli,
Berachoth 49a. Rashi commentary. *Tanhuma* 58:17, ed.
Buber, p. 44. Psalms 147:2. *Yalkut Shimoni, Psalms* 888,
147. Psalms 132:2. *Midrash Tehillim* 122:4, ed. Buber,
p. 508. Isaiah 54:2–3.
177. *JERUSALEM IN THE FUTURE: Yalkut Shimoni, Isaiah*
550. *Pesikta de-Rab Kahana,* p. 143. *Sifri, Deuteronomy* 1.
Isaiah 54:11–12. Babli, Baba Bathra 75b. *Midrash Tehillim* 48:4, p. 138.
178. *THE CELESTIAL JERUSALEM:* Babli, Taanith 5:1;
Baba Bathra 75b. *Tanhuma*, ed. Warsaw, p. 130b. *Sefer
Raziel* 24:1. "Sefer Eliyahu," *Beit ha-Midrash* (ed. Yellinek), III, p. 67. Jeremiah 30:18.
179. *LIVING WATERS IN JERUSALEM:* Psalms 46:5. Zech-

ariah 14:8. Ezekiel 47:1, 5, 7. Babli, Yoma 77b–78a. Joel 4:18.

180. *THE PILGRIMAGE IN THE FUTURE:* Isaiah 60:8. Nahum 2:1, 5.

181. *THE EVERLASTING WALL: Koheleth Rabba* 2:22. *Eicha Rabba* 1:32.

182. *THE WALL AND THE SULTAN:* M. Haggiz, *Parshath Eleh Massai.* Moshe Yerushalmi, *Yedei Moshe,* ed. Haberman, 1938.

183. *UNCOVERING THE WAILING WALL: Abboth de-Rabbi Nathan* (A) 31. Eliezer Nahman Puah, *Medrash Bahidush,* 1641, p. 31a. Psalms 113:7.

184. *THE RING AND THE DIVINE PRESENCE: Eicha Rabba, Petihta* 2. *Midrash Tehillim* 105:1. *Sefer Eliyahu Rabba* 38, p. 149.

185. *WHO SAW THE DIVINE PRESENCE?: Midrash Tehillim* 105:1. Y. M. Sofer, *Mahaze Eretz ha-Kedosha,* 1891, p. 8. Yevi Hirsh Kaidnover, *Kab ha-Yashar,* 1732, chapter 93. Letter of Shelomo Shelumel, 1608. *Kobetz al-Yad,* III, 1940, p. 123. Haim Yosef David Azulai (Hida), *Shem ha-Gedolim,* ed. Ben-Yaacob, p. 5. Reisher, *Shaarei Yerushalaim,* p. 48.

186. *GOD IS BEHIND THE WALL:* Song of Songs 2:9. Nahmanides commentary. *Shir ha-Shirim Rabba* 2:24. *Ha-Yad Kettana,* 1868.

187. *THE HILL OF GOD:* Yerushalmi, *Yedei Moshe,* ed. Haberman.

188. *"MY HOUSE" ENGRAVED ON THE WALL:* "Sundrie the personall voyages performed by John Sanderson," *Purchas His Pilgrims,* II, p. 1632.

189. *THE WALL SHEDS TEARS:* Babli, Berachoth 32b. This legend is well known among the Jews of Jerusalem; I heard it in 1920.

190. *A LAMENTATION: Kinot Hakotel Hamaaravi.*

191. *A PRAYER AT THE WAILING WALL:* From a pamphlet called *Peduei Yashuvun Va-Bahu Be-Zion be-Rina;* Kiriath Sefer, 26, 1946–47, p. 140.

192. *THE MOURNING DOVE: Shir ha-Shirim Rabba* 6:5. *Yerushalaim* (ed. Lunz), X, p. 33. Babli, Berachoth 3a.

193. *RABBI SHALOM AT THE WAILING WALL:* I heard this in the Bethel Synagogue in the Old City, Jerusalem.
194. *THE WALL AND THE NAILS:* Isaiah 22:23. Ezra 9:8. *Va-Yikra Rabba* 5:5. *Aruch ha-Shalem,* ar. Gal. N. Poggibonsi, *Libro d'Oltramare,* 1945, p. 46.
195. *A MISSIVE TO THE WALL:* Moshe Goldstein, *Masaoth Yerushalaim,* 1931, p. 26.
196. *THE MERITS OF A MISSIVE:* Yaacob Sofer, *Sipurei Yaacob,* 1904, p. 5.
197. *THE WALL OF THE POOR:* I heard this from a Jewish youth in the Old City, Jerusalem, in 1922.
198. *THE STONE OF IDOLATRY: Kobetz al-Yad,* IV, p. 32.
199. *THE STONE WHICH HINDERS REDEMPTION:* Found in a manuscript, "Toei Ruah," in the library of the Jewish Theological Seminary, New York; Enelow Memorial Collection, no. 2223, fol. 185–189. G. Shalom, *Zion,* VII, 1942, p. 173.
200. *GOD PRAYS IN JERUSALEM: Midrash Tehillim* 76:3, ed. Buber, p. 171a. *Bereishith Rabba* 56:10. *Yalkut Shimoni, Psalms* 813. Babli, Berachoth 7a. Psalms 76:3. Isaiah 56:7.
201. *ALL HEARTS TOWARD JERUSALEM:* 1 Kings 8:44–48. Yerushalmi, Berachoth 4:5.
202. *HOW MANY SYNAGOGUES?:* Isaiah 1:21. Rashi commentary. Babli, Ketuboth 105a. *Pesikta de-Rab Kahana,* ed. Buber, p. 121b. *Eicha Rabba, Petihta* 1. L. Ginzberg, *Genizah Studies,* I, 1928, p. 261.
203. *THE IMPORTANCE OF PRAYER IN JERUSALEM: Midrash Tehillim* (Shoher Tob) 76:3. *Bereishith Rabba,* 56:10. Exodus 3:9. *Tub ha-Aretz,* p. 16b.
204. *THE MERITS OF PRAYER IN JERUSALEM:* Le Strange, *Palestine under the Moslems.*
205. *JERUSALEM OPPOSITE THE "HOLY OPENING":* Abraham Azulai, *Hesed Le-Abraham,* Salzbach, 1685, p. 30.
206. *THE WINDS WORSHIP IN JERUSALEM:* Obadiah of Bertinoro, *Otzar Massaoth,* p. 121.
207. *THE SYNAGOGUE OF RABBI YOHANAN:* Yerushalmi, Megillah 3:1. *Tanhuma,* ed. Buber, p. 120. *Eicha Rabba,*

Petihta 13. I heard about the shofar from the sexton of
the synagogue. See Shneior Zalman, *Zichron Yerushalaim*,
Jerusalem, 1876, p. 3b.

208. *THE SYNAGOGUE OF ELIJAH THE PROPHET*:
Yerushalmi, Megillah 3:1. This legend is widespread
among the Jews of the Old City of Jerusalem. A letter sent
from Jerusalem to Sir Moses Montefiore informs him:
"His prayer is permanently before the cave of our master
Elijah the prophet"; "An open letter to Sir M. Montefiore,"
p. 32, 1877. Moshe Reisher, *Shaarei Yerushalaim*, p. 46.
Haim Horowitz, *Hibat Yerushalaim*, 1835, p. 2b.

209. *THE MIRACLE IN ELIJAH'S SYNAGOGUE: Abboth
de-Rabbi Nathan* (A) 41. This legend is well known to
the inhabitants of Jerusalem's Old City. Zev Vilnay, *Holy
Shrines in the Land of Israel*, 1951, p. 414 (Hebrew).

210. *THE ISTANBULI SYNAGOGUE*: A. M. Lunz, *Ha-
Zefirah*, II, 1877, no. 7.

211. *BETHEL—CENTER OF THE MYSTICS: Abboth de-
Rabbi Nathan* (B), 48. Issachar and Zebulun, 1913, p. 37.

212. *THE FIG TREE IN THE COURTYARD*: Given in several versions, Shneior Zalman, *Zichron Yerushalaim*, Jerusalem, 1876. A. Shenkil, *Noraot Anshei Maaseh*, 1900.

213. *THE BIRTHPLACE OF HA-ARI THE HOLY*: Elhanan,
Emek ha-Melech, p. 10a. Simha ben Yehoshua, *Ahavat
Zion. Kobetz al-Yad*, III, 1940, p. 129. H. Azulai, *Shem
ha-Gedolim*. Horowitz, *Hibat Yerushalaim*, 1844, p. 43.

214. *THE KING AND THE DOME*: A well-known legend
among the Jews of the Old City in Jerusalem.

215. *THE SYNAGOGUE OF THE KARAITES*: Reisher, *Shaarei Yerushalaim*, p. 94. Hutzin, *Maaseh Nissim*, p. 4b.
O seh Pelé, 1866, p. 76. A. Fraenkel, *Yerushalaim*, p. 187.
Yerushalaim, (ed. Lunz), VI, 1902. Frumkin-Rivlin, *Toldoth Hachmei Yerushalaim*, III, p. 89.

216. *SOIL FROM JERUSALEM*: Babli, Megillah 29a, and
Rashi commentary; Rosh ha-Shanah 24b; Nidah 13a;
Abodah Zarah 43b. *Igereth Rab Shrirah*, ed. Levin, 1921,
p. 72. *Shaarei Teshuba*, 1858, p. 8. B. M. Levin, *Otzar
ha-Geonim*, 1939, *Rosh ha-Shanah*, p. 43; *Megillah* p. 54.

J. Mann, *The Jews in Egypt and in Palestine*, II, 1922, p. 333. A. Ben-Yaacob, *Toldot Ha-Rabb Abdallah Somech*, 1948, p. 57. *Midrash Talpioth*, 1909, p. 302.

217. *STONE FROM JERUSALEM:* Babli, Megillah 29a; Sanhedrin 32b; Pesahim 3b. Deuteronomy 16:20.

218. *THE SYNAGOGUE "ALTNEU-SHUL":* A well-known legend among the Jews of Prague. I heard while visiting the synagogue in 1932. Babli, Megillah 21b. Y. V. Zikernik, *Sipurim Nehmadim*, 1903, p. 7. (David ben Shimon), *Shaar ha-Hatzer*, 1862, p. 39.

219. *THE TURKISH CONQUEST:* S. A. Rosanis, *Dibrei Yemei ha-Yehudim Be-Tugarmah*, 1, p. 90. It is told in the name of Joseph Sambari. Micah 5:4. Isaiah 19:4. *Sefer Yohasin*, p. 165b.

220. *ENTRANCE INTO JERUSALEM:* Hagiz, *Parashath Eleh Massai*, 1733. Ahmad Ibn Zunbul (died in 1543), *Risala Mushtamilah*, p. 2. H. Jansky, "Die Eroberung, Syriens durch Sultan Salim I," *Mitteilungen zur Usmanischen Geschichte*, II, 1926, p. 200.

221. *FATE OF THE ARCHITECTS:* Hanauer, Folklore, p. 96.

222. *HANNAH'S LANE:* A legend known to the elders of the Old City, Jerusalem. I first heard it in 1922. Another legend locates the graves of Hannah and her sons on a hill in the Jewish cemetery of Safed. See Vilnay, *Holy Shrines of the Land of Israel*, 1951, p. 242.

223. *ZELA—THE KARAITE QUARTER:* Joshua 18:28. *Sefer Zerubbabel*. Eben Shemuel, *Midrashei Geulah*, p. 88. Mann, *The Jews in Egypt and in Palestine*, II, p. 374.

224. *DROUGHT IN JERUSALEM: Otzar Massaoth*, p. 118. See the description of a journey in 1491, *ZDPV*, 1898, p. 57.

225. *THE PROTRUDING STONE:* I heard this from a Jerusalem youth during a survey of the wall of Jerusalem in 1928. This is according to a Talmudic legend in Babli, Baba Mezia 59b.

226. *IN THE SHOPS:* Babli, Shabbath 15a; Rosh ha-Shanah 31a; Abodah Zarah 88b.

227. *THE BATH OF HEALING:* This was told to me by one of the attendants of this bath in 1925.

228. *GOLGOLTHA—GOLGOTHA:* J. Jeremias, *Golgotha,* 1926. A Aptowitzer, "Les éléments juifs dans la légende du Golgotha," *REJ,* 79, 1924, p. 147. Origen the Greek, in the beginning of the third century in Caesaria, was apparently the first to tell about the skull of Adam in Jerusalem as an Hebrew tradition. See his commentary to Matuwes, *Migne, Patrologie Graeca,* XIII, col. 1777; XXVIII, col. 208.

229. *GOLGOTHA—CENTER OF THE WORLD:* A legend found in the writings of Christian pilgrims at the end of the Middle Ages. Psalms 74:12.

230. *MELCHIZEDEK AND ABRAHAM:* Genesis 14:18. Fabri, *Evagetorium* (1484), p. 386, 371.

231. *WHY WERE THE GATES CLOSED?:* Reisher, *Shaarei Yerushalaim,* p. 22.

232. *THE GATE OF LIONS:* Hanauer, *Folklore,* p. 94. The German S. Schweigger, who visited Jerusalem in 1581, attributes the wall and the Gate of the Lions to Sultan Salim and tells the legend in a slightly different version: *Reiz-Beschreibung . . . nach Jerusalem,* 1665, p. 307. The traveler Zuallardo, who visited Jerusalem in 1576, tells of the lions, which were made contrary to the Turkish law: *Il Devotissimo Viaggio di Gerusalemme,* 1587, p. 169. Horowitz, *Hibat Yerushalaim,* 1844, p. 40a.

233. *THE DUNG GATE:* Nehemiah 3:13–14; 12:27–31. Babli, Baba Kama 82b. *Abboth de-Rabbi Nathan* (A) 35.

234. *THE GATE OF FLOWERS:* Koran 79:14. Al-Mukaddasi, *Ahsan al-Takassim,* p. 171. Nasir Khosrau, *Sefer Nameh,* ed. Shefer. Mujir ed-Din, *Kitab a-Uns.*

235. *THE TOWER AND THE POOL:* Song of Songs 4:4. 2 Samuel 2–27. *Two Journeys to Jerusalem,* 1695, p. 67. Al Mukaddasi, *Ahsan al-Takassim.* Babli, Sanhedrin 107a. Haim Vital, *Etz ha-Da'at Va-Yetze. Bereishith Rabba* 39:11. *Yalkut Shimoni, Genesis* 64. About the grave of Uriah the Hittite in Rabbath Ammon, see Vilnay, *Holy Shrines in the Land of Israel,* 1951, p. 185.

236. *GOLIATH'S FORTRESS:* Flavius, *Wars*, VIII, 3. *Itineraires Jerusalem*, 1882, p. 184. 1 Samuel 17:54. *PEQS*, 1901, p. 403.

237. *WHERE EZRA WROTE THE TORAH:* Babli, Sukkah 20a. Ezra 4:14. E. Pierotti, *Jerusalem Explored*, I, 1864, p. 230.

238. *THE STONING PLACE:* Mishnah, Sanhedrin 6:1–2. Warren-Conder, *The Survey of Western Palestine*, Jerusalem, 1884, p. 430.

239. *ASHES OF THE SACRIFICE:* Jeremiah 31:38–39. Leviticus 4:12, 21; 6:4. Babli, Yoma 68a; Zebahim 106a. Ha-Parhi, *Kaphtor Va-Perah*, ed. Berlin, p. 14.

240. *THE MONASTERY OF THE CROSS:* This legend was told to me by the Greek superior of the Monastery.

241. *WHY WAS IT CALLED MEAH SHEARIM?:* Genesis 26:12. Y. Brill, *Yesod ha-Maalah*, p. 217. Isaiah 54:13.

242. *AGRIPPAS STREET-BEILEH PATH:* I heard this from older people who live in the neighborhood.

243. *THE ASSYRIAN CAMP:* 2 Kings 19:35. Isaiah 37:36. Flavius, *Wars*, V, 7, 3; 12, 2. Rashi on Babli, Berachoth 54b; Sanhedrin 95b. Exodus 8:15; 14:31. 2 Chronicles 32:21.

244. *THE FINGER OF OG:* A legend known among the children of Jerusalem. I first heard it in 1928. Flavius, *Wars*, V, 5, 6. *Tanhuma*, ed. Buber, addition to Debarim, p. 6.

245. *WHY THE NAME MAMILLA?:* Mujir ed-Din, *Kitab a-Uns.*

246. *WHY IS IT CALLED ABU-TOR?:* Mujir ed-Din.

247. *MOUNT OF ABRAHAM:* Genesis 22:4–5. *Yehus Aboth We-Nebiim.*

248. *VALLEY OF REPHAIM:* Deuteronomy 2:11. *Bereishith Rabba* 26:9. Isaiah 17:4–5.

249. *THE VALLEY OF BACA:* Psalms 84:3, 7–8, and the Aramaic translation. 2 Samuel 5:17–24. 1 Chronicles 1–14. Babli, Eirubin 19a. *Midrash Tehillim*, ed. Buber, p. 186. David Yellin, "Emek ha-Baca, Becaim," *Kobetz ha-Hebrah ha-Ibrith Le-Hakirat Eretz Israel*, I, 2, 1925, pp. 103–5.

250. *HOSTEL FOR THE ONE HUNDRED AND FORTY-FOUR THOUSAND:* Revelation 7:2–4.

251. *TENT OF THE MESSIAH:* Malachi 3:1. H. M. Michlin, *Berei Hadorot*, 1950, p. 113.

252. *ROD OF THE MESSIAH:* Psalms 110:2. *Midrash Yilamdenu.*

253. *THE CAVE OF ZEDEKIAH:* Jeremiah 39:4–5. The cave is first mentioned in Babli, Eirubin 81b. See the commentary of Rashi on 2 Kings 25:4.

254. *THOSE WHO DARED ENTER THE CAVE:* Reisher, *Shaarei Yerushalaim*, p. 49. Hutzin, *Maaseh Nissim*, p. 8. Y. S. Parhi, *Moraim Gedolim*, 1914, p. 80.

255. *KING SOLOMON'S QUARRIES:* This was told to me by the president of the Masons in Jerusalem.

256. *WHERE DOES THE CAVE LEAD?:* Koran 28:76–81. Al-Mukaddasi, *Ahsan al-Takassim*, p. 185.

257. *JEREMIAH'S COURT OF THE GUARD:* Jeremiah 38:6, 10, 13. Horowitz, *Hibat Yerushalaim*, 1854, p. 46b.

258. *THE CAVE OF HA-RAMBAN: Shaarei Dima a ha-Shalem*, p. 15b. The letter of Ramban was first published in the book *Shaar ha-Gemul*, 1490. Pierotti, *Jerusalem Explored*, I, 1864, pp. 38, 136. G. Dalman, *Jerusalem und sein Gelaende*, 1930, p. 180.

259. *THE CAVE OF THE LION: Otzar Massaoth*, p. 67. *Yerushalaim* (ed. Lunz), 1928, p. 57. Eugesippus *MPCC*, CXXXIII, 1864, p. 1002. *La Citez de Jherusalem*, ed. Tobler, p. 215.

260. *THE CAVE OF THE AMORITES:* Amos 2:10. Tosefta, Shabbath 7:25. *Tanhuma*, ed. Buber, addition to Debarim, p. 9.

261. *THE WONDROUS CAVERN:* Zakaria Kazwini, *Kitab Ajaib al-Mahlukat*, 1849, p. 154.

262. *THE MONUMENT OF ABSALOM:* 2 Samuel 18:18. Menahem Mendel, *Koroth ha-Itim*, 1835. Reisher, *Shaarei Yerushalaim*, 1867.

263. *THE FATE OF ABSALOM'S MONUMENT: Abboth de-Rabbi Nathan* (A) 36. Yaacob ben Nataniel, ed. Gruenhut, p. 13. *Otzar Massaoth*, p. 196. Bernardin Surius, *Le Pieux Pélerin*, 1664, p. 404.

264. *THE SHELTER OF KING AZARIAH (UZZIAH):* 2 Kings 15:5. Commentaries of Radak and Rashi. I Chronicles 24:15. Psalms 88.5.

265. *THE WELL OF THE MAIDS:* Bassola, *Massaoth Eretz Israel,* ed. Ben-Zvi, p. 54.

266. *KING PHARAOH IN KIDRON:* I heard this from an Arab passerby at the Brook of Kidron in 1932. See Ahmad Sameh al-Khaldi, *Rihlat fi Diar esh-Sham,* 1946, p. 32.

267. *KING SOLOMON'S MINT:* Bassola, *Massaoth Eretz Israel,* ed. Ben-Zvi, p. 54.

268. *KIDRON—PLACE OF REFUSE:* 2 Chronicles 29:16; 30:14. 1 Kings 15:12. Mishnah, Yoma 5:6; Middoth 3:2; Meilah 3:3.

269. *OPHEL AND KIDRON:* Leviticus 26:4. Micah 4:1, 8. Tosefta, Taanith 3:1. Yerushalmi, Taanith 3:11. Babli: Taanith 22b.

270. *THE JUDGMENT IN THE END OF TIME:* Joel 4:2–12.

271. *THE JUDGMENT OF THE NATIONS:* Isaiah 60:1–4. *Eliyahu Zutta* (chap. Rabbi Eliezer), 1904, p. 34.

272. *ISRAEL IN THE VALLEY OF JEHOSHAPHAT:* Isaiah 60:1–4. Psalms 12:6. "Nistaroth Rabbi Shimon," *Beit ha-Midrash,* III, p. 80.

273. *THE TWO BRIDGES:* A folk tale popular among Jews.

274. *FROM THE SEA TO THE VALLEY: Sefer Zerubbabel,* ed. Kashta. Eben Shemuel, *Midrashei Geulah,* p. 138.

275. *WITNESSES IN THE VALLEY OF JEHOSHAPHAT:* English translation, Fabri, *Evagetorium,* (1484), *PPTS,* IX, p. 129. Genesis 31:46–48.

276. *THE PILLAR OF MUHAMMAD:* Mentioned in the writings of Christian pilgrims: Tschudi. Fuerer von Heimendorf (1566), *Itinerarium Palestine,* 1620, p. 63. Fabri, *Evagetorium* (1484) *PPTS,* IX, pp. 125, 130. Tobler, *Topographie von Jerusalem,* I, p. 61.

277. *VALLEY OF JEHOSHAPHAT-GEHENNA:* Nasir Khosrau, *Sefer Nameh.* Bassola, *Massaoth Eretz Israel,* ed. Ben-Zvi, p. 54.

278. *VALLEY OF DECISION:* Joel 4:14. Septuagint: Valley of Judgment; Vulgate: Valle concisionis; English: Valley

of Decision. Isaiah 10:22–23. "Othoth ha-Mashiah, VIII," Beit ha-Midrash (ed. Yellinek), II, p. 61. *Midrash Tehillim* (Shoher Tob), p. 234.

279. *THE GATE OF HELL:* Deuteronomy 18:10. Isaiah 31:9. Babli, Eirubin 19a; Sukkah 32b. Zechariah 14:2. *Pesikta de-Rab Kahana*, p. 186b. Bassola, *Massaoth Eretz Israel*, ed. Ben-Zvi, p. 53. *Mechilta, Yithro*, 9.

280. *VALLEY HINNOM—TOPHET:* Jeremiah 7:31–33. 2 Chronicles 33:6. Tosefta, Abodah Zarah, VI, 4. *Yalkut Shimoni, Jeremiah*, 277.

281. *IDOLATRY IN THE VALLEY HINNOM:* Jeremiah 19:11–12. Isaiah 30:33. "Masechet Geihinom," *Beit ha-Midrash* (ed. Yellinek), I, p. 147. Rashi on Jeremiah 7:31. *Yalkut Shimoni, Jeremiah*, 277.

282. *WHY IS IT CALLED TOPHET?:* Jeremiah 19:11–13. Lamentations 1:9. Isaiah 30:33. *Eicha Rabba* 1:36.

283. *VALLEY OF SLAUGHTER:* Jeremiah 19:6. Hanauer, *Folklore*, p. 84.

284. *ADAM IN THE WATERS OF GIHON: Pirke Rabbi Eliezer* 20. *Zohar*, I, p. 55b. *Zohar Hadash. Midrash Ruth*, 1870, p. 86b.

285. *SOLOMON BY THE FOUNTAIN OF GIHON:* 1 Kings 1:45. Tosefta, Sanhedrin 4:10–11. Babli, Horioth 12a.

286. *WHO SEALED UP THE GIHON?:* 2 Chronicles 32:30. Babli, Berachoth 10a; Keritoth 8b; Pesahim 56a. *Abboth de-Rabbi Nathan* (A) 2.

287. *WHO UNSEALED THE GIHON?:* H. Azulai, *Shem ha-Gedolim*, ar. Haim Vital.

288. *THE BATH OF THE HIGH PRIEST:* Leviticus 16:4. Babli, Yoma 31a, and Rashi. Yaacob ben Nataniel, ed. Gruenhut, p. 5. S. Hornstein, *Gibeath Shaul*, 1893, p. 15.

289. *THE POOL OF SILOAM:* Nehemiah 3:15. Yerushalmi, Taanith 2, 1. *Abboth de-Rabbi Nathan* (A) 38.

290. *SILOAM IN THE END OF DAYS:* According to the story of Eliyahu ha-Cohen, *Midrash Talpioth*, 1903, p. 203. *Emek ha-Melech*, p. 14.

291. *SILOAM ON THE SABBATH: Itinerarium Burdigalense.* Babli, Sanhedrin 65b, and Rashi. Josephus, *Wars*, VII, 5, 1.

292. *WHENCE THE WATERS OF SILOAM?: Al-Mukad-dasi, Ahsan al Takassim.*

293. *EIN ROGEL—FULLER'S SPRING:* 1 Kings 1:9 and the commentary of Rabbi Isaac Abarbanel.

294. *THE WELL OF JOB:* Hanauer, *Folklore.*

295. *WELL OF JOB—WELL OF JOAB: Otzar Massaoth,* 1927, pp. 196, 208. Moshe Poriyath, *Darkei Zion.* H. M. Mohr, *Mebasereth-Zion,* 1881, p. 47a.

296. *THE WELL OF NEHEMIAH:* According to the Book 2 of the Maccabees 1, 22–30.

297. *THE PLACE OF RESURRECTION:* Zechariah 14:1–11. 1 Chronicles 8:38; 9:44. Josephus Flavius, *Antiquities,* IX, 10, 4.

298. *THE WANDERING OF THE DIVINE PRESENCE: Eicha Rabba, Petihta* 25. Ezekiel 11:23. Jeremiah 3:14. Malachi 3:7. Hosea 5:15. Isaiah 55:6. *Abboth de-Rabbi Nathan* (A) 34.

299. *THE CONSOLER ON THE MOUNT OF OLIVES:* Zechariah 14:1–11. Eliezer ha-Kalir.

300. *PRIVILEGES ON THE MOUNT OF OLIVES:* A. Azulai, *Hesed Le-Abraham,* ed. Amsterdam, p. 33b.

301. *NO WORMS IN THE MOUNT OF OLIVES:* Mishnah, Abboth 4:4. Babli, Berachoth 18b; Baba Kama 17a. J. Parhi, *Tub Yerushalaim,* 1844, p. 6a. R. Trivish, *Zach Ve-Adom,* 1600, p. 41b.

302. *JUDGMENT ON THE MOUNT OF OLIVES:* Ha-Parhi, *Kaftor Va-Perah,* ed. Berlin, p. 35; ed. Lunz, p. 211. *Beit ha-Midrash* (ed. Yellinek), I.

303. *EARTH FROM THE MOUNT OF OLIVES:* Frumkin-Rivlin, *Toldoth Hachmei Yerushalaim,* III, pp. 177–78. Additions, p. 25.

304. *THE LAND OF THE LIVING:* Psalms 72:16, 142:6. Babli, Ketuboth 111b.

305. *THE ROLLING IN TUNNELS:* Isaiah 26:19. Babli, Ketuboth 111b. *Pesikta Rabbati* 31.

306. *RESURRECTION ON THE MOUNT: Beit ha-Midrash* (ed. Yellinek), II (1853), p. 58.

307. *THE PROCESSION ON THE MOUNT: Sefer Hasidim,* ed. Friman, 1891, p. 169.

308. *MOUNT OF ANOINTMENT—MOUNT OF CORRUPTION:* Mishnah, Horioth 3:4. 1 Kings 11:7. 2 Kings 23:13, and the Aramaic translation. Jeremiah 51:25.

309. *THE DOVE AND THE OLIVE:* Genesis 8:11. *Bereishith Rabba* 33:11.

310. *FLARES ON THE MOUNT:* Babli, Sanhedrin 42. Mishnah, Rosh ha-Shanah 2:4. Yerushalmi, Rosh ha-Shanah 2. Tosefta, Rosh ha-Shanah 2:2.

311. *CEDARS AND CINNAMON TREES:* Isaiah 14:8. Babli, Shabbath 63a. Yerushalmi, Peah 7. Leviticus 5:7, 14:11.

312. *JEREMIAH ON MOUNT SCOPUS:* "Alfa Beta de Ben Sira," *Otzar Midrashim* (Eisenstein), p. 34. *Koheleth Rabba* 1:2. *Pesikta Rabbati* 26, 1880, p. 131. Jeremiah 20:7. *Eicha Rabba, Petihta* 19.

313. *WHOEVER SEES JERUSALEM:* Isaiah 64:9. Yerushalmi, Moed Kattan 3:7.

314. *DAUGHTERS IN THE VINEYARDS:* Song of Songs 3:10. Mishnah, Taanith 4:8 and the commentary of Rabbi Obadiah of Bertinoro. Proverbs 31:30. Babli, Taanith 31a.

315. *THE ROADS OF ZION MOURN:* Babli, Hagigah 3. *Eicha Rabba* 1:9. Isaiah 33:8. *Midrash Tehillim* 42:1. See Ginzberg, *Genizah Studies,* I, 1928, p. 272. Lamentations 1:4. Psalms 42:5–7.

316. *THE HIGHWAYS LIE WASTE:* Isaiah 33:8.

317. *THORNS ON THE ROADS:* Isaiah 29:1. *Eicha Rabba, Petihta.* Babli, Eirubin 34b; Baba Kama 119b.

318. *WHERE ARE THE STONES FROM?:* I heard this from a Jewish tourist in 1950. Psalms 102:14–29.

319. *YE MOUNTAINS OF ISRAEL:* Joel 4:18. Ezekiel 36:4–12. *Pesikta Rabbati,* p. 161.